a world *more* bright

The Life of Mary Baker Eddy

a world *more* bright

The Life of Mary Baker Eddy

by Isabel Ferguson
and
Heather Vogel Frederick

The Christian Science Publishing Society
210 Massachusetts Avenue, Boston, Massachusetts 02115 USA

The Christian Science Publishing Society
210 Massachusetts Avenue, Boston, Massachusetts, 02115 USA
www.christianscience.com

Several abbreviations appear in credits and
copyright notices throughout this book:
CSPS: The Christian Science Publishing Society
TMBEC: The Mary Baker Eddy Collection
TMBEL: The Mary Baker Eddy Library
LM: Longyear Museum

Book cover photos of Mary Baker Eddy from the collections of The Mary Baker Eddy Library, Left: by J. Photo H. F. Currier, Center: Courtesy TMBEC, Right: © TMBEC; Cover photo Goodshoot/Thinkstock
Book design by Jerry Rutherford

Library of Congress Cataloging-in-Publication *(Provided by Quality Books, Inc.)*
Ferguson, Isabel
A world more bright : the life of Mary Baker Eddy /
by Isabel Ferguson and Heather Vogel Frederick, – 1st ed.
p. cm.
Includes bibliographical references and index.
LCCN 2013941259
ISBN 978-0-87510-494-2

1. Eddy, Mary Baker, 1821-1910.
2. Christian Scientists—United States—Biography.
I. Frederick, Heather Vogel. II. Christian Science Publishing Society. III. Title.

BX6995.F475 2013 289.5'092
QBI13-600094

G750B50860EN

Printed in the United States of America
1 3 5 7 9 8 6 4 2

First Edition

Table of Contents

1
Early Days

On a cold winter day in the 1820s, Mary Baker came home from school without her coat.

It wasn't the first time that articles of the girl's clothing had vanished. Hats, scarves, mittens—even hair ribbons—all had disappeared before, when tender-hearted Mary gave them away to other children in need.

She knew she shouldn't; she was well aware of how hard her mother worked on their family's New Hampshire farm, and how long it took to make a warm winter coat. But the sight of a shivering schoolmate had touched Mary's heart and sparked her to action.

"You must not give away your clothes," her mother scolded gently, reminding Mary that she'd given away so much it wouldn't be right to ask her father for more. Abigail Baker couldn't have remained upset for long, however. The Bible anchored their family's life, just as it did the lives of so many New England families in those days, and Jesus had instructed his followers, "It is more blessed to give than to receive." Young Mary had obviously taken the lesson to heart, if perhaps a bit too literally.

Mary may have given her coat to one of the White children. They'd recently lost their father, and Mrs. White was having a hard time keeping her family clothed and fed. Mark Baker, Mary's father, had already made them some shoes. Mary was likely just trying to do her part, for in the small town of Bow where the Bakers lived, neighbor helped neighbor.

Born on July 16, 1821, Mary Morse Baker was the youngest of six. She had three older brothers—Samuel, Albert, and George, whom the family often called by his middle name of Sullivan—plus two older sisters: Abigail (nicknamed Abi) and Martha. They were a close-knit, happy family, and

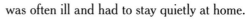

COURTESY TMBEL

▲ Artist's depiction of the Baker homestead in Bow, New Hampshire

Mary was the resident peacemaker, always quick to step in when her siblings squabbled.

Mary had a keen sense of justice, too, and was also quick to step in at school if someone was in trouble or being treated unfairly. Once, she stood up to a bully who was forcing some of the younger students into drinking muddy water from a hollowed-out cucumber, and another time she invited a girl whom everyone else had shunned to sit beside her, a kindness her schoolmate would remember for the rest of her life.

A frail but pretty girl with chestnut hair and deep blue eyes, Mary loved life on her family's upland farm. There were woods to explore and berries to pick and meadows bright with wildflowers to roam. There were animals, too, and Mary loved them all, including her family's Newfoundland dog, Hunt, and the horses whose broad backs she enjoyed scrambling up on for a ride now and then.

Mark Baker was well aware of his daughter's love for animals, and if one of the lambs was weak, he'd often bring it home to her. "Here is another invalid for Mary," he'd say, giving it to her to nurse back to health. Mary may well have felt a special sympathy toward her woolly charges, as she herself was often ill and had to stay quietly at home.

Like her brothers and sisters, Mary was responsible for a number of chores on the farm, one of which was picking out dried corn for the chickens to eat. Mary and her mother were busy at this task one evening when a kernel slipped from Mary's fingers onto the floor. She started pushing it toward the fireplace with her foot.

EVERYDAY LIFE

WORDS OF WISDOM

Abigail Baker shared a number of her favorite sayings with her children. Here are two that Mary later recalled:

Count that day lost whose setting sun finds no good done.

A word that's flown is in your hearer's power and not your own.

"Mary, get down and pick up that corn," chided Mrs. Baker, ever the thrifty Yankee housewife.

"It's only one grain!" Mary protested.

"Never mind — it will help make a meal for a little chick."

Short, plump, and blonde, with eyes as blue as her daughter's, Abigail Ambrose Baker's loving heart warmed her family the way the fire in the hearth warmed their home. "Her presence, like the gentle dew and cheerful light, was felt by all around her," wrote Reverend Rust, a family friend. And Mary would later recall how her mother "was always thinking of ways that she could help an ailing friend or neighbor."

The two were especially close, and Mary spent her days following her mother around and helping with the housework. There was much to do in the busy household, including cooking for their large family and for the friends and relatives who often came to visit.

When the evenings turned cool, Mrs. Baker began the work of spinning. Like other children growing up at that time, Mary would have been lulled to sleep by the whir of the wheel and her mother's steady, rhythmic tread — forward and back, forward and back, as she spun the soft wool into yarn and thread. Later, the beat of the loom may have sounded, too, as some of the wool was woven into cloth.

During the day, Mary and Martha and Abi were kept busy helping with other household chores, including making soap, dipping candles, churning butter, and pressing cheese. Like other New England girls, the Baker sisters also learned to do needlework such as sewing, darning, and embroidery.

There was no work on Sundays, though. The devout Bakers kept the Sabbath as a day

COURTESY OF LONGYEAR MUSEUM CHESTNUT HILL, MASSACHUSETTS

▲ A needlepoint sampler made by young Mary Baker

▼ Grandmother Maryann Baker's spinning wheel. A woman could walk many miles in the course of a day's spinning, so spinning wheels were sometimes called "walking wheels."

COURTESY OF LONGYEAR MUSEUM CHESTNUT HILL, MASSACHUSETTS

of rest and worship, often attending both morning and afternoon church services. Mary's parents were members of the Congregational Church in Bow, which held services in the town's meetinghouse. Later, after that church was dissolved, the family would either travel across the river to Pembroke to the church that Mary's grandfather Nathaniel Ambrose had helped build, or make the five-mile journey to Concord to the large First Congregational Church there.

Much of Sunday's remaining free time would be spent reading the Bible, something young Mary loved to do. She was particularly fond of the Psalms and the stories of Jesus' healings, and Daniel was another of her favorites. When she read that he prayed three times a day, she resolved to do even better, and for a while she slipped off to the woodshed seven times a day, marking her devotions with chalk on the side of the wall.

When she felt well enough, Mary walked to the school at the crossroads a mile away with Abi and Martha. In those days, girls went mostly in the summer as the roads were less muddy and the schools less crowded, what with the older boys out working in the fields.

On her first day, Mary followed her sisters down the hill, through the orchard and neighboring woods, and into the schoolhouse where the teacher was waiting for them at her raised desk. All eight grades were taught together in one room.

Abi and Martha could hardly wait until lunch when they could show off their little sister. They sat her on a table while the others crowded around.

"Mary, what are you going to do when you

EVERYDAY LIFE

HANDSPUN AND HOMEMADE

Sewing machines didn't come into use until the mid-19th century, so when Mary was growing up, most clothing was made by hand. While the Bakers may have purchased fabric from peddlers or a store, some would likely have been woven at home, too. To do so, the sheep had to first be shorn and then the fleece washed. The locks of wool were then separated by hand and the fibers gently teased apart. "Carding" the wool between two hand-held brushes to remove any remaining tangles was a task often assigned to the youngest children. Afterwards, the smoothed fiber would be shaped into rolls and spun into yarn. The spinner would attach the end of the roll to the spindle and then, while the wheel was turned with one hand, step backward, maintaining just the right tension on the wool with the other hand to stretch the fiber into the desired thickness. After the wheel was reversed, stopping the spindle, the spinner would take a few steps forward and begin turning the wheel in the original direction again, winding the newly-formed yarn onto the bobbin. Depending on the thickness of the result, the yarn could then be woven into cloth on a loom, or knitted into sweaters, hats, mittens, and other garments.

are grown up?" someone asked. Most of the girls wanted to be mothers or teachers, while the boys planned to be farmers like their fathers.

"Write a book," Mary answered, and everyone laughed.

The walk home from school was through neighbor Gault's woods. One day, Mary picked up a pitch pine knot, something children loved to find because it blazed blue when thrown on the fire. It also kept the flame burning longer, which adults valued.

Had Mary asked Mr. Gault for it? Mrs. Baker asked when she saw it.

"No," Mary admitted.

"Carry it right back again, Mary. It is stealing for you to do that, and God forbids you to steal."

Mary balked. She was tired—couldn't she do it later?

"Would you have God and Mother thinking until tomorrow that you had broken His commandment?"

Mary took it back.

By the time Mary was eight, her older brother Samuel, then 21, had already left home for Boston to learn the building trade. Albert, 19, would soon be off to Dartmouth College. Only 17-year-old Sullivan remained at home to work on the farm and laugh with his younger sisters as they joked and teased

ONE-ROOM SCHOOLHOUSES

SIGNS OF THE TIMES

One-room schoolhouses were common in rural America in the 19th century. When the Baker family lived in Bow, the town had seven of them. Mary and her siblings attended School #3, a mile from their home. It was a simple structure, typical of that era in New England, just 22 feet square with walls of white-washed plaster. A fireplace served to heat the single room, and Mark Baker often supplied the wood.

There were generally two school sessions each year, with each term running from 10-20 weeks, depending on the availability of teachers and the town's budget. Schoolteachers boarded with local families as part of their pay. Mary's brother Albert and sisters Abi and Martha all taught school at one point; records show that Albert earned $3.35 a month.

In the fall of 1829, Albert took a job teaching at Bow School #3 to help earn college tuition money, and Mary must have been delighted to have her favorite older brother nearby for an entire term.

One-room schoolhouses have all but vanished, but a few are still in operation today in a handful of remote rural communities.

➤ The Baker children attended a Bow Schoolhouse that probably looked like this one.

COURTESY OF LIBRARY OF CONGRESS, PRINTS AND PHOTOGRAPHS DIVISION

SIGNS OF THE TIMES

"SCOTS WHA HAE"

Scottish poet Robert Burns wrote the lyrics to this song in 1793, imagining it as a speech given by Scots nobleman Robert the Bruce to his army before the Battle of Bannockburn in 1314, when Scotland won its freedom for a time from English rule. "Wallace" refers to Sir William Wallace, a leader during the Wars of Scottish Independence, while "Edward" is England's king. The song served for a long time as Scotland's unofficial national anthem. Here is the first stanza:

Original lyrics in Scots

Scots, wha hae wi' Wallace bled,
Scots, wham Bruce has aften led,
Welcome tæ yer gory bed,
Or tæ victorie.

English translation

Scots, who have with Wallace bled,
Scots, whom Bruce has often led,
Welcome to your gory bed
Or to victory.

around the kitchen table. Abi was 13 by now and bossy. Ten-year-old Martha was good at telling stories and would go on to write lively letters. Once, a few years later when Sullivan was away, she wrote him how Abi and Mary "keep shaking the table and making me laugh all the time, and now they have brought on a bowl of apple sauce and a plate of nuts and turnovers and a pitcher of sap beer [maple sap boiled down and flavored with spruce twigs]. Now do you wonder I cannot write."

Like her favorite brother Albert, Mary was a bookworm. Sometimes when her siblings went out to play, she'd stay at home reading. Other times when she joined them, as often as not she'd eventually slip away to a secluded spot where they'd find her later, engrossed in a book.

Grandmother Baker, whose ancestors originally came from Scotland, lived with the family. Mary was devoted to her, and loved to hear her tell stories about their Scottish forebears. These daring men and women were Covenanters who had fought for religious freedom. Among her grandmother's treasures was a heavy sword in a brass scabbard that had been given to a kinsman by Sir William Wallace, immortalized for his bravery in the rousing song "Scots Wha Hae."

Mary's grandmother told her about the American side of her family, too—General Henry Knox, who fought in the Revolutionary War, and Captain John Lovewell of Dunstable, New Hampshire, a gallant militia leader who perished during hostilities with the Abenaki tribe of Maine. His exploits were immortalized in story and song, and for his brave service to King and country his heirs were given a grant of land, part of which the Baker family now farmed.

Mary very likely often heard about the time her great-grandmother

Hannah Baker, Captain Lovewell's daughter, was washing clothes by a spring one day in 1747. Suddenly, she heard the alarm—hostiles were coming! While everyone else ran to the nearest garrison house, Hannah calmly finished her laundry. A rescue party sent out to save her found the unruffled woman walking to the fort, her basket of clean clothes balanced on her hip. These tales of her courageous ancestors must have thrilled Mary, and they left a deep impression on the girl.

Grandmother Baker would also have told her about clearing the land and building their farmhouse in Bow. The house and two barns stood on the rise of a hill. If Mary looked out on one side, she saw fields where in summer the wind whispered through the tall grain. Beyond lay the smooth, glassy face of the Merrimack River with its canal boats laden with freight. If Mary ran to the lower part of the hill, she came to a rocky ledge that she and her brothers and sisters called "the playground." From here she could look down on the turnpike, where stagecoaches swirled by on their way to Concord, the capital of New Hampshire, or to faraway Boston.

One time when Mary was about eight, her 23-year-old cousin Mehitable Huntoon, whom the family called "Mitty," came to visit. The two were sitting together when they both heard: "Mary! Mary! Mary!" Mehitable looked up, but Mary paid no attention. She had been hearing this call for about a year now. It sounded like her mother's voice, but whenever she ran to her, Mrs. Baker would shake her head—no, she hadn't called.

Again the call came, repeating Mary's name three times in an ascending scale.

"Why don't you go? Your mother is calling you!" Mehitable said sharply.

Mary obediently ran to the kitchen. "What is it, Mother?"

Puzzled, Mrs. Baker replied that she hadn't called for her.

Mary persisted. "Mitty heard it this time, Mother."

Abigail Baker led the way back to where Mary's cousin was waiting. She took Mehitable into the next room, but left the door open. Mary heard her mother tell Mehitable all about the mysterious voice, and then ask, "Did you really hear Mary's name being called?"

Mary held her breath.

"Yes," her cousin answered quickly, to Mary's relief. This was the first time someone else had heard the voice. No one had believed her before.

That night, before Mrs. Baker tucked Mary into bed, she read her the Bible story of young Samuel, who had also heard a voice calling his name.

"When the voice comes again, Mary," her mother told her, "answer the way Samuel did: 'Speak, Lord; for thy servant heareth.'"

Mary was alone when the voice came again, "but I was afraid, and did not answer," she later recalled. Afterwards, her cheeks wet with tears, she asked God to forgive her. Next time, she promised herself, she would do as her mother had instructed. And when the call came again, that's exactly what she did, answering: "Speak, Lord; for thy servant heareth." That was the last time she heard the mysterious voice.

When Mary was 10, her oldest brother Samuel married Eliza Ann Glover from nearby Concord. Eliza's brother, Major George Washington Glover, came to the wedding. His title was an honorary one, and he had such a long name that his friends just called him "Wash." With his sandy red hair and easy manner, Wash reminded Mary very much of her brother George Sullivan. At some point during the festivities, Wash swept her up on his knee.

"I shall wait for *you* to be *my* wife!" he told Mary, who scrambled down shyly and ran away to hide.

Mary loved school and was a diligent student, but her parents worried about her delicate health and frequent illnesses. The family doctor told Mr. Baker that his daughter's brain was "too large" for her body, and counseled removing her from school and letting her spend more time outdoors.

Mary's parents did just that, and for much of her childhood she was homeschooled. Her brother Albert helped tutor her whenever he came back to the family farm to visit, teaching her a little of what he was studying at Pembroke Academy, the private high school he attended, and later at Dartmouth College. Under his watchful eye, Mary studied Latin, Greek, Hebrew, and philosophy, among other things, and she read Shakespeare and wrote poetry, too.

One of Mary's favorite spots to write was under an apple tree. She'd sit in its cool green shade composing her poems, then take them to her mother to read. Here's an excerpt from one she wrote when she was 12:

Resolutions for the Morning

I'll rise in the morn and drink in the dew,
From flowers that bloom in the vale—
So mildly dispensing their charms ever new,
Over hillocks, and flowery dales.

I'll gaze on the orb in yon eastern sky,
For loftier thoughts 'twill invite!
His beams can enlighten the spiritual eye,
And inspire my pen as I write.

Mary looked up to her tall, scholarly brother with his chestnut hair and clear brown eyes full of intelligence and love. She must have admired his desire to make something of himself, his determination to obtain a college degree, and the uncomplaining way in which he worked to pay for his education, for it was to him that she confided her dreams of being a writer someday.

Just like Albert, young Mary Baker had plans. Unexpected changes lay ahead for them both, however.

2
What's Right?

Mary's father, Mark Baker, was a man of strong character. Highly respected in the community, he was a clear and forceful speaker whose opinion was valued, and who was often asked to help settle neighbors' disputes. In addition to running his farm, he served as a selectman and justice of the peace, moderated town meetings, sat on the school board, recorded deeds, worked as surveyor of roads for Bow, and occasionally as chaplain for the local militia. He treated everyone with kindness and respect, and was known to be generous and fair.

"At Christmastime," Mary would later recall, "father would fill the democrat [all-purpose] wagon with turkeys, chickens, and vegetables and go with them to the poor of the neighborhood. Every present was nicely done up and there was something for every needy neighbor."

Mark Baker, who was the youngest of ten children, had inherited the family home and, along with his older brother James, about five hundred acres of land. On their farm the Bakers cultivated fields of grain, lush green pastures, and orchards of apples, peaches, pears, and cherries.

Mark Baker, father of Mary Baker Eddy

COURTESY OF LONGYEAR MUSEUM CHESTNUT HILL, MASSACHUSETTS

Mary's hard-working father was a man of many talents, ably juggling the manual labor required to run a farm with such neighborly concerns as making shoes for a family in need or arguing for a friend in court when they faced a legal battle. He also put a great deal of time into helping run the school, the town, and the church.

Mark became clerk of the Congregational Church in Bow the year after Mary was born. In clear, precise handwriting he wrote in its record book "... it is the duty of heads of families to train up the children under their care for GOD, by all good precepts and examples and by praying with and for them night and morning."

True to his word, every morning and evening Mary's father opened the old Bible that had been a wedding present from his own father and read a chapter to his family. He also prayed out loud for them, and Mark Baker's prayers were long. Dark storm clouds might fill the sky while tons of hay lay waiting in the fields—precious food for livestock that most farmers hurried to protect—but it didn't make a speck of difference. Mary's father never skipped nor shortened his devotions.

Once, when all the Baker family had been down on their knees for quite a while, young Mary opened her eyes and spotted the nearby pincushion full of long pins her mother used to keep her shawls in place. Quietly, she reached out for one of them and then inched her way behind her father. One quick poke in the rear accomplished what nothing else could: the praying finally stopped! Years later, Mary would recount with amusement how she made her escape in the confusion that followed.

The Bakers were a generous family, and Mary saw many visitors come to the house. "My childhood's home, I remember as one with the open hand," she later wrote. Her parents often shared meals with those who were less fortunate and, like many other families in the community, they welcomed ministers to their home and table. Mr. Baker liked nothing better than to discuss religion with his guests, and Mary would lie awake in bed at night, listening to the rise and fall of their voices as they debated Bible verses and doctrine.

Mark truly loved his six children and acted for their good, but he ruled them with an iron hand. A Calvinist, he thought that God must be believed, feared, and obeyed. His religion taught that unbelievers would suffer endless punishment, with no mercy or forgiveness, and that most people were predestined to go to a place called hell after death and there be damned forever.

As Mary listened to what she would later refer to as her father's "relentless theology," many questions troubled her, particularly the "horrible decree" of predestination, as John Calvin himself called this grim theological point.

None of Mary's brothers and sisters had publicly accepted their father's stark faith, and as Mary later explained, "I was unwilling to be saved, if my brothers and sisters were to be numbered among those who were doomed to perpetual banishment from God."

Mark Baker held his ground stubbornly, and so did his daughter, for Mary refused to accept the idea of a God less loving than her mother. She and her father argued over these points from time to time, and after one heated exchange when she was about 12, Mary developed a fever. The family doctor was called to the house.

As Mrs. Baker bathed her daughter's burning forehead, she told her to lean on God's love. Her heavenly Father would give her rest if Mary prayed to Him for an answer, she said. Obediently, Mary stopped listening to the argument raging inside her and turned to God. As she prayed, a light, joyful feeling flooded over her. The fever was gone. She got up and dressed, calm and well. Her mother was overjoyed; the doctor quite amazed. Mary was no longer afraid of that harsh teaching, and never again did it have any power over her.

About two years later, in January of 1836, Mark Baker decided it was time to sell the Bow farm and move to a smaller one near the town of Sanbornton Bridge, some 20 miles away. Grandmother Baker had died the year before, and Mark's three sons had all left home, none of them wanting to be farmers. At 17 and 20, Martha and Abi were nearing marriageable age, and living closer to town would give all three girls an opportunity for better schooling and more social life.

Their friends gave the Baker girls a going-away party, but leaving "the dear old farm," as Mary called it, was bittersweet, especially for 14-year-old Mary and her mother. The homestead in Bow was at the heart of what Mary would always fondly remember as "the golden days of childhood," and she and her mother both fell ill shortly before the move.

For Martha and Abi, it was a different story. The two older girls could hardly wait to taste all that Sanbornton Bridge had to offer. Eager to make a good first impression, they wanted to arrive at their new home in style. They dragged their feet at the thought of being seen in the family's humble wagon, and begged their father to buy a chaise, something the frugal Mr. Baker refused to do.

"We like to had a dreadful fight about it," Martha reported afterwards to Sullivan, though whether the spat was over the wagon itself, or over the young men at the reins of the respective carriages their mother eventually arranged

COURTESY OF PEARSON SCOTT FORESMAN

▲ A 19th-century chaise

for them to ride in, isn't entirely clear. In the end, Abi rode with Daniel Gault in a much-coveted chaise and Martha with a "gentleman from New York," while Mary was left to trundle along with her parents in the old family wagon.

"Father is as happy as a clam," Albert wrote to Sullivan the following summer. The new home and new town were proving very much to Mark Baker's liking—and to that of his pretty daughters as well.

Mary impressed the local girls when she introduced the new "French Twist" hairstyle, and she quickly made two fast friends: Priscilla Clement and Augusta Holmes, a mill owner's daughter whose brother had been at Dartmouth with Albert. All three Baker sisters were soon swept up into Sanbornton Bridge society, and they received many invitations to balls and parties.

Some had to be turned down, however.

"Balls and dancing schools we have not frequented," a miffed Abi reported to Sullivan. Their strict father didn't allow it. Still, Martha managed to slip out to at least one—a Fourth of July ball—when Mr. Baker was away. Later that year their father must have relented, for when the girls received another invitation, Martha told her brother, "he did not forbid us and of course we went ... next day I felt a slight inconvenience from friction in the joints—the usual effects of such exertions."

Abi especially liked her new life. "We find society very agreeable and refined," she told Sullivan, although the lack of proper transportation still clearly chafed. "If our buildings and furniture were a little more splendid, and we had a chaise, I think we could appear to much better advantage."

STEPPING OUT IN STYLE

EVERYDAY LIFE

A two-wheeled carriage with a convertible top, the chaise was the sports car of its day. This pleasure vehicle so coveted by the Baker girls was much less practical than their family's sturdy wagon, but oh, how much more elegant it would have been to be seen in one!

"It is extremely mortifying, to my pride, to push off to meeting in a waggon [sic]," Abi grumbled to her brother Sullivan in the spring of 1836.

Alas, Mr. Baker would have had to pay tax on a chaise, and being a frugal New Englander, the answer was no.

Even Mary had something to say to him on the subject. "Hopeing [sic] time still continues to glide smoothly as in former years," she wrote, adding slyly, "it continues to do so with us only when we are obligeed [sic] to ride in a wagon, and then it is rough...."

The old farm wagon couldn't have impeded the Baker girls' social life all that much, for as Abi noted happily, "The young gentlemen have not been slow in their attentions."

Their male visitors may have been surprised at dour Mr. Baker's wet blanket approach to courtship, on the other hand. Mary's father had a habit of stepping into the room when "young gentlemen" came to call and announcing, "Let all conversation and pleasure be in harmony with the will of God."

Even that solemn pronouncement couldn't dampen the spirits of the potential suitors, who included the town's most eligible bachelor. Alexander Tilton was a successful businessman in Sanbornton Bridge, which would later be renamed Tilton in honor of one of his relatives. When Alexander and Abi married the following year, in 1837, who should show up at the wedding but Wash Glover! Mary was a lively almost-16-year-old by now, well thought of in her new community.

"Bright, good, and pure, aye brilliant!" her pastor, Reverend Enoch Corser, said of her.

More used to young men and not as shy as she had been at 10, Mary was still no doubt surprised when Wash asked if she would write to him so that they could get to know each other better. She couldn't have helped smiling at the persistence of this handsome young man.

Months passed in a flurry of activity. There was school, of course, and Mary excelled at her studies. She attended Sanbornton Academy in Sanbornton Bridge, and likely Woodman Sanbornton Academy at Sanbornton Square as well. At some point Sarah Bodwell, one of her teachers at Sanbornton and later principal of Woodman Sanbornton, told her, "Mary, some day you will be a distinguished author."

Reverend Corser, Mary's minister, was a Middlebury College graduate who also taught at Sanbornton Academy. He once remarked to his son Bartlett, "I never before had a pupil with such depth and independence of thought. She has some great future, mark that. She is an intellectual and spiritual genius."

In the summer of 1838, Mary and her parents joined the local Congregational Church. At 17, Mary was one of its youngest members, and she was allowed to join despite her disagreement with the doctrine of predestination.

© TMBEC

▲ Mary joined the Congregational Church in Sanbornton Bridge (later Tilton) at 17, and taught Sunday School here.

She framed her protest in the words of the Psalmist: "Search me, O God, and know my heart: try me, and know my thoughts: and see if there be any wicked way in me, and lead me in the way everlasting." Her sincerity melted the hearts of the other church members, as well as Rev. Corser, and they "received me into their communion, and my protest along with me," Mary would later recall.

She became a Sunday School teacher and was given charge of the youngest class. Mary was popular with her little students, many of whom would remember her with great affection years later.

"She always wore clothes we admired," noted one. "We loved her particularly for her daintiness, her high-bred manners, her way of smiling at us, and her sweet, musical voice."

Still an avid reader, Mary kept up with newspapers and magazines, and she loved novels and poetry, copying poems by Byron and Burns, among others, in her notebooks or quoting them in letters she wrote during this period. She was especially fond of the stories of Sir Walter Scott, and she read Charlotte Brontë's novels as they rolled off the press.

Mary continued to write, too, and experienced the thrill of seeing what was probably her first published poem in the December 23, 1840 issue of *Hill's New Hampshire Patriot.* Its saucy tone and lilting rhymes hint at the 19-year-old's sunny disposition:

Excerpt from *When I Was a Wee Little Slip of a Girl*

When I was a wee little slip of a girl,
Too artless and young for a prude;
The men as I passed would exclaim "pretty dear,"
Which I must say I thought rather rude;
Rather rude, so I did;
Which, I must say, I thought rather rude.

However, said I, when I'm once in my teens,
They'll sure, cease to worry me then;
But as I grew older, so they grew the bolder—
Such impudent things are the men;
Are the men, are the men,
Such impudent things are the men.

When she wasn't writing poems or essays for school, Mary wrote letters to friends and family, including her brother Albert, who had graduated Phi Beta Kappa from Dartmouth College in 1834 and was now working hard at his new job. Earlier in 1840 he'd written to his sisters, "If you knew how much satisfaction I take in reading your letters, you would write oftener.... If there is a brother in the world, who is happy in the love of his sisters, it is I. Indeed, it is to me the oasis in the desert of life, the only spot upon which I rest with entire safety.... But my joy was saddened upon reading in your postscript that Mary's health is again in danger. I pray she will be careful."

After Albert's graduation, General Benjamin Pierce and his wife had invited him to come and live with them in Hillsborough, New Hampshire, while he studied law with their son, Franklin. The Pierces were old family friends, and the General had often stopped at the Baker house when he visited Bow. Their son was a successful attorney, and he later asked Albert to join his law practice.

PORTRAIT BY GEORGE PETER ALEXANDER HEALY, 1853
NATIONAL PORTRAIT GALLERY

▲ Franklin Pierce, Albert Baker's friend and employer. In 1852 he was elected 14th president of the United States, an occasion Mary would mark with a sonnet published in the *New Hampshire Patriot and State Gazette.*

READING LAW IN THE 19TH CENTURY

SIGNS OF THE TIMES

Before law schools were common in the United States, men like Mary's brother Albert (along with Thomas Jefferson, Abraham Lincoln, Clarence Darrow, and many others) got their start in the legal profession by what was called "reading law"—apprenticing with an established attorney or judge. During the day, the aspiring lawyer would intern as an office assistant, helping with whatever work there was to be done, and then at night he would study or "read" law books. Once fully prepared, the candidate would sit for the bar examination, which would qualify him as a practicing attorney. In a handful of states, it's still possible to take this path to becoming a lawyer today, instead of earning a law degree.

© TMBEL

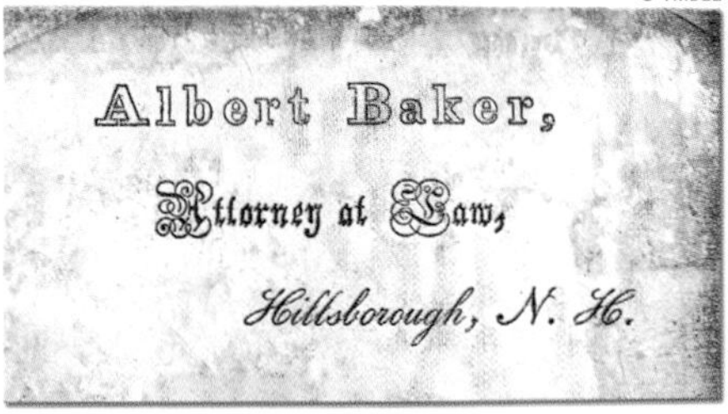

▲ Albert Baker's business card

In 1836, Franklin Pierce was elected to the United States Senate from New Hampshire. Albert, meanwhile, passed the bar exam in both Massachusetts and New Hampshire. The following year, Franklin was very glad to turn over his law office and the care of his parents to Albert while he went off to Washington, D.C. In December 1838 Franklin wrote to Albert, "I am very anxious to hear again from my dear father. Do write me two or three times each week in relation to the state of his health." Fourteen years later, Franklin Pierce would become President of the United States.

Albert himself entered politics in 1839 and served two years in the New Hampshire legislature. Having been raised on a farm, he was quick to stand by old neighbors like the Gaults, whose land was being cut up for the new railroads without proper payment. He also spearheaded legislation abolishing imprisonment for debt. It wasn't long before Albert earned a reputation for fairness, justice, and support of individual rights, and he received many invitations to speak in public. His workload in the law office also increased.

"I have some eight or ten jury trials—double what I ever had before," he told his two younger sisters in a letter home early in 1840, adding with brotherly concern, if not grammatical accuracy: "Take care of your healths." And in another letter later that year, he again urged Mary, "Your health is of paramount importance ... I beg of you be careful."

Albert's own health was troublesome. By 1841, his political star was on the rise. An acknowledged party leader, he was well-respected in the legislature and likely under consideration for his party's nomination to Congress. Before this could happen, however, he fell ill—so seriously that Sullivan went to be with him. Sadly, Albert died on October 17th. He was only thirty-one years old.

The Bakers were proud of Albert, but until his death even they didn't realize how much he was liked and admired by his peers. He was buried in the Pierce family plot in Hillsborough, and as Sullivan sifted sorrowfully through his brother's belongings, he found many letters from Albert's fellow politicians. Sullivan wrote to these men, asking them to return Albert's letters so that the family could preserve them. Many heartfelt responses came in reply.

"Your lamented brother," wrote one legislator, "was emphatically one of the best friends of the rights of the people."

Tributes flowed in the press as well. "He was no stickler for expediency," noted a longtime friend from Maine. "His only question was—what is RIGHT? and that which in his idea was the right, he would pursue fearless of consequences. His maxim was that what is right must be politic."

Even Albert's political opponents were complimentary. In an obituary in the *New Hampshire Patriot,* Governor Isaac Hill, one of his fiercest rivals, had this to say about Albert: "Mr. Baker was a young man of uncommon promise .... Had life and health been spared to him, he would have made himself one of the most distinguished men in the country. As a lawyer, he was able and learned.... In his legislative career he was noted for his boldness, firmness, and powerful advocacy of the side he deemed right." Albert's death, concluded Hill, "is a public calamity both to the town of Hillsborough and to the State."

The Baker family was in shock, and for 20-year-old Mary it was an empty, desolate time. All her life Albert had watched over, guided, and encouraged her. Now, he was gone.

3

Mountains and Valleys

Mary had much in Sanbornton Bridge to keep her from sinking into a mire of grief. She would spend the next year finishing up her schooling, for one. Higher education for women was almost non-existent in those days, as most colleges and universities wouldn't open their doors to female students until after the Civil War, and women's colleges such as Mount Holyoke, Smith, Vassar, and Wellesley were still decades away from being chartered. Mary's formal education was coming to an end.

In addition to her studies, Mary took comfort in writing and reading, including, of course, her beloved Bible.

"The Bible and I are inseparable," she would note many years later. "It has always been so."

It was a Bible verse that inspired a poem she published in October 1842 in a local literary magazine, the *Belknap Gazette*, whose title "The Summer is Past the Harvest is Ended," comes from Jeremiah 8:20 ("The harvest is past, the summer is ended, and we are not saved"). In it, Mary muses on the fleeting nature of time, perhaps thinking of her brother Albert.

Excerpt from *The Summer is Past the Harvest is Ended*

O! time forever on the wing
Why float ye noiseless by?
Life must have lost its genial spring
When hours so swiftly fly.

Borne on, on eagle's pinions, thought
Roams free o'er fancy's bowers,

Stealing that boon the Monarch sought
Who cried, "I've lost an hour."

And thus with dreams of empty bliss
Ye tempt; then onward fly,
Whispering mortal join the chase
Tomorrow ends your sighs.

The verses continue in this vein until the end, when a ray of hope shines through:

And this is life so quickly flown
More transient than a flower,
Born of a summer's breath at morn
To wither in an hour.

Yet if, as when the rose bud dies
A glory hath been shed,
Its perfume rises to the skies
Tho' beauteous tints are fled.

Although Mary had been writing for her own pleasure for many years, these first published poems marked the modest beginnings of the career she'd been dreaming of since she was a small girl, and must have been encouraging.

There was more to cheer her, too, including the excitement and distraction of a pair of weddings—that of her sister Martha to Luther Pilsbury, and also of her friend and former schoolmate Augusta Holmes, who in November of 1842 became Mrs. Samuel Swasey.

"As to my being married," Mary had written to Augusta loftily several years earlier, "I don't begin to think much of that 'decisive step,' neither do I intend to be 'married' at present. I am sure, I feel as though I should like my liberty a while longer."

That was soon to change.

Quick-witted and lively, Mary had grown into an attractive young woman. She was medium height and slim, with curly chestnut brown hair and a ready laugh. Her deep-set blue eyes were one of her most arresting features, and people would remark on them throughout her lifetime, describing them as "soulful," "brilliant," "expressive," "luminous," and the like.

Mary had no lack of admirers, including her friend John Bartlett, who helped found the Young Ladies' Literary Society at Sanbornton Academy. The two of them had been in a wedding together a few years earlier, John as a groomsman and Mary as a bridesmaid. "We had a fine time," Mary assured her brother George Sullivan, in a letter describing the event.

But there was one "young gentleman" in particular who had made a lasting impression on her. While on an errand in Sanbornton Bridge during the summer of 1841, Mary had caught sight of her brother looking particularly sharp. She went up and slapped him on the back, saying, "Oh, you're dressed up!" When he turned around, it was a George all right, but not the one she'd been expecting. George Washington Glover had surprised her again! Mary was mortified, but if anything, her high spirits seemed to pique Wash's interest, and from that time on his letters came more frequently.

Mr. Baker was not happy about this correspondence, despite the fact that Major Glover was by all accounts an enterprising young man. Back in 1838, he'd been working for Mary's oldest brother Samuel in his contracting business in Boston when news came of a fire in Charleston, South Carolina. Generous loans were offered by city officials to encourage rebuilding, and Wash decided to try his luck. He sailed on the *Mohawk*, one of the first ships to leave Boston harbor, and three weeks later, an advertisement in the Charleston *Mercury* announced that he and a partner were ready to "contract and build to the satisfaction of all who may favour them."

The sore point for Mark Baker wasn't Wash necessarily, but rather the prospect of his frail daughter moving to the South. Reports of fever epidemics in

DEAR PENPAL

EVERYDAY LIFE

Long before the invention of emails, cell phones, text messages, instant messages, and videoconferencing, handwritten letters were the only means of connecting with far-off friends and loved ones. Mary enjoyed putting pen to paper so much that she even wrote to her good friend Augusta Holmes, who just lived across town! Letters were an important part of courtships, too, allowing couples to get to know each other.

"In this way we got acquainted," Mary said about her correspondence with Wash. "For in writing to him I became very fond of him."

Mary would remain a prolific letter-writer throughout her lifetime, and fortunately for historians many of those letters have been saved. Reading them offers a window into her daily life and her relationships with family and friends.

the hot, humid summer months convinced Mary's father that the climate was unhealthy, and he didn't want his delicate daughter living so far away from home.

Early in 1843, Wash's letters stopped coming. Mary didn't know what to make of it. Had she written something to offend him? Had his feelings toward her changed? The two might have lost all contact if her brother hadn't stepped in to help.

Sullivan liked Wash Glover. He was convinced that his friend was still writing to Mary, but that their father was intercepting the mail. He explained his suspicions to his dejected sister and proposed a plan. He was going on a business trip to the White Mountains in New Hampshire. Would she like to come along? Sullivan promised to let Wash know in advance where they were going and where they would be staying, so that he could write to her there.

At the first stop, Mary wrote in a journal she kept of the trip: "The lonely night-wind sighs a dull requiem to my spirits the rain is pelting the windows and I am thinking of home and thee."

Could "thee" have been Wash? Most likely. Her entry for the next night was equally dreary. Then suddenly the young woman was in "much better health and spirits." Perhaps a letter or two from Wash had finally come through! Her brightened outlook continued, for after jouncing along in a stagecoach the following day on a solo trip to Haverhill to visit her newlywed friend Augusta, a giddy Mary wrote to Sullivan "... such a sky rocket adventure I never had," adding that she felt "at least midway between heaven and earth."

She also told him that she and Augusta had stayed up all night talking. No doubt handsome Wash Glover was one of the topics of discussion between the two fast friends.

Meanwhile, Wash had been corresponding with Sullivan as well.

"I beleve [sic] among 7 Builders I am Duing [sic] one half the Buiseness [sic] in the Citty [sic]," he boasted in one of his letters. "Last Saturday Bills to my workmen was $1267.00 [nearly $40,000 in 2013 dollars]."

Working in both Charleston and Wilmington, North Carolina, Wash and a new partner also had plans to build a cathedral in Haiti. But first, Wash wanted to marry the youngest and loveliest Baker daughter, for whom he had waited 12 long years.

It was slowly dawning on Mary's parents that she was going to marry

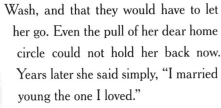

COURTESY OF
LONGYEAR MUSEUM
CHESTNUT HILL, MASSACHUSETTS

◀ George Washington Glover

Wash, and that they would have to let her go. Even the pull of her dear home circle could not hold her back now. Years later she said simply, "I married young the one I loved."

The wedding was held at the Baker home in Sanbornton Bridge on Sunday, December 10, 1843. Family and friends came by sleigh from near and far for the festivities. The day was "some cloudy" as a local diary recorded, words that might have summed up 22-year-old Mary's mood, too, for her excitement must have been mixed with sadness at the thought of leaving home. After the wedding, the newlyweds traveled over the snowy roads to Concord, stopping there to visit Wash's elderly parents. Mary and Wash made a farewell trip to the old Baker homestead in Bow, then took the newly established train to Boston, where they saw Mary's brother Samuel and his wife Eliza, Wash's sister. Finally, the young couple traveled to New York, and on Christmas Day they set sail for Charleston.

Mary was as eager to take up her new life in the South as Wash's friends were to welcome her. Wash had joined the Freemasons, an old, well-established fraternal organization that strove to follow the teachings of the Bible through charitable works and upright business practices. He was well-known and well-liked by this network of friends, and his pretty northern bride was immediately admired and accepted.

The Glovers didn't linger long in Charleston, but headed north later that winter to Wilmington, where Wash had business. The newlyweds moved into a hotel, and Mary was soon caught up in a social whirl. She went horseback riding and attended parties and took a boat trip up the Cape Fear River to Fayetteville with her new friend Mrs. Cook. A teenage girl who was present at a dinner held there for Mary recalled her as "brilliant in conversation and most gracious in her manner."

PEOPLE AND PLACES

THE OLD MAN OF THE MOUNTAIN

The Old Man of the Mountain was a striking natural rock formation in the White Mountains of New Hampshire. Before its collapse in 2003, the Franconia Notch marvel was a popular tourist attraction and proud symbol of the Granite State, featured on postage stamps and coins.

Mary wasn't the only writer to find inspiration in its features. Nathaniel Hawthorne would describe the formation as "a work of Nature in her mood of majestic playfulness" in his 1850 short story "The Great Stone Face," and famous statesman Daniel Webster once wrote: "Men hang out their signs indicative of their respective trades; shoe makers hang out a gigantic shoe; jewelers a monster watch, and the dentist hangs out a gold tooth; but up in the Mountains of New Hampshire, God Almighty has hung out a sign to show that there He makes men."

Mary worshiped at St. James Episcopal Church with her new husband, and continued her practice of writing for local newspapers.

"She had no sooner come to Wilmington than she began contributing rhymes to the local paper," recalled the daughter of one of Wash's Masonic Lodge brothers, who attended the same church as the Glovers and remembered Mary as one of the prettiest young women she'd ever seen. "Her enthusiasm about the local scenery amused us."

Mary's strong interest in politics and skill with a pen soon became known, and she was asked by Michael Hoke, the candidate for governor, to write the toasts for one of the Democratic dinners.

The Glovers went to the theater as well, and Mary wrote a glowing review of the play *The Death of Rolla* for a Wilmington paper. Once, when her thoughts turned homeward, she sent "The Old Man of the Mountain" to a new Charleston magazine called *The Floral Wreath*. She had written the poem on her trip to northern New England with her brother Sullivan the year before.

Excerpt from *The Old Man of the Mountain*

Gigantic sire, with proud unfallen crest;
Primeval dweller on yon hoary cliff;
Beyond the ken of mortal, o'er to tell
What power sustains thee in thy rock-bound cell.

Or if, when erst creation vast began,
And loud the universal fiat rang

"Let there be light" — from chaos dark set free,
Ye rose a monument of Deity!

As she often did, Mary would later revise this poem for an anthology.

Letters from home brought news of a new niece, her sister Martha's "little fat beautiful Daughter" Ellen, and showed Mary she was not forgotten.

"Dear Child:" her mother wrote, "Are you happy as anticipated[?] ... We miss your good cheer. I look out at the window and say how I wish I could see George and Mary coming over the hill.... Mary, everything reminds me of you..."

Happy? Yes, Mary could reply, for in many ways she was. In addition to a new husband, she had new friends, new activities, and a new corner of the world to explore, where gardens bloomed even in winter. And Mary had an additional reason to be joyful, too, for she was expecting a baby.

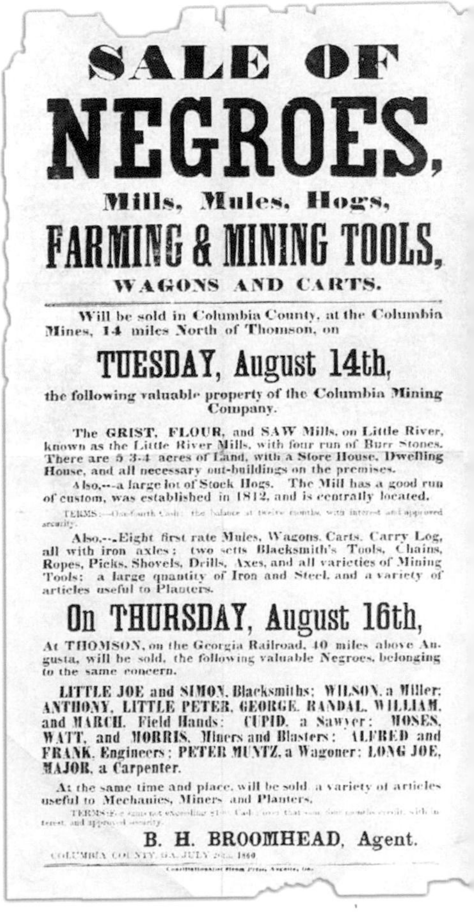

Advertisement for a slave auction

Yet there was something that troubled her about her new home — slavery. From early childhood, tender-hearted Mary had championed victims of injustice, and she would later speak of her opposition to slavery. The house that Wash had built on Hasell Street in Charleston may have had slave quarters in the rear, and slave auctions were held regularly in both Charleston and Wilmington, just blocks from where the Glovers lived. This must have shocked Mary, as would the local newspapers, which carried ads such as "Negros and Furniture for Sale."

"My father was a strong believer in States' rights," Mary would eventually write, "but slavery he regarded as a great sin."

So did she. Two decades later, Mary composed a poem entitled "The Liberty Bells," to celebrate the day that Massachusetts ratified the 13th Amendment to the Constitution.

"To-day," she added in a note to the editor of the *Lynn Reporter* accompanying her submission, "by order of Governor Andrew, the bells are ringing to celebrate the passing of a resolution in Congress prohibiting slavery in the United States." Her poem reads in part:

Righteousness ne'er—awestruck or dumb—
Feared for an hour the tyrant's heel!
Injustice to the combat sprang;
God to the rescue—Liberty, peal!

Joy is in every belfry bell—
Joy for the captive! Sound it long!
Ye who have wept fourscore can tell
The holy meaning of their song.

Meanwhile, though, back in the Carolinas, Wash and Mary were preparing to travel to Haiti, where Wash had apparently received a contract to build or supply the lumber for a proposed cathedral. Mary again picked up her pen, and the result was "The Emigrant's Farewell," a poem that envisions her as "a rover on the sea," heading "o'er the white foam dashing high/ home fading from my sight," as she thought back to her family circle in New England and wondered if she'd ever see them all again.

It wouldn't be published for some time, however, because Mary and Wash never made the voyage. Instead, in June of 1844, disaster struck. Wash had put nearly all his money into the necessary building supplies, and while these materials lay unprotected (and uninsured) on the dock, they were lost—either burned or stolen.

The Glovers were facing financial ruin. Worse, Wash fell ill with yellow fever. Mary prayed desperately for her husband to get better, but after 12 long days he passed away. With his parting breath, Wash begged his brother Masons to transport his beloved wife to her relatives. Mary was carrying his child, and he wanted her safely back home with her family. They had been married for only six months.

As always, Mary poured her heart out in verse, and this sad couplet from a poem she wrote that year reflects her grief:

"Dead is he who loved me dearly:
Am I not alone in soul?"

After the funeral—which was attended by the Governor of North Carolina and his staff, a testament to the regard in which Wash was held—Mary stayed shut up in her room, eating very little and turning away all visitors. Finally, a kindly Freemason insisted on seeing her. He found the young widow tear-stained and distraught, and asked, "What would your husband say to you if he came now and looked at you? What would he say to you for this action, and yielding to your agony of grief?"

His words roused Mary, and she thanked him. She spent the next few weeks settling her husband's affairs, and Wash's good friends did everything they could to help. They even bought mourning clothes for her and, true to their word, saw her safely home. A Mason by the name of Cook, whose wife had taken Mary to Fayetteville, traveled with her as far as New York, where Sullivan was waiting. Even though New Hampshire was still several hundred miles further north, just seeing her brother must have brought Mary the comfort of home. The steamy four-day, 1400-mile inland journey, which required changing back and forth from train to steamboat to horse-drawn carriages numerous times in the oppressive summer heat, had made the pregnant young widow weak and ill.

Mary's family opened their arms wide and welcomed her back in. When her baby boy was born that September, though, she was still too feeble to care for him. Mr. Baker sat for long hours by her bedside, and the family feared she might not live.

George Washington Glover II, on the other hand, grew sturdy and full of energy like his father. Mahala Sanborn, a longtime friend and helper in the Baker home, had looked after Mary many times when she had been ill, and was fond of this loud little baby. She seemed a godsend to Mary and her beleaguered family, and Georgy spent a great deal of time at her house.

In the meantime, Mary worried about what she could do to support herself and her little son. She had no money of her own. As the months passed and she grew stronger, the young Mrs. Glover decided to try a new venture.

4
Two Goodbyes

We will go to Mrs. Glover
And tell her we love her.

Mary Glover couldn't have helped smiling as the children marched around the room singing their version of a popular song. She had opened a school. Encouraged by a minister friend, Reverend Rust, she had started a kindergarten, one of the first of its kind in New England. Her sister Abi and her husband had a small building on their property in Sanbornton Bridge that had once been a shoemaker's shop. They had it painted red and fitted with little chairs and desks. Forty children flocked to the new one-room schoolhouse with its plaster walls and central brick chimney.

COURTESY TMBEL

Mary Glover as a young widow

Sarah Clement, who lived in the house opposite, remembered running over to see her teacher as often as she could. Mary liked to work in her flower garden in the evenings, and the little girl would climb the gate and talk to her. To Sarah, Mrs. Glover, "tall, slender, exceedingly graceful, was altogether one of the most beautiful women I have ever seen." Sarah's mother and Mary were friends. "I often used to hear her talking to my mother and laughing. Her laugh was very sweet."

Mary was equally fond of Sarah, but one day when the girl misbehaved at school, she had to lay down the law. "Mrs. Glover said she would have to whip me so to go out and choose a stick," Sarah later recalled. "I went out in fear and trembling and brought in a little twig, the smallest I could find."

The contrite look on Sarah's face, along with the ridiculous twig she handed over, made Mary smile. The punishment was forgotten, and she sent the girl back to her seat.

Although the children liked her school, Mary was unable to keep it going for long. There were a number of reasons, including the fact that she wasn't strong enough. Plus, teaching didn't provide her with enough of a salary. There was also Georgy to look after, as well as her sister's son, Albert, when Abi fell ill at one point. Mary and her mother watched over the two boys as they romped and played in the Baker home.

"I feel as if I must begin something this summer, if my health is sufficient," Mary fretted to her sister Martha in 1848. Still longing to be independent, she turned again to writing, producing a steady stream of poetry and prose. A stanza from "The Bible," one of her poems that was published during these years, shows that she was still "inseparable" from the Scriptures, to which she habitually turned for comfort and guidance:

Oracle of God-like wonder,
Frame-work of His mighty plan,
Chart and compass for the wanderer,
Safe obeying thy command.

Mary wrote lighter fare as well, including short stories ("Emma Clinton, or a Tale of the Frontier" and "The Test of Love"). Her efforts didn't bring in a dependable income, however.

"Tis like looking down through the transparent waters of the sea of life, checkered with sunshine and shade," Mary wrote forlornly to a friend.

There were occasional sunny patches, to be sure, including a "spree" in the winter of 1848 that sounds like a modern-day girls' night out. "There has been some sleigh riding," Mary reported to Martha, "I and Miss Lane the Sem. Teacher and Miss Rand invited our Driver and took a ride to Concord! after driving, returned to Loudon; supped, then came home, had a real spree with ourselves no Gents. Made the driver (Sleeper) foot the bill and laugh at the joke."

COURTESY OF THE LIBRARY OF CONGRESS, PRINTS AND PHOTOGRAPHS DIVISION

▲ Lombard Farm Poorhouse in Barnstable, Massachusetts. After the Social Security Act took effect in 1935, institutions such as this one faded from use, disappearing altogether by about 1950.

(The "Sleeper" Mary referred to here was William Sleeper, principal of the Woodman Sanbornton Academy and clearly a good sport.)

Another ray of light in Mary's life was her renewed friendship with John Bartlett. John was fond of Georgy, and even fonder of Mary, who traveled to Cambridge, Massachusetts, in the summer of 1848 to see him graduate from Harvard Law School. The two became engaged, and the future looked bright. But first, before they married, John wanted to go West to seek their fortune. Gold had recently been discovered in California.

SIGNS OF THE TIMES

POORHOUSE BLUES

Immortalized by Charles Dickens in *Oliver Twist*, poorhouses (or workhouses, as they were known in Great Britain) were a stark reality for much of the 19th century. At that time there was no federal safety net for the poor in the United States—no social security to provide for widows like Mary with small children, no welfare system, no daycare centers or homeless shelters. Impoverished people had to rely on the generosity of friends and relatives or face the prospect of being sent to live in poorhouses or on poor farms, where paupers were kept at county expense.

Whether he meant it or not, Mark Baker's threat must have alarmed Mary, for she would have had no choice in the matter. Just like other women in the first half of the 19th century, Mary had few rights. Considered the weaker sex and therefore in need of male protection, women were by custom and law subservient to the men in their lives—their husbands, fathers, and other male relatives.

Legally, a married woman couldn't own property, and any that she did bring to a marriage became the property of her husband. She wasn't allowed to sign a contract or make a will, nor could she control any wages she might earn. Divorce and child custody laws favored men, too. This began to change with the passage of equity laws regarding women's rights—first in Mississippi, with the Married Women's Property Act of 1839. Other states would eventually follow its lead, and by 1857 the Married Women's Property Bill passed in the U.S. Congress.

Divorce often doomed a woman to poverty, however, as almost no colleges or universities accepted female students, and employment opportunities were few. Professions such as medicine and law were closed to women, and those not fortunate enough to find work as a teacher or domestic servant would most likely be dependent on the kindness of relatives. A few, like Mary, might eke out a precarious living with their pen. It wasn't until after the Civil War, when

Meanwhile, Mary's parents purchased a lot in town near Abi, and planned to build a new house on it. Early in November 1849, Sullivan came home and married his long-time sweetheart, Martha (nicknamed Mathy) Rand. The joy of the wedding festivities had barely faded when Mary had to write to her brother a few weeks later with the sad news that their mother had died. "This morning looks on us bereft of a Mother! Yes, that angel on earth is now in Heaven! ... what is left of earth to me! But oh, my Mother! ... I cannot write more. My grief overpowers me."

There was more to come. In December, Mary received word that her fiancé had died in Sacramento. It was a bitter blow.

The move to her father's new house later that winter brought additional woes. After more than 40 years of marriage, Mark Baker felt lonely and sad. His new surroundings must have seemed cold and empty without the cheery

industrialization expanded rapidly in the United States, that factories opened their doors to women, and even then female workers earned a fraction of what their male counterparts did.

Mary would later write, "Our laws are not impartial, to say the least, in their discrimination as to the person, property, and parental claims of the two sexes." And, "If a dissolute husband deserts his wife, certainly the wronged, and perchance impoverished, woman should be allowed to collect her own wages, enter into business agreements, hold real estate, deposit funds, and own her children free from interference."

Though many of these restrictions were loosened and lifted during Mary's lifetime—and she herself would break many of the barriers—it wasn't until the 19th Amendment to the Constitution was passed in 1920, granting women the right to vote, that more rapid progress toward full equality was made.

ILLUSTRATION BY GEORGE CRUIKSHANK CA. 1837

▲ Frontispiece to first edition (1838) of *Oliver Twist*

presence of his wife, and his rambunctious young grandson was proving to be a handful. At one particularly low point, Mr. Baker threatened to send Georgy to the poorhouse if Mary wouldn't send him away herself.

Mary had nowhere to go. The following year, in 1850, when her father decided to remarry, she knew both she and her son had to leave. Abi offered to have Mary come and live in her house, but not Georgy—he was too rough-and-tumble. Redheaded Georgy was tall for his age, and he liked the outdoors. Albert was slight and delicate. Abi worried that his bigger cousin would overpower him.

What should be done with Georgy, now a sturdy six-year-old? Again the family thought of Mahala Sanborn, who had married Russell Cheney by now and was living some 40 miles away in North Groton. Mahala had no children of her own and had always loved Mary's son. She was delighted at the thought of having Georgy come and live with them. Both Abi and Mr. Baker thought this an excellent solution, but Mary dreaded the separation. What else could she do, she wondered?

She sent the boy on a short visit to Wash's brother Andrew and his wife, who lived in nearby Concord, and explained the plan to send their nephew away to the Cheneys.

"Oh! How I miss him already! There seems nothing left me now to enjoy," she told them in a letter. "I want very much to know how you have succeeded with him and if he has been a good boy (some naughty things of course) ... is he not a pretty good and very dear boy?... Will dear little Sully [the Glovers' son] be sorry to have him leave?"

Was she dropping a hint to her in-laws, hoping they'd ask Georgy to live with them instead?

They didn't. Nothing, it seemed, could prevent the boy's move to North Groton.

The night before Georgy was to leave, Mary knelt by his side all the dark hours, praying for a last-minute reprieve. None came. By morning, she knew she had no other choice. Georgy would have to go.

As was her habit, Mary poured her heart out on paper. "Written on the 9th day of May [1851] on parting with my babe," she wrote in a notebook, beside a poem that began:

Go, little voyager, o'er life's rough sea—
    Born in a tempest! Choose thy pilot God.
The Bible, let thy chart forever be—
    Anchor and helm its promises afford…

As she packed his small belongings and said goodbye to her son, Mary felt as if her heart would break.

5

Another Marriage

Mary lived with her sister Abi for two long years. Losing Georgy made her feel worse, not better, as her father and Abi had hoped. Often ill and bedridden, Mary had plenty of time to think about her son. How she missed him and wanted him back!

When her father remarried, a distant relative of his new wife came to live in Franklin, a town three miles away. Dr. Daniel Patterson was a dentist, an outgoing man who had an eye for the ladies. He rode his horse from town to town in his black silk top hat and kid gloves, doing whatever dental work was needed by the people there.

COURTESY TMBEL

Mary was one of his patients. As their friendship grew, she wrote him little notes and even made up a funny poem about a toothache. At first, Daniel tried writing flowery letters back, but he knew he couldn't keep it up for long. He was a plainspoken man. Better that Mary should know him as he really was, especially as he was beginning to hope she would marry him.

The prospect of marriage opened up a new world for Mary. To once again have a devoted husband, a home of her own, and a place for Georgy! But Mark Baker did not consider Daniel to be the right man for his daughter. In his view Daniel went to the wrong church—

◀ Dapper dentist Daniel Patterson

Baptist, not Congregational—and then there were rumors, "dark things," about his character.

Mary was filled with misgivings. She felt she couldn't switch churches, and the objections to Daniel's morals were troubling. She decided to break off the relationship.

"I beg you to remember that we will be friends.... Farewell, May God bless you and protect you," she wrote.

Daniel wanted to prove that he was worthy of her, but in the end simply replied, "It seems that I have lost you at last...."

All was not as lost as he thought, however. As a dentist, Dr. Patterson still worked on Mrs. Glover's teeth, and that gave him a chance to work on her heart. He knew she longed to be reunited with Georgy, and promised to provide a home for the boy, if only she would agree to marry him. Mary's doubts were swept away.

The two were married in June 1853. Mary would turn 32 the following month; Daniel was 34. On her

PHOTO
W. G. C. KIMBALL
COURTESY TMBEL

▲ Mary's sister Martha Baker Pilsbury helped the Pattersons purchase a home in North Groton, New Hampshire.

▼ Mary and Daniel's home in North Groton, New Hampshire

COURTESY OF CLIFF LEEKER

wedding day, Mary signed a paper before the ceremony naming her future husband as Georgy's guardian. Daniel and Mark Baker both signed a guardianship bond the same day, but in order to make the bond legal, Daniel had to appear in court.

He never went.

Daniel wanted to please his wife, but he didn't always carry through on his promises, including his promise to provide a home for Georgy. More than a year passed, and still Mary hadn't regained her son. Finally, in March of 1855 she persuaded her husband to move to North Groton, where Georgy lived with the Cheneys. Her sister Martha — now a widow herself with two daughters to support — dipped into her meager resources and loaned Mary and Daniel money for a house.

North Groton, in the foothills of the White Mountains, was a remote but bustling community of about a thousand people. Agriculture and a mica mine were the backbone of the local economy. The town had a white church and an overcrowded one-room school. Mary and Daniel found a small cottage built on a high rock-and-granite foundation that had once been the site of a gristmill. A rushing stream flowed swiftly past, right under the kitchen window.

It wasn't exactly peaceful, however. A sawmill in which Daniel purchased part-ownership lay a stone's throw from their front door. The constant screech and whine of sawblades, coupled with the shouts of workers, must have been unsettling to Mary, who was still so often ill. Concerned for her comfort, Daniel would have a thick layer of sawdust strewn across the nearby bridge at times to muffle the clop and rattle of horses' hooves and wagon wheels.

Here in this new home, Mary looked forward to reuniting with her tall, active, nearly-eleven-year-old son. He, in turn, wanted to be with his mother. Mahala had taken him from time to time to visit Mary since they'd moved away, and he vividly remembered the cookies and cakes she always had waiting for him, and the time he'd spent sitting on her knee, listening to Bible stories and memorizing verses. Now here she was, living only a mile away.

Mary hoped to teach Georgy to read stories on his own, but he balked at the lessons. He disliked the village school and didn't fit in with the other children, who found him too rough and teased him because of his red hair. He preferred hanging around the blacksmith's shop, or fishing, or hunting for rocks. In addition to mica, of course (which among other things was formed into isinglass for use in stoves and lanterns), North Groton had many gemstones—amethysts, aquamarines, garnets, rose quartz, and crystals. Georgy kept his rock collection hidden in the Cheney's barn.

COURTESY OF LONGYEAR MUSEUM CHESTNUT HILL, MASSACHUSETTS

Abigail Baker Tilton came to North Groton in 1856 to check on Mary and Georgy, and very likely helped finance the Cheneys' move to Minnesota.

Daniel and Mary argued about the boy. Daniel felt his wife's efforts were wasted on her son, and that his visits only left her tired and weak. She, in turn, grieved and worried that Georgy wasn't getting the education he needed, for Russell Cheney, Mahala's husband, made him work on the farm. Hadn't she left her family and circle of friends to be with Georgy? She must be allowed to see him and teach him! In spite of her pleas, Daniel insisted it was best for her that the boy stay away.

One day Mahala and Georgy slipped in to see Mary while Daniel was gone. As they were leaving, he unexpectedly returned. Furious to find his stepson in the yard, he went after the boy with a stout stick. Georgy ran around the house, picked up a stone, and threw it hard. It glanced off Daniel's shoulder, shattering a window.

The break that followed was much harder to fix than a windowpane.

Abi had her hands full at home, but in early 1856 she made the 40-mile trip north in her carriage to see what was going on with Georgy. Mary was delighted to see her, and didn't suspect the real purpose behind her visit. It's very likely that Abi and Daniel cooked up a scheme, and may have spoken to Mahala and

Russell about the Cheneys' hopes to go out west to Minnesota. Russell's brother and several other New Hampshire families were already successfully farming there, but lack of money had prevented the Cheneys from joining them. Now, after Abi's visit, they suddenly found the means to go, taking Georgy with them.

The first that Mary heard of this was when her son came to say goodbye. He started to cry—he didn't want to leave his mother, and Mr. Cheney had made him throw away his whole rock collection. Mary was overcome by this news of another separation. She and Georgy were being forced apart again. She felt as if the family was plotting against her.

The Cheneys returned to Sanbornton Bridge to say farewell to relatives and friends (including Georgy's grandfather, Mark Baker), then made the long, six-day journey by train to the Mississippi River, where they took the riverboat to Winona County, Minnesota. Georgy, still rebellious and unhappy about leaving his mother, insisted he was going to try and find her. Later, Mary would learn that in order to keep him quiet, Russell Cheney told Georgy it was no use—his mother was dead. Mary, in the meantime, was told that her son had gone missing.

"Every means within my power was employed to find him, but without success," Mary later recalled. A storm of sorrow engulfed her. She lapsed further into illness, and could barely sit up. To add to her distress, Daniel told her that he had to travel again to find work to support them. Mary was left in the care of Myra Smith, a young blind woman from town.

Myra was devoted to Mary. On pleasant days, she'd wrap blankets carefully around her and pull Mary in her rocking chair onto the piazza, a small wooden porch on the side of the house. Here, Mary would sit as long as she could. From the piazza she became friendly with Daniel Kidder, her closest neighbor. Kidder was 18 when Mary and her husband moved in. He was impressed by this "fine looking woman," calling her "intellectual and stately in appearance." He noted that she kept her house "in the most perfect order," and he was intrigued that she was a published writer whose poetry appeared in newspapers and magazines. Mary, unable to help her own son to read, "took a great interest in the education of the young then living near her," Kidder later wrote. "She was a great help to me in my studies at that time. I remember her as a sincere friend."

Myra Smith's sister, Marcia, who was 10 in 1859, was also a frequent visitor. She recalled that Mrs. Patterson was ill nearly all the time, lying in bed with a book for her constant companion. "I remember well her beautiful eyes, her soft voice and how she would put down her book and lay her white hand on my head. She did it to comfort me, for I had lately lost a good father...."

Once, Mary couldn't help exclaiming, "Oh, you dear little girl. You are worth your weight in gold. I wish you were mine!"

The children in the neighborhood were fascinated by the "poor sick lady," as they called Mary, and loved to bring her berries and flowers. But the adults were more skeptical. It was hard work wresting a living out of the rocky New England soil, and it wasn't easy for them to understand or sympathize with a bedridden woman.

Though they may not have known it, Mary was busy, too. She read her Bible almost constantly, and during a particularly severe bout of illness around this time she made a solemn promise to God: If He would restore her to health, Mary vowed she would devote the rest of her life to helping sick and suffering humanity.

6
Prison Breaks

Desperately seeking a way to cure herself and others, Mary delved into homeopathy, a popular system of treatment in the 19th century. She learned about it from Dr. Alpheus Morrill, a homeopathic physician who was her cousin by marriage and a graduate of Dartmouth Medical School. Mary studied *Jahr's New Manual of Homeopathic Practice* as she investigated the system thoroughly, exploring its theory that "like cures like," or as she would later explain it, "that symptoms, which might be produced by a certain drug, are removed by using the same drug which might cause the symptoms."

Homeopathic remedies, she learned, were created through attenuation, or repeated dilution of a drug. The more diluted the drug, the more powerful it was seen to be. Mary's medical experiments led her to an unexpected conclusion at one point, when she treated a neighbor who was severely ill.

The woman had been under the care of a homeopath who gave her up as incurable. As Mary later recalled, "I prescribed the fourth attenuation of *Argentum nitratum* [silver nitrate] with occasional doses of a high attenuation of *Sulphuris* [sulfur]. She improved perceptibly."

When Mary discovered that the woman's physician had prescribed the identical remedy, however, she began to worry that its prolonged use would aggravate the symptoms. She told her patient this, but the woman refused to abandon the treatment. "It then occurred to me to give her unmedicated pellets and watch the result," Mary noted. To her surprise, the woman began to feel better. "She went on in this way, taking the unmedicated pellets,—and receiving occasional visits from me,—but employing no other means, and she was cured."

From the way her neighbor responded, Mary began to glimpse that perhaps there was something beyond homeopathy, "a mental standpoint not understood," as she later put it, but that brought "phenomenally good results." It wasn't the drug, but the woman's *faith* in the drug that brought about a cure.

The experience "was a falling apple to me," Mary later wrote, referring to the apple that Sir Isaac Newton saw fall from a tree, leading him to discover the law of gravity. "It made plain to me that mind governed the whole question of her recovery." She would eventually call this important step "my first discovery of the Science of Mind." Mary didn't know it at the time, but the soil of her thought was being prepared for the seed of a major breakthrough.

In the meantime, though, she was unable to help herself, and eventually, Dr. Patterson had to stay home and nurse his "Very Dear Wife." With no work and no income, the Pattersons could no longer repay Mary's sister Martha the money they owed on the house. Tensions between the family members rose. In September of 1859, with the country suffering an economic depression, Mary's sister Martha was forced to foreclose. Mary had to auction off some of her possessions—gold jewelry, her large dictionary, and pieces of furniture that had come from her mother—to cover their debts.

The Pattersons were allowed to remain in the house for another six months, but Daniel continued to have money problems. At one point, he bargained for a load of wood from a neighbor, Joseph Wheet. Weeks passed and Daniel still hadn't paid for it. One day, as he was in the yard splitting the wood, Wheet and his son Charles happened to drive by. Joseph stopped his wagon, walked over to Daniel, and asked for his money. Mary heard angry voices, then the sound of blows. Horrified, she watched the two men grapple as Charles stood by, axe in hand, ready to strike at her husband. Conscious only of the need to save Daniel, Mary sprang up, ran out, and seized the axe from the boy. Under the headline "Female Bravery," the *Nashua Gazette* published a dramatic account of the story in its March 15, 1860 issue, ending with: "Help soon came, the assailants fled, and the feeble but brave wife was carried back to her bed."

When the Pattersons finally left North Groton, it was a terrible day for Mary. Daniel was away, leaving her to face the humiliation alone, for as she left the village the Wheets tolled the church bell in spiteful triumph. Abi had

SIGNS OF THE TIMES

ONE BIG HAPPY FAMILY

In the 19th century, many families supplemented their income by taking in lodgers, who received a room of their own plus meals in exchange for a fee. A convenient arrangement for all involved, it provided a steady source of income for the homeowners (often widows) and a reasonable lifestyle for those with limited incomes. Boardinghouses were larger operations along the same lines, and lodgers usually had access to shared living rooms and parlors. Meals would be taken together, family-style. The downside, as Mary soon found out, was that living in close quarters meant little privacy, which could fuel gossip and criticism.

come to accompany her, but even her presence was cold comfort.

"It was spring and the roads were very bad—in spots deep snow—other places mud," recalled Myra.

Mary's faithful companion trudged behind the carriage for six long miles down the steep mountain road to Rumney, their destination. Abi walked partway with her, both of them unable to bear the sound of Mary's anguish.

In Rumney, Mary was installed at the depot boardinghouse, most likely at Abi's expense. Her sister had to leave to return to her family, but Myra stayed on to help. Daniel eventually rejoined Mary and started up his dental practice again. He found a house to rent for the two of them, away from the gossip and curiosity of the other boarders.

▼ Mary and Daniel's home in Rumney, New Hampshire

COURTESY OF LONGYEAR MUSEUM CHESTNUT HILL, MASSACHUSETTS

The new house lifted Mary's spirits. Situated on a hillside on the outskirts of town, it had a pretty view of Stinson Mountain. Mary's writing, which had languished in North Groton, began to blossom again. A poem she wrote in her notebook during this time reflects a more upbeat frame of mind:

Excerpt from *Ode to Adversity*

Am I to conflicts new to be innured [sic]?
No! I have long the utmost wrongs indured [sic]
And drawn fresh energies from sharpest blows
Thus from rude hammer strokes or burning heat
With each successive change refined complete
The gold is purged of dross and brightly glows.

Mary had endured more than her fair share of "rude hammer strokes" and "burning heat" in the recent and not-so-recent past, but it's clear from her words that she was resolved to "draw fresh energies" from the experiences as she went forward.

It was here in Rumney that Mary accomplished a significant early healing. She'd grown disenchanted with homeopathy, telling Myra "not to mind as they were no good anyway" when the girl accidentally broke a bottle of pellets while making the bed one day. It was around this time that a young mother brought her baby to Mary. The little one's eyes were inflamed to the point that "neither pupil nor iris" were discernible.

"I gave the infant no drugs," Mary later wrote, "held her in my arms a few moments while lifting my thoughts to God, then returned the babe to her mother healed."

The grateful woman embroidered a petticoat for Mary as a thank you, and named her little daughter after her.

This healing was one more step in a journey that Mary would later describe as a twenty-year effort "to trace all physical effects to a mental cause," and it must have given her much food for thought.

Her attention was also riveted by events unfolding on the national scene. Though Rumney was no bigger than North Groton, because it had a train station there were more connections to the outside world. News of the growing divide between North and South reached Mary through the papers, along with rumblings of a coming war. She read of the secession of South Carolina and the upheavals in Charleston, where she had lived with Wash as a young bride. In December of 1860, she read of Major Anderson's secret withdrawal with a small command of Union troops to Fort Sumter, in the middle of Charleston's harbor. She held her breath along with the rest of the country as the siege dragged on through the early months of 1861, and Anderson bravely withheld from firing on the Southerners in hopes of preventing a civil war.

Stirred by this news, Mary wrote a long poem, "Major Anderson and Our Country," which was published in *The Independent Democrat* of Concord on February 14, 1861. One verse reads:

> Yet would I yield a husband, child, to fight,
> Or die the unyielding guardians of right,
> Than that the life blood circling through their veins,
> Should warm a heart to forge new human chains.

Little did Mary know that both her husband and her child would soon be involved in the war, and because of this she would finally have news of Georgy.

In the end, Major Anderson and his troops were forced to fire back on the Confederate forces in self-defense. Fort Sumter's capture on April 13th was a triumphant first victory for the South, but for the North a sad surrender. At the time it occurred, the governor of Minnesota happened to be in Washington. He immediately went to see President Lincoln and was the first state governor to offer assistance. Back in Minnesota, patriotic fervor ran high. Rallies were held. Flags flew off the store shelves, quickly selling out. Young men rushed to enlist in the army.

Georgy Glover, two days shy of seventeen, was one of them. The Minnesota quota of men was already filled by the time he applied, so he crossed the Mississippi River to Wisconsin, whose Eighth Regiment was just being organized. Initially turned down because he was underage, he got into a scuffle outside the recruiting office with a pair of older boys who were teasing him.

"If you're old enough to take those two big fellows like that, you're old enough to go into the army," observed one of the recruiters, and Georgy's pluck earned him a spot in the ranks.

Along with his fellow recruits in Wisconsin's "Eagle Regiment," Georgy marched 179 miles from La Crosse to Camp Randall in Madison. In his inside coat pocket, the new infantryman placed the Bible his mother had inscribed to him years earlier. Although he couldn't read, he remembered the Bible verses she had helped him memorize, and they gave him strength and comfort. Carefully tucked between the book's pages was Mary's picture. Georgy would lose other equipment during the battles to come, but these cherished possessions remained with him the entire time he was in uniform.

COURTESY OF LONGYEAR MUSEUM CHESTNUT HILL, MASSACHUSETTS

Georgy Glover at the time of his first enlistment in 1861

Perhaps because he was going to war, Georgy may have finally been told that his mother wasn't dead, but living in New England. What is clear is that when he joined his regiment, a young man named David Hall enlisted at the same time. David wrote letters home for illiterate soldiers like Georgy who couldn't write themselves, and it was he who inquired of Mary's whereabouts, and then wrote Georgy's first letter to her for him. Mary cried tears of joy when she received it in October of 1861. Her son wasn't lost—he was alive! Although the two wouldn't see each other for another eighteen years, mother and son could now keep in touch through letters.

COURTESY TMBEL

One of Georgy's sons would later identify this tintype of Mary as most like the one his father carried with him as a young soldier.

Gladdened as she was at this news from Georgy, it must have been bittersweet, too. So many years spent apart! And now here he was, a soldier, facing danger at every turn. Two months after receiving her son's letter, Mary wrote a poem called "The Heart's Unrest." The first stanza reads:

O give me wings and the flight of a dove
Unfasten these fetters of clay
And sing me the song of a seraph's love
While the spirit is passing away
I gaze on the beautiful orbs of night
Hung out on the boundless blue
And long to inhabit a world more bright
And say to this false one Adieu

Mary's restless longing for "a world more bright"—one unshadowed by illness and separation and loss—would be a theme she'd return to again and again in future years.

Meanwhile, though, there was a war on, and Daniel was about to get involved in it. Money had been collected in New Hampshire for Southerners who supported the North. The Governor commissioned Mary's husband to take the funds down to Washington in March of 1862. When Daniel arrived, he went sightseeing with some companions at Bull Run, where the famous battle had been fought the previous summer. Pockets of Confederate soldiers

▼ Bull Run (also known as Manassas) battlefield, then and now.

COURTESY OF THE LIBRARY OF CONGRESS, PRINTS AND PHOTOGRAPHS DIVISION

PHOTO: CAROL HIGHSMITH, COURTESY OF THE LIBRARY OF CONGRESS, PRINTS AND PHOTOGRAPHS DIVISION

still lingered in the area, and Daniel ran into a band of them. They promptly captured him and confiscated the funds.

"You will be amazed to learn that I am in prison," Daniel wrote to his wife on April 2, 1862. "I was taken one week ago to-day." His letter ended with, "My anxiety for you is intense but be of as good cheer as possible and trust in God."

Mary's concern for her husband, who was locked up in the Confederacy's infamous Libby Prison in Richmond, Virginia (he was later transferred to Salisbury, North Carolina), was equally great. Hoping to secure his release through an exchange of prisoners, she wrote letters to everyone she could think of, including her brother Albert's friend and former employer, ex-President Franklin Pierce, but with no success.

Mary spent several weeks with Daniel's family in Maine during this period, and she also published a poem ("To a Bird Flying Southward") in *The Independent Democrat* that mirrors her anxiety over her absent husband, yet ends, as her poetry so often did, on an uplifted note—that of a heart trusting in God. It reads in part:

Oh! to the *captive's* cell I'd sing
A song of hope—and *freedom* bring—
An olive leaf I'd quick let fall,
And lift our country's blackened pall;
Then homeward seek my frigid zone,
More chilling to the heart *alone*.
Lone as a solitary star,

BULL RUN

SIGNS OF THE TIMES

The First Battle of Bull Run is also known as the Battle of First Manassas, the name used by Southern (Confederate) forces and the U.S. National Park Service. It was the first major battle of the Civil War, taking place near Manassas, Virginia, on July 21, 1861.

Expecting an easy victory for the Northern (Union) troops, many people from nearby Washington, including some congressmen and their wives, set out by carriage and on horseback to picnic and watch the battle. Instead, they witnessed a crushing defeat as the green recruits panicked and ran. Fortunately for the North, the Confederate army was too disorganized to follow up on their success, and the Union army got away.

New York lawyer George Templeton Strong, on hearing of the battle's outcome, had this to say in his diary: "Today will be known as BLACK MONDAY. We are utterly and disgracefully routed, beaten, whipped by secessionists."

There would be a second battle at Manassas in late August of 1862, and it was during the interval between the two that Mary's husband Daniel Patterson was captured.

Lone as a vacant sepulcher,
Yet not alone! my Father's call—
Who marks the sparrow in her fall—
Attunes my ear to joys elate,
The joys I'll sing at Heaven's gate.

Daniel wasn't the only captive during this time. Mary was still working on her own release from illness.

Letters tell of a number of ailments, including digestive difficulties and a recurring back problem which prevented her from sitting comfortably or walking. That summer, as the war raged on, Abi insisted on sending her to Dr. William T. Vail's Hydropathic Institute in Hill, New Hampshire, to try a popular remedy of the day. It didn't do any good, though, and in fact left Mary worse than when she started.

"I have been at this Water Cure between 2 and 3 months, and when I came could walk ½ a mile, now I can sit up but a few minutes at one time," she wrote in a letter that August, clearly discouraged.

Before Daniel left for Washington, he'd heard of a man named Phineas Quimby in Portland, Maine. Quimby, a clockmaker by trade, had become interested in hypnotism as a means to help sick people, and his fame for remarkable cures was widespread. Daniel had written to Quimby, hoping to arrange a meeting between him and Mary, but nothing came of it. While Mary was at Vail's, a patient who was considered incurable left, "and in a few weeks returned apparently well," Mary later recalled. The patient gave Quimby the credit.

Phineas Quimby

COURTESY TMBEL

Intrigued, Mary decided to go to Portland and see Quimby for herself.

In October of 1862, her oldest brother Samuel and his wife came from Boston to accompany her on the journey. Mary, still an invalid, had to be carried up to her room at Portland's International Hotel, where Quimby lived and worked. Yet her hopes were high. Perhaps this treatment would finally cure her.

Small and energetic, Quimby was called a "magnetic healer," because he believed that energy—in the form of electricity—passed from himself to his patient. In his opinion, dipping his hands in water and rubbing parts of the patient's body aided this effect, a method that today might be called therapeutic touch.

Charles Norton, a medical student whose mother was a patient of Quimby's, made notes on how the doctor worked. According to Norton, Quimby walked among those seeking his help and "in a loud voice demanded that each patient look him straight in the eye. An assistant followed him about the room holding a large dish of water. In most cases not a question was asked, in some, however, Mr. Quimby would say, 'Where is your pain ... What ails you?' In some [cases], he would wet both hands in the water and gently press or stroke the face, neck or head of the person being treated. In a number of incidences he would say, in a quick, sharp voice: 'Get up and walk away! You can walk, walk!' the patient almost always doing as bid."

When it was Mary's turn, Quimby told her that she was held in bondage by the opinions of her family and physicians. He dipped his hands in water and vigorously rubbed her head.

"I well remember the fearful tangle which Mrs. Patterson's hair was in after her treatments," wrote Martha Hunter, landlady of the Portland boardinghouse that Mary eventually moved to, "and often helped her to comb it out." Undergoing this treatment, Mary was free from the pain in her spine for the first time in years. In a week, she was able to climb the 182 steps leading to the dome of Portland City Hall. This must have felt like flying after being bedridden so many long years.

Mary wrote enthusiastically about Quimby in the *Portland Evening Courier.* She tried to find out how he healed people, and made many notes. Was he, as residents of his hometown of Belfast, Maine, claimed, merely a mesmerist and hypnotist? Or were his healings the same as those of Jesus in the Bible?

Unlike Jesus, though, Quimby based his cures not on faith in God but in himself. Many of his patients, including Mary, found that while they were with Quimby, they felt better, but when they left him, old ills returned. His patients needed constant reinforcement from the doctor.

Quimby's methods may well have been "the essence of quackery," as Mary's brother and sister-in-law saw it, but they probably underscored for Mary one thing that she had been thinking about since her experience in North Groton — the connection between physical effects and a mental cause. She remembered the woman she had healed with unmedicated pellets in North Groton, and her own sudden strength when the Wheets had threatened Daniel. And over the next few years she would continue, as she later put it, "assiduously pondering the solution of this great question: Is it matter, or is it Mind [God], that heals the sick?"

In the late fall of 1862, Mary was about to go to Washington to press for Daniel's release, when she heard that he had escaped from prison and was heading home. Daniel joined Mary in Portland in November, where he tried lecturing on his experiences as a prisoner of the Confederacy, with no success. Eventually, he decided to start up his dental practice again in Lynn, Massachusetts, a busy factory town nine miles north of Boston.

Right around the same time that Daniel made his escape, Georgy was swept up in the Vicksburg Campaign. In October, while helping man a cannon during the Battle of Corinth in Mississippi, he was severely wounded in the neck. Mary prayed diligently for him and wrote him comforting letters while he was hospitalized. She was overjoyed when he recovered.

The following couple of years found Mary dividing her time between Portland, Maine, where she continued her treatments with Quimby, Sanbornton Bridge, New Hampshire (soon to be renamed Tilton), where she visited Abi and the rest of the Baker family, and Swampscott, Massachusetts, the quiet little fishing village next door to Lynn where Daniel had rented a small apartment for the two of them. The marriage was unraveling by this point. Daniel was often absent for long periods of time, and he was a woefully erratic provider. Most disturbing was the fact that those "dark things" Mary's father had heard years ago about his character had proved true. Dr. Patterson was unfaithful to his marriage vows.

Through it all, Mary continued to write, including a bittersweet poem entitled "Christmas Day," published in the *Portland Daily Press* on December 31, 1863, in which she reflects sadly on her absent soldier son who would soon sign up for a second tour of duty. Part of Mary's poem reads:

> In the camp, or at the battle,
> Weary on the march, or guard,
> Know, my brave boy, hearts are with thee,
> Love and glory thy reward.

By this time, Mary had accumulated quite a portfolio of published articles, essays, poems and stories from newspapers and magazines. She was contributing regularly to a local paper, the *Lynn Weekly Reporter*, and to national publications as well, including *Godey's Lady's Book* (forerunner to the modern-day *Ladies' Home Journal* and quite a feather in a writer's cap in those days) and *The Independent*, a popular New York weekly. Still, finances were a constant struggle.

In the fall of 1865, Mary's father passed on. Mark Baker's will left the bulk of his money and property to his youngest son George Sullivan. Although Martha and Mary were both desperately poor, each of Mark's three daughters

© TMBEC

PHOTO J. H. PHILLIPS COURTESY TMBEL

▲ Mary Glover and her son, around the time of Georgy's re-enlistment.

received only $1.00. This was common practice in those days, and not necessarily a reflection of Mr. Baker's affection for his family, but still, it may have come as yet one more disappointment to Mary.

A few months later Quimby, who had been ill for some time, also died. Mary felt abandoned. One by one, her supports were all vanishing.

Now in her mid-40s, Mary had suffered through decades of invalidism, deprivation, betrayal, and almost unimaginable loss. Looking back in hindsight she would later be able to write, "God had been graciously preparing me during many years" for something which at this point still lay ahead. But at this moment in time, her prospects must have looked relentlessly bleak.

Just around the corner, however, was an experience that would change the course of her life.

7
A Turning Point

On a cold February night in 1866, Mary was walking to a temperance meeting with some friends in Lynn when she slipped on an icy sidewalk and fell, striking her back and head. She was carried unconscious to the nearest house, the home of Samuel Bubier. Dr. Alvin M. Cushing, a popular local homeopath and surgeon, was called. He came twice that evening. Mary had a concussion and possible spinal dislocation, he said gravely. All that night she lay speechless and unmoving. Some of her friends stayed and watched over her, along with Mrs. Bubier.

The next day, Mary "came to consciousness," she later wrote, "amid a storm of vapors from cologne, chloroform, ether, camphor etc., but to find myself the helpless cripple I was before I saw Dr. Quimby." She insisted on being taken home. Those who had kept watch were afraid for her, and the doctor was very reluctant to let her go. He gave her an eighth of a grain of morphine, and while she was plunged into sleep, took her by sleigh to her apartment in neighboring Swampscott.

Daniel was away at the time, and two of Mary's friends telegraphed him about the accident. They remained at Mary's side, as did Dr. Cushing, until Mary regained

Mary and her husband Daniel had an apartment on the second floor of this house on Paradise Road in Swampscott, Massachusetts. In winter, Mary liked to feed the birds from her windowsill.

COURTESY TMBEL

SIGNS OF THE TIMES

TEMPERANCE MOVEMENT

Between the Revolutionary War and the Civil War, the abuse of alcohol in the United States increased dramatically, reaching a peak around 1820. Concerned with the terrible toll this was taking on individuals, families, and society, a social reform movement sprang up to encourage either moderation ("temperance") or complete abstinence from the use of alcohol. Supported by churches and individuals nationwide, the movement had many offshoot organizations, including the Women's Christian Temperance Union, which would launch Carrie Nation to fame in the late 19th century, and the Order of the Good Templars, founded in Utica, New York, in 1851. Mary was on her way to the Linwood Lodge of the Order of the Good Templars when she slipped on the icy sidewalk.

The Lodge, which favored total abstinence from alcohol, was organized by men, but there was a women's auxiliary called the Legion of Honor. Mary served for a time as the Lynn chapter's presiding officer. She "had a quiet way about her of commanding attention," recalled Dr. E. J. Thompson, the Lodge president, "and in the delivery of an address she was impressive."

The temperance movement had a positive affect, according to historians at Old Sturbridge Village, as per capita alcohol consumption in the United States has never gone back to pre-1820 levels.

consciousness a second time. The doctor came to see her again later that day, but there was still no improvement in her condition. Since there was nothing more he could do for her, Mary's friends asked George Newhall, the milkman, to fetch their minister.

Rev. Jonas B. Clark soon came to pray with Mary and prepare her for the worst. A close friend, Rebecca Brown, also paid a visit, bringing her nine-year-old daughter Arietta with her. Arietta later recalled that as they were leaving, Mary astonished them by saying, "When you come down the next time, I will be sitting up in the next room. I am going to walk in."

"Mary, what on earth are you talking about!" Arietta remembered her mother exclaiming.

Lying helpless in bed that afternoon, Mary asked to be left alone. As always, she turned to her Bible for comfort, and opening it at random to the New Testament, she found

FAMILY TEMPERANCE PLEDGE

TEMPERANCE LEADS TO VIRTUE & HAPPINESS

INTEMPERANCE TENDS TO POVERTY AND RUIN.

"WINE IS A MOCKER, STRONG DRINK IS RAGING: AND WHOSOEVER IS DECEIVED THEREBY IS NOT WISE."

We the undersigned Family of ______ Agree with each other that we will not Buy, Sell or Use intoxicating Liquors as a beverage and will use our Best Endeavors to Curtail and Prevent the Sale and use of the Same by others.

Signatures. Signatures. Signatures.

COURTESY OF THE LIBRARY OF CONGRESS, RARE BOOK AND SPECIAL COLLECTIONS DIVISION herself reading from one of the gospels the story of a man who couldn't walk, and how Jesus healed him, commanding "Arise, and walk."

"As I read, the healing Truth dawned upon my sense," Mary later explained. Jesus' words, "I am the way, the truth, and the life," came to her with such a blaze of understanding that she felt a power and strength not her own. When next she thought about her body, she found that the coldness and pain had ceased, and she was able to get up and walk into the next room.

Her friends, who were gathered waiting for what they had been told was her imminent death, were amazed, as was Reverend Clark. Mary felt as if she had been made anew. The next day, she sent for Dr. Cushing to show him she was well.

"What! Are you about?" The doctor was astounded. Was it his medicine that had healed her?

"Come here and I will show you." Mary took him to her bedside table and opened the drawer. Every bit of the medicine he had left her was still there, untouched.

"If you will tell me how you cured yourself, I will lay aside drugs and never prescribe another dose," he told her.

But Mary had no idea how she had been healed, or if other people could be helped in this way. All she knew was that she had glimpsed something wonderful, "namely, Life in and of Spirit," as she later explained, an entirely different, brighter reality than the one presented by the material senses.

After the doctor left, his fear at seeing her up and about shook Mary's confidence. She momentarily felt weak again until, as she later explained, "it all seemed to come to me again with such a light and presence" that she "rose right up" with the feeling that she could never again be conquered.

Was this the presence she had known as a little girl, when she'd heard a voice call her name and she had answered? Was this the same pure, lifting divine love—only stronger now, and more vivid—which had freed her so quickly from the childhood fever and healed the baby in Rumney?

Mary was filled with questions.

8
"I found him"

Mary felt herself being led, like a little child, "into a new world of light and Life," as she would later describe it.

There were still times when she looked back at past troubles and felt afraid. At one point she wrote urgently to Julius Dresser, one of Quimby's patients who had taken an interest in healing: "I am constantly wishing that <u>you</u> would step forward into the place he [Quimby] has vacated. I believe you would do a vast amount of good ... I confess I am frightened ... Now can't <u>you</u> help me?"

But Julius refused, saying, "I do not even help my wife out of her trouble."

With that path blocked, there was no turning back. Mary could no longer depend on another person. She had only one familiar guide from the past—her Bible. She searched it every day for answers. What did the Scriptures teach about God, and what was it, exactly, that had brought about her healing?

Meanwhile, her husband was no support. By this time the couple had moved to Lynn, closer to Daniel's dental practice. In the Spring of 1866 he disappeared with one of his patients, the wife of a local businessman.

Mary forgave Daniel, and he returned home. But that summer he deserted her yet again, and this time the Pattersons' marriage was over. Daniel had betrayed his wedding vows once too often. There'd been too much "disappointment and tears," Mary told her sister Martha after she and her husband parted ways.

Daniel blamed himself for their separation and eventual divorce, and years later told an acquaintance that "if he had done as he ought he might have had as pleasant and happy a home as one could wish for."

With Daniel gone for good, Mary felt very much on her own. In September 1866, she wrote a poem, "I'm Sitting Alone," that was later printed in the *Lynn Reporter.* In it she thinks of her mother, "parting the curls to kiss my cheek;" of her first husband, Wash; of herself as a "fair young bride; and of Georgy's "glad young face upturned to his mother's in playfulness." All that had gone. Yet as was so often the case with some of her more melancholy poems, Mary again ended on an upbeat note:

> And wishing this earth
> more gifts from above,
> Our reason made right
> and hearts all love.

Mary asks for right reasoning and a heart full of love. The child who had given away her winter coat to a schoolmate in need had grown into a woman who yearned to reach out and help others. Mary hadn't forgotten her promise to God, that if somehow her health were restored she would devote herself to helping her fellow man. Despite the fact that she had very little money and no settled place to live—she was forced at this point to live mainly off the kindness of friends and relatives—Mary still had two thoughts uppermost in mind: finding the source of her own healing, and relieving the sufferings of others.

And Mary quickly found herself doing just that. There was young Dorr Phillips, for instance, the son of a Quaker couple whose home was Mary's refuge during that tumultuous summer of 1866. Dorr had a painfully infected finger that was keeping him up at night and out of school. Mary healed it overnight through prayer alone, much to Dorr's joy and his family's amazement.

It wasn't a miracle, Mary explained. "Nor would it be if it had been a broken wrist or a withered arm. It is natural, divinely natural. All life rightly understood is so."

Around this time Abi, who had always looked out for her younger sister, offered to build a house for Mary and give her an allowance. But there was one condition—Mary must give up her strange ideas about spiritual healing.

PEOPLE AND PLACES

RED ROCK

Now part of Red Rock Park in Lynn, Massachusetts, the shoreline's famous red-hued outcropping was a favorite spot of Mary's. As a child, she loved roaming the woods and fields of her family's farm in Bow, New Hampshire, and spent many happy hours on the granite ledge above the Merrimack River that she and her brothers and sisters dubbed "the playground." Perhaps Red Rock reminded her of those carefree days, for this dramatic rock formation was sometimes her destination after a long day of writing and study. Accessible at low tide, it's still a popular spot today, and visitors can explore the tide pools and scramble over the craggy boulders, or just sit and look out to sea at the same beautiful view Mary would have enjoyed when she lived nearby.

Mary was now 45, at a time when the average life expectancy for a female born in 1821 was 37. She had no money and no home. Her marriage was over; her only child far away. She was lonely for her family and a familiar circle of friends. Abi's offer must have been tempting, but Mary couldn't accept it. In the past, she had often listened to her older sister. Now, convinced she must do the work that God had called her to do, she had to turn Abi down.

How could she do otherwise, given what she was witnessing first-hand?

There were other healings that summer, including one that occurred when she went for a walk on one of the beaches in Lynn. Mary often slipped away to the shore, and especially loved sitting at Red Rock looking out over the sea. On this particular day, a woman had left

▼ Red Rock in Lynn, Massachusetts

her seven-year-old son sitting on the sand while she went to hitch up their horse and get some water. The boy had never walked, as both of his feet were severely deformed. When his mother returned, her son had vanished. To her astonishment, she spotted him down by the water, with a stranger holding both his hands. As she watched, Mary let go, and the boy stood on his own for the very first time in his life. Then he took a few steps by himself. The mother ran over to them. Tears of joy streamed down the two women's faces as they gave thanks to God.

Later, a family friend wrote down the boy's description of what happened. He told of an unfamiliar lady walking by, and seeing him with his feet covered, "asked why he was not playing with the other children there. He told her he had never walked, and she lifted the shawl and saw why. She put her hands under his arms, and while he protested his inability to do so, told him to stand, and when he was lifted to an upright position, she guided his feet with her own, supporting him the while he took his first feeble steps into freedom." The size and shape of the boy's feet soon became completely normal, and he grew up to become a mechanical engineer and lead a happy and productive life.

Experiences like this one convinced Mary she must be on the right track.

She pondered deeply the source of these healings. "When I came to the point that it was mind that did the healing, then I wanted to know what mind it was," she would explain. "Was it the Mind which was in Christ Jesus, or was it the human mind and human will?"

Mary grew more confident that "the Divine Mind was the Healer." Looking back on her years of investigation into homeopathy, she would point out, "After these experiments you cannot be surprised that we resigned the imaginary medicine altogether, and honestly employed Mind [God] as the only curative Principle."

But she still had so many questions. She knew from reading her Bible that many people had been cured through "holy, uplifting faith," and certainly Jesus had taught others to heal. Was there a principle behind his method? Could it be used by anybody? Mary hungered for answers.

"I must know the Science of this healing," she later wrote, looking back on this period of her life.

"I sought God diligently," she explained, "and with the Bible in my hand searching its precious pages I found Him...."

The Bible answered her questions as to how she was healed. "But the Scriptures had a new meaning, a new tongue; their spiritual signification appeared, and I apprehended for the first time their spiritual meaning, Jesus' teachings and demonstration, and the Principle and rule of metaphysical healing...."

Mary began to glimpse that these Biblical accounts which had always seemed miraculous were "divinely natural and possible to understand. It was the uninspired interpreter whose ignorance of Christ's healing had named it a miracle instead of divine law."

She was eager to share the ideas that were being revealed to her with anyone who would listen. They were so different and so startling, however—Christian healing as a present-day possibility, not just a miraculous gift granted only to Jesus and his disciples?—that even her most spiritually-minded friends feared people would think her deluded if she persisted. So she turned to the new acquaintances she met.

That autumn of 1866, Mary boarded with a Mrs. Ellis and her school-teacher son, Fred. He later recounted how she would spend all day in her room writing, and in the evening, "would read the pages to Mother and me, inviting, almost demanding, our criticism and suggestions."

Thirty years later, Fred wrote to Mary of his "cherished remembrance of those precious evenings in the little sitting-room at Swampscott, when the words of Jesus, of Truth, were so illumined by your inspired interpretation."

And she wrote back, "Do you forget your Christmas present to me—that basket of kindlings all split by your hand and left at my door? I do not."

Few of the places Mary stayed were as warm and friendly as the Ellises. Most people in the boardinghouses where she lodged worked hard all day, and just wanted to relax around the supper table in the evenings. They didn't understand what Mary was up to with her Bible study, and they didn't want to hear her revelations about God and healing.

A handful were interested in Mary's spiritual discoveries, though, including a young shoemaker in Lynn.

9

A Shoemaker Learns a New Trade

Mary thought it would take "centuries of spiritual growth" before she could teach others the spiritual laws of healing she was discovering in the Bible. To her surprise, she found herself being asked to teach right away.

Hiram Crafts, a young shoemaker, came with his wife to work in the shoe factories in Lynn for part of each year. In early winter the two would return to their home in East Stoughton, Massachusetts, where Hiram would join others working in backyard shoe shops. The couple were both Spiritualists. They believed that the spirits of people who had died could control those who were living. They thought that a medium, someone sensitive and tuned in to the "spirit world," could receive communications from the dead about the past and the future and in this way guide and direct the living.

Mary met Hiram and his wife while they were all staying at the same boardinghouse in Lynn. When she talked about spiritual healing at the supper table, Hiram, who sat next to her, was a ready listener.

In November of 1866, the Crafts invited Mary to come back to East Stoughton and live with them, so that Hiram could learn to be a healer. Mary took what was left of her furniture to help furnish their front parlor, and began teaching Hiram in return for her room and board.

COURTESY OF LONGYEAR MUSEUM CHESTNUT HILL, MASSACHUSETTS

➤ Hiram Crafts, Mary's first pupil

SIGNS OF THE TIMES

SHOE CAPITAL OF THE WORLD

When Mary was growing up, her jack-of-all-trades father once made shoes for a needy family. It's likely he shaped the leather with the help of a wooden "last," or form, and sewed the shoes by hand, just as cobblers had done for centuries. By the time Mary moved to Lynn in the 1860s, however, the Industrial Revolution was well under way, and the trade had been transformed. Small cobbler shops run by individual shoemakers were rapidly being replaced by large-scale mechanized production of ready-made goods.

The Civil War brought further growth and prosperity to the industry. Soldiers needed boots, and they needed them quickly and cheaply. There wasn't time to wait for individually hand-crafted orders to be filled. Shoe sizes were standardized for the first time during this period, too, helping to ensure that the troops received their army boots in the correct sizes.

Lynn factories pioneered the use of sewing machines in stitching "uppers" to shoe soles, and from around 1870 to 1920, the city was considered the "shoe capital of the world," producing more shoes than anywhere else in the United States.

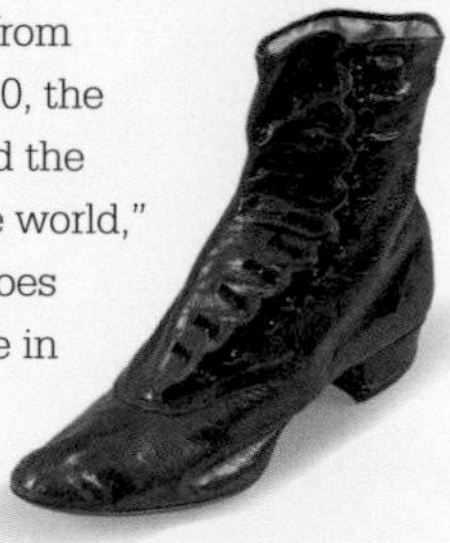

COURTESY OF LONGYEAR MUSEUM CHESTNUT HILL, MASSACHUSETTS

▲ One of Mary's button shoes

➤ Advertisement, circa 1872

Hiram wrote later that he changed his views and gave up spiritualism as a result of Mary's teaching. "We used nothing outside of the New Testament, she had no manuscripts of any kind until after I had been studying six months," he explained.

Both teacher and student did well, and in a few months the Crafts family and Mary moved to a more comfortable house in nearby Taunton. As this was a much larger town, Hiram expected more patients. He advertised in the newspaper offering a money-back guarantee and addressed it, "To The Sick."

I buy my Boots at the
"UP-TOWN" SHOE STORE

COURTESY OF THE LIBRARY OF CONGRESS, PRINTS AND PHOTOGRAPHS DIVISION

"*I can cure you,*" he asserted, and then gave a list of diseases. "If you give me a fair trial and are not helped, I will refund your money." At the end of the ad was a statement from Abigail Raymond of Taunton, who had been healed of a longstanding illness by Hiram. Mary helped Hiram by taking the more difficult cases herself.

James Ingham, who was suffering from consumption, was one such case. "I had not received her attention but a short time, when my bad symptoms disappeared, and I regained health," he wrote. "During this time, I rode out in storms to visit her, and found the damp weather had no effect on me. From my personal experience I am led to believe the science by which she not only heals the sick but explains the way to keep well, is deserving [of] the earnest attention of [the] community; her cures are not the result of medicine, mediumship, or mesmerism, but the application of a Principle that she understands."

Ingham meant that Mary didn't employ drugs, didn't rely on a medium (someone directed by spirits of the dead), or on mesmerism, which is a form of hypnotism. She relied solely on God.

As she herself would later explain, "Metaphysics, as taught in Christian Science, is the next stately step beyond homœopathy. In metaphysics, matter disappears from the remedy entirely, and Mind [God] takes its rightful and supreme place."

Mary wrote to her sister Martha about her own and Hiram's success: "All that come to him sick he cures." Perhaps that is why when Ellen, Martha's twenty-one-year-old daughter, lay ill with typhoid fever and enteritis in the summer of 1867, Martha sent for her sister.

Ellen's case had been given up by three doctors, and she was said to be dying. Bark and straw had been spread on the road outside the house to prevent her from being jolted by carriages or wagons rolling by. Anyone going into the young woman's room stepped on tiptoe. Ellen could only be moved from bed to bed on a sheet. Most of the time she lay silently with her eyes closed.

Mary went into the room and stood beside her niece quietly for a while, praying. In a few minutes she heard Ellen say, "I am glad to see you, Aunty." Mary kept on praying and then told her niece to get up and walk, and to stamp her foot on the floor. Ellen did so, and felt no ill effects. The next day she dressed and went down to the table.

"Such a change came over the household," a family member wrote later. "We all felt 'the angel of the Lord appeared and glory shone round.'"

Abi was away at a fashionable resort, where the wealthy went to drink mineral water for their health, so she missed Mary's visit. The eldest sister, whose pride had been hurt when Mary rejected her offer of a home, had mixed feelings when she heard how Mary had healed their niece. She wrote to Martha a few days later, "I have my private opinion that in the end no real good will result from all the stir she has made about Ellen, but hope I am mistaken and great benefit will result from her efforts yet."

Ultimately, the family itself would not choose to benefit from Ellen's experience, but great good for others, in the form of healing, would indeed result from Mary's efforts.

Ellen joined her Aunt Mary when she returned to the Crafts household in Taunton. They arrived to find the couple in turmoil. Mrs. Crafts was tired of "doing" for her houseguest, and the niece was just an added burden. She wanted Hiram to go back to shoemaking, a more respectable trade.

The plan was for Hiram to give Ellen continued treatments until her health was on a firm basis, but he didn't know what to do with his angry wife. With the house in such an uproar, Ellen felt confused. The joy of her sudden recovery evaporated. She was ashamed that Mary lived with such poor, uneducated people, and decided that the only way to maintain her own dignity was to return home and forget the whole thing. And so she left, and would later become resentful that she even owed her aunt gratitude for the healing.

Mary also left, and Hiram and his wife returned to East Stoughton, where Hiram went back to shoemaking. When Mary wrote to him a year later to see if he would like to resume working with her, he answered: "I should be willing to do all you ask if I was in different circumstances.... I feel the same interest in the developing of Truth and its principles.... But it would be impossible for me to come over there to help you at present. I should have no peace at home if I did."

In spite of this setback with Ellen and the Craftses, Mary felt compelled to continue with her work. Her teaching seemed to have a polarizing effect on people—on the one hand, great gratitude for healing and a desire, from those like Hiram, to learn more; on the other, anger and open hostility, from those like Ellen and Mrs. Crafts.

Mary's own life had two very different aspects as well: an inner spiritual force fueled by a Bible search that she would later describe as "sweet, calm, and buoyant with hope," and outer circumstances — no settled home, few friends, barely enough money to live on — that were very discouraging.

For three years following her accident on the icy sidewalk in Lynn, Mary was forced to move many times, as the things she was learning about God and Christian healing often stirred up her landlords and fellow boarding-house guests. Still, she pressed on, all the while searching the Bible for answers and pondering her mission.

One stormy summer night in 1868, while staying in Amesbury, Massachusetts, Mary was evicted — turned out in the rain with her trunk. She had no place to go until a neighbor named Sarah Bagley took pity on her. Sarah was interested in what Mary had to say, and offered her room and board and a modest percentage of her earnings as a healer in exchange for instruction.

Mary stayed three months. Late that August, she submitted a poem to the local newspaper, the Amesbury & Salisbury *Villager.* A slightly different version had been printed earlier that

© CSPS

▲ Mary in 1867

▼ Mary's niece Ellen Pilsbury

COURTESY OF LONGYEAR MUSEUM CHESTNUT HILL, MASSACHUSETTS

▼ Mary worked on this poem for nearly 40 years, revising and republishing it from time to time. Set to music in 1892, it was one of the first official Christian Science hymns. In 1909, Mary made one final edit, changing the word "wait" to "wake" in the third verse.

CHRIST MY REFUGE
(August 1868 version)

Over the voice harp of my soul
There sweeps a hand—
Beyond this mortal, weak control,
From some soft band.

Of ministries, a white-winged throng
Of thoughts illumed
By God, and breathed in raptured
song
By love perfumed.

And in this unveiled presence grew
A ladder bright,
Rising to bear me upward to
A world of light.

Not from this earthly home afar,
But nearer Thee,
Father, to shine a loving star
O'er crystal sea.

Over the waves of error here—
Time's Galilee,
Aid me to walk, Christ ever near,
To strengthen me.

And fix my sight on God, the rock
Upon my shore,
'Gainst which the waves and winds
may shock,
O nevermore!

I am no reed to shake at scorn,
Or from it flee.
I am no medium but Truth's, to warn
The Pharisee

'Gainst their oppression and
their wrong,
To crucify
The Christ, whose deeds they
must prolong
To hold Him nigh.

CHRIST MY REFUGE
(present-day version)

O'er waiting harpstrings of the mind
There sweeps a strain,
Low, sad and sweet, whose
measures bind
The power of pain.

And wake a white-winged
angel throng
Of thoughts, illumed
By faith, and breathed in
raptured song,
With love perfumed.

Then His unveiled, sweet mercies
show
Life's burden's light.
I kiss the cross, and wake to know
A world more bright.

And o'er earth's troubled, angry sea
I see Christ walk,
And come to me, and tenderly,
Divinely talk.

Thus Truth engrounds me on the rock,
Upon Life's shore,
'Gainst which the winds and waves
can shock,
Oh, nevermore!

From tired joy and grief afar,
And nearer Thee,—
Father, where thine own children are,
I love to be.

My prayer, some daily good to do
To Thine, for Thee;
An offering pure of Love, whereto
God leadeth me.

year in the *Lynn Reporter*, and it gives readers some insight into what Mary may have been thinking during this period, particularly her yearning for a refuge, or safe haven, from the storms of life. It shows, too, how she was continuing to turn to God for strength and for the inspiration that lifted her to "a world of light"—perhaps that same bright world of spiritual reality she had glimpsed when she was so quickly healed after her accident in Lynn, and for which she had expressed such a longing in her earlier 1861 poem, "The Heart's Unrest."

When his unveiled
sweet mercies show
Life's burdens light.
I kiss the cross, and wake
to know
A world more bright.
And o'er earth's troubled,
angry sea
I see Christ walk,
And come to me, and tenderly
Divinely talk.

PHOTO TMBEC ILLUMINATION BY VIOLET OAKLEY

▲ Image from an illuminated edition (1939) of Mary's poem "Christ My Refuge."

With God's help, Mary was riding out the "winds and waves" that continually tried to shock her, and in the fall she accepted an invitation to the home of a family named Wentworth, whom she had met through Hiram Crafts. They gave her a warm welcome.

"When Hiram Crafts brought her to our fireside, we just felt as if an angel had come into our home," the Wentworth's daughter Lucy later wrote.

Alanson Wentworth loved listening to Mary's comments on Scripture. Part farmer, part shoemaker, he was devoted to his Bible, and grateful when she healed him of an addiction to tobacco and of sciatica in his hip, freeing him to work again. With Mary's help, the health of the Wentworth's older daughter, Celia, who was suffering from consumption, greatly improved, and she cured Lucy of a hearing impairment. Sally Wentworth, who enjoyed tending the sick, was impressed, and looked forward to learning about healing from Mary.

Mary called 13-year-old Lucy "little Lue," and let the young girl wear her pearl ring, which thrilled Lucy no end.

"Her manners were beautiful and I imitated her in everything," she would recall.

The Wentworth family welcomed Mary into their home in Stoughton, Massachusetts.

Often, Mary went to meet her on her way home from school, and the two of them would walk across the fields to call on Lucy's aunt. Visits to the spacious old house with the brook flowing by were a welcome change for Mary, after being cooped up in her room all day writing.

Evenings were spent with the Wentworth family. They loved music, and Mary often joined them in singing. She bought a backgammon board and taught them all how to play, and subscribed to two fiction magazines, *Saturday Night* and *Chimney Corner*, when she discovered that Lucy's seventeen-year-old brother Charles loved stories. Charles later described Mary as cheerful and sprightly, "a woman of culture and refinement" who was a brilliant conversationalist. He looked back on the 18 months she spent with his family as "one of the brightest spots in my life."

PHOTOS COURTESY OF LONGYEAR MUSEUM CHESTNUT HILL, MASSACHUSETTS

Charles Wentworth

It was a bright spot for Mary, too, who thoroughly enjoyed young people's company. "She was lively and entered heartily into our fun and made herself one of us," said Lucy, who admired the way Mary walked—"a sort of graceful glide." Although her older friend had few fine clothes, Lucy noted that "it made no difference what she wore, there always seemed to be a certain style about her."

Lucy also noticed "a faraway look" in Mary's expressive eyes, and remembered times when her new friend told her sadly about Wash, her dashing first husband of only six months, and Georgy, their son, who had been taken from her. She let her know about her separation from Daniel Patterson, too, whose name she had dropped by now, reverting to "Mrs. Glover."

Although Mary still frequently felt lost and alone, she was learning to trust God completely for everything she needed. The Bible remained her "chart and compass," and she was energized by her research. Her days were spent absorbed in the Scriptures as she searched and pondered. "The revelation of Truth in the understanding came to me gradually and apparently through divine power," she later wrote, describing this period of her life.

COURTESY OF
LONGYEAR MUSEUM
CHESTNUT HILL, MASSACHUSETTS

Lucy Wentworth adored Mary, and followed her around like a pet lamb.

As Mary set her thoughts and findings down on paper, she wrestled to articulate what was being revealed to her. At times, dissatisfied with what she had written, she would tear everything up at the end of the day.

Still, she pressed forward. "I won my way to absolute conclusions through divine revelation, reason, and demonstration," she would explain. From the very beginning, Mary understood the vital importance of demonstrating what she was discovering. Just as Jesus offered his healing work to John the Baptist's disciples as verification of his identity as the promised Messiah, so Mary felt that the healing works effected by herself and her students would prove that the ideas she was recording weren't mere theory.

"The question, What is Truth, is answered by demonstration,—by healing both disease and sin," she later wrote.

Mary was working on another project during this time, too, a manuscript that would help explain this method of healing more clearly, and keep her students from mixing in other, more physical methods, the way Sally Wentworth insisted on doing. She wanted to make it clear that it was spiritual power alone, not personal willpower or physical manipulation, that accomplished real Christian healing.

PHOTO MARK THAYER © TMBEL

▲ For three years after her fall on the ice in Lynn, Mary wrote hundreds of pages of notes on the book of Genesis, some of them pictured here.

Mary loved to discuss her discoveries, and William Scott, one of Charles's friends, recalled that two or three nights a week, he "used to visit Mrs. [Glover] with other young people of the town ... to listen to her talks, for even then she was regarded by those who knew her as a wonderful woman. Some of the most pleasant recollections of my youthful days center in that little room at the Wentworths."

Mary received many requests for healing while she was living in Stoughton, including one in 1869 from William's father. Mr. Scott was suffering from severe intestinal trouble, and had been given up by his regular physician. After Mrs. Wentworth's efforts failed to alleviate the painful condition, young William was sent to hitch up the team and fetch Mary. She came at once, prayed for his father, and restored him to health within the hour.

When Mary left the Wentworth home in the spring of 1870, little Lue's heart ached. For older family members, though—in particular Mr. Wentworth, who felt that Mary was monopolizing too much of his wife's and daughter's time—there may have been some relief mixed with their genuine regret at her departure. Mary's single-minded vision was a demanding one.

10
Writing Her Book

In August of 1870, Mary placed an advertisement in the *Lynn Semi-Weekly Reporter.* She'd spent the early spring teaching and writing in Amesbury, but come mid-May had been persuaded to move to Lynn and go into partnership with Richard Kennedy, one of her students. The manufacturing hub was just a short train ride from Boston, and offered wider opportunities than did the sleepy mill town on the New Hampshire border.

While Richard put what he was learning from Mary into practice by seeing patients who came to him for healing, Mary focused mainly on writing and teaching.

Many of Mary's new students were in the shoe trade and had to work in the factories during the day. They came to her class that summer with their hands stained and worn, but with their minds open to something new. Sitting around a plain wooden table, with only a single lamp casting long shadows and their lessons accompanied by the sound of insects banging up against the windows, Mary's students found to their surprise that learning to heal meant learning about God.

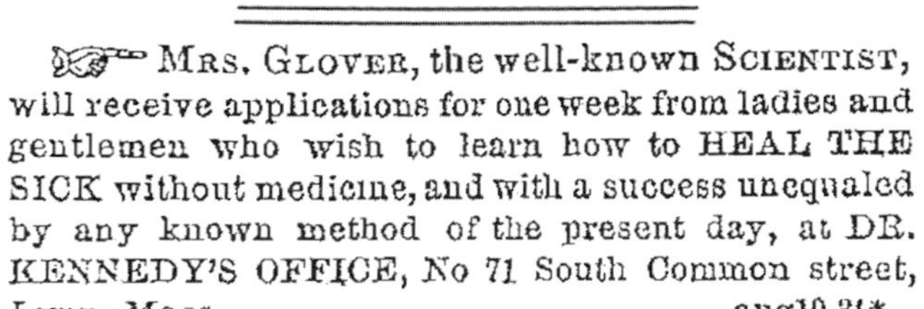
☞ MRS. GLOVER, the well-known SCIENTIST, will receive applications for one week from ladies and gentlemen who wish to learn how to HEAL THE SICK without medicine, and with a success unequaled by any known method of the present day, at DR. KENNEDY'S OFFICE, No 71 South Common street, Lynn, Mass. aug10-3t*

"What is God?" was the first question they were asked. Many imagined God as a man with a beard somewhere up in the sky. Mary had come to understand God to be "Principle, wisdom, love, and truth," an infinitely intelligent Being who never created disease, and whose law led naturally to healing and peace. What authority did she have for such a claim?

"If sickness was truth Christ would not have destroyed it," Mary told them firmly, "and I would not teach a student such presumption."

One of the manuscripts she'd been working on at the Wentworth's — entitled *The Science of Man* — was soon complete. Each student received a handwritten copy, which he or she was required to study thoroughly. Mary's teaching method involved questions and answers, the same format she'd learned in her religious training as a child from the *Westminster Catechism*. This let her see just what each student was thinking. Everyone participated; everyone felt their thoughts stirred up, their old beliefs challenged.

"While we may have been unable to fully grasp the truths she uttered," one student wrote, "we could not fail to realize the inspiration."

If matter and its conditions were superior to God, Mary explained to them, "then we admit that effect is superior to cause and can save or destroy the works of God." On the contrary, she reasoned, just as "discord is not caused by the principle of music," so any discordant human condition could not be caused by a wholly good God, and therefore had no reality.

PHOTO © TMBEL

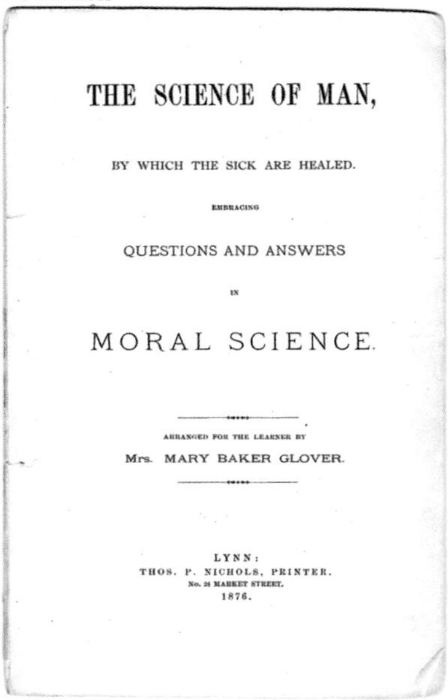
THE SCIENCE OF MAN,

BY WHICH THE SICK ARE HEALED.

EMBRACING

QUESTIONS AND ANSWERS

IN

MORAL SCIENCE.

ARRANGED FOR THE LEARNER BY

Mrs. MARY BAKER GLOVER.

LYNN:
THOS. P. NICHOLS, PRINTER.
No. 24 MARKET STREET.
1876.

▲ This pamphlet was first copyrighted October 10, 1870, under the name "Mrs. Mary Baker Glover," and later published in 1876.

Among many other things that Mary pointed out to her students was the fallibility of the material senses (the same ones that would fool them into thinking that the sun revolved around the earth, instead of the other way around), and the importance of holding thought calmly and persistently to the spiritual sense of God's allness and goodness. Doing so was like letting in "the sunlight that melts away darkness," she said, and opened the door to healing.

Her students were to mentally cast out error with truth, just as Jesus taught his disciples, "Ye shall know the truth, and the truth shall make you free."

Mary's course consisted of twelve lessons and cost $300—roughly equivalent to $5,000 today and quite a sum, considering it was about half the average annual income for shoe workers at that time. Initially, she wasn't sure what to charge "for an impartation of a knowledge of that divine power which heals" and "shrank from asking" the sum she felt was God-impelled, "but was finally led ... to accept this fee." In the end, few paid the full tuition, as Mary was always quick to lower or waive the fee for those in need. Plus, she freely gave additional classes and private instruction to her pupils, who would gather each week for refresher meetings and advice from their teacher.

WHAT IS GOD?

FOOTSTEPS OF PROGRESS

Mary would continue to refine her teachings over the years, but she always began her classes by giving her students a clear understanding of God, whom she would eventually come to define by seven synonymous terms. This definition comes from the glossary of the Christian Science textbook that she would later write:

"God. The great I AM; the all-knowing, all-seeing, all-acting, all-wise, all-loving, and eternal; Principle; Mind; Soul; Spirit; Life; Truth; Love; all substance; intelligence."

(from *Science and Health with Key to the Scriptures*)

"We learned that our success or failure in healing depended on the purity of our lives, as well as on the instruction she gave us," noted Samuel Putnam Bancroft, who studied with Mary that year.

Mary expected her students to obey the Ten Commandments and the Sermon on the Mount, and to follow Jesus' example just as she endeavored to do. Additionally, she told her students that they must seek the truth as a means of doing good. This pure motive would lead to better healing. If they were simply looking to make money, she warned, their patients would not recover as well.

Daniel Spofford, whose wife was in the first class, was very impressed with Mary's manuscripts. He studied them carefully on his own, and understood enough to do some healing work. Mary later heard of this, and invited him to take her class free of charge.

Spofford was so moved by the experience that he wrote to her during the course: "Many, many times each day I ask myself, do we students realize what is held out for our possession?" He felt that the difference between Mary's writing and teaching was like the difference between "the printed page of a musical score compared to its interpretation by a master." He hoped he was worthy to give back to her a little of what she had given to him.

Mary found that teaching students was like raising a family—her work was never done. She watched over her growing flock carefully, counseling and encouraging them in letters and in person.

Mary was healing steadily during this time, too—muteness, deafness, rheumatism, and heart disease, among many other conditions. But while some pupils left Mary's class and became successful healers themselves, others found the discipline too hard and turned against their teacher. Wallace Wright, the son of a Universalist minister, came to class full of questions. At the end, he told Ellen Locke, a fellow classmate, that the last lesson alone was worth the price of the whole course. In June of 1871, Wright left New England for Knoxville, Tennessee, where another of Mary's students was located, to practice what he had learned. At first he had good success. Then he got into a quarrel with the other student and started to rebel against the strict morals and self-discipline needed for the healing work. He began to have doubts about what he was trying to do, and eventually lost his ability to heal. In anger, he wrote to his teacher demanding his tuition money back, along with two hundred dollars extra in compensation.

She refused, telling him, "To be happy and useful is in your power, and the science I have taught you enables you to be this, and to do great good to the world."

Returning to Lynn, Wright again demanded a refund and the extra two hundred dollars. Mary still said no, so he wrote a letter to the *Lynn Transcript* blasting Moral Science, as Mary then called her teaching, as being nothing more than mesmerism.

PHOTO W. T. BOWERS © CSPS

◀ Mary Glover in Lynn around 1871. Caring for her students was much like raising a family, and many of Mary's early followers called her "mother," both as a term of endearment and out of respect. Interestingly, the term "mother" was also sometimes used by Civil War soldiers for their nurses, and is thus associated with the ministry of healing.

Mary was quick to respond to this attempt to discredit her. Moral Science, she maintained, had nothing to do with mesmerism, a form of hypnotism in which one person yields his thoughts to another. On the contrary, her teaching originated with God, not with man, and "enables us to determine good from evil, and to destroy the latter by understanding first, what is error and what truth ... undertaking this great work 'in the name of Almighty God.'"

Wright fought back. "Mrs. Glover and her Science [are] practically dead and buried," he scoffed on February 24, 1872. Some of Mary's other students rose to her defense. Copies of the *Lynn Transcript* sold briskly as the controversy flared. Mary put up a strong front, but confided to her old friend Mrs. Ellis that she felt keenly the mental anguish of the very public debate.

Wright's attempt to seek revenge by putting Mary out of business did not succeed. His attack did push her to make an important change, however. In the past, although she herself had never done so, she had allowed her students to rub their patients' heads while praying for them. Now, she realized that this led to confusion, and prevented both practitioner and patient from full reliance on God as the only healing power. She told her students to stop this practice.

Richard Kennedy refused. Their business partnership soured because of it and eventually dissolved in the spring of 1872. Richard went off in a huff. Like Wright, he too would later turn on his teacher.

As Mary pondered how she might best strengthen her students in their healing work, and ensure that they understood the importance of relying on prayer alone, she turned once again to her Bible. Opening it at random one day, she found this inspiration in Isaiah: "Now go, write it before them ... and note it in a book." And so, after teaching one more class in March of 1872, she stepped back from the classroom to concentrate all her energies on doing just that. The project would occupy her attention for the next three years.

George Barry, one of her young students in Lynn, was like a son to her. While Mary wrote, he ran errands, found her places to stay, watched over her finances, and spent long hours copying and recopying her manuscript. Mary had to deal with constant distractions, among them the continual search for a quiet refuge. She moved at least nine times during these years.

"There was no good reason for my moving except the antagonism that was felt to the ideas, and to me for voicing them," she would later tell a friend.

Mary's pupils also clamored for her attention. Although she wasn't officially teaching, Mary was in constant demand for counsel and support. Sick people continued to flock to her, too, and her tender heart wouldn't allow her to turn them away.

There was the local woman, for instance, whose baby was suffering from a bowel obstruction. The child had been given up by physicians, who told the distraught mother that there was nothing more they could do. "He was reduced to almost a skeleton," the woman reminded Mary in a letter two years later. After Mary paid a visit to the family and prayed for the baby, he was healed "in less than an hour," his mother noted, adding, "all his symptoms changed at once."

In 1873, Mary completed a draft of her book and submitted it to a publisher. It was rejected with such severe criticism that she felt she had to revise the whole thing. She spent many more months doing so, then tried submitting it again the following year. Once more she met with rejection. The publishers, she later said, "could not understand it, and would not attempt to publish it."

Mary refused to give up. She continued to revise her book to make the meaning clearer. She hadn't found just the right title yet either—she originally thought of calling it *The Science of Life*—but trusted that God would reveal it to her.

He did.

"Its title, Science and Health, came to me

▲ Called the "Morning Star of the Reformation," John Wycliffe was a 14th-century religious reformer persecuted by the Roman Catholic church for translating the Latin Vulgate Bible into English.

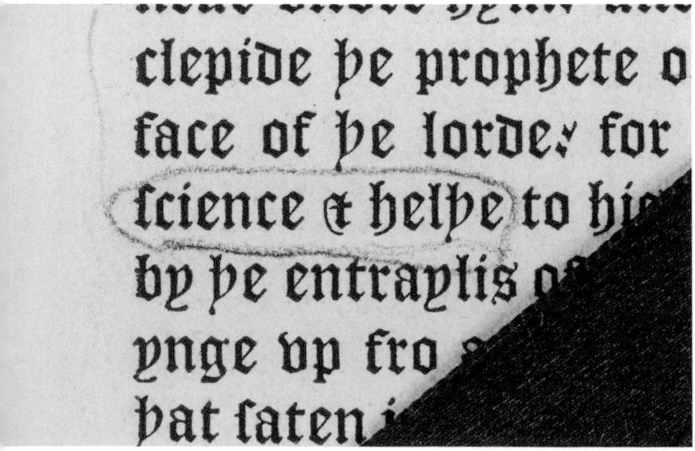

clepide þe prophete o
face of þe lorde: for
ſcience & helþe to hi
by þe entraylis o
ynge vp fro
þat ſaten

PHOTO © TMBEL

◀ This copy of the Wycliffe Bible, shown here open to Luke 1:77, is just one of the dozens of Bibles that Mary would own over the years.

in the silence of night, when the steadfast stars watched over the world," Mary would recall.

She got right up and wrote it down. When she told some of her literary friends about it, though, they advised her "to drop both the book and the title. To this, however, I gave no heed, feeling sure that God had led me to write that book, and had whispered that name to my waiting hope and prayer."

Six months later, one of her students brought Mary a copy of Wycliffe's translation of the New Testament "and pointed out that identical phrase, 'Science and Health,' which is rendered in the Authorized [King James] Version 'knowledge of salvation,'" Mary noted. She was amazed to find the title of her book embedded in her Bible all along!

Mary also realized that the term Christian Science more accurately described her subject than did Moral Science. "I named it *Christian*," she would explain, "because it is compassionate, helpful and spiritual."

As she wrote, inspiration poured into her thought. "Such a flood tide of truth was lifted upon me at times it was overwhelming," Mary recalled, "and I have drawn quick breath as my pen flew on...."

Referring to herself as "a scribe under orders," she saw her work as a divine revelation, and asked "who can refrain from transcribing what God indites...?"

When Mary's book was finally ready, she talked things over with her students. Some of them agreed to subscribe to a fund to help finance the project, and in July of 1874 a printer, W. F. Brown of Boston, was found. Mary gave him her manuscript in September. She had to pay all the costs and supervise the work; in effect, she was self-publishing the book. In a letter to "Putney" (her student Samuel Putnam Bancroft), she explained what this meant:

"After two years and a half incessant labor seven days in a week I have now the part of proof reader to take or my book will be spoiled and go over again the four hundred pages correcting it because they have made the plates from proofs in which they made many blunders.... Tired to death, broken down with persecution, no home to rest in, invalids all around me, one room only, etc, etc., to work in, this is my present lot...."

In spite of all the setbacks, Putney had never known his teacher so continuously happy in her work as during this time. "Although she was writing, teaching and preaching, and occasionally treating some severe case beyond a student's ability to reach, her physical and mental vigor seemed to be augmented rather than depleted."

He was awed by her persistence, too. "I have known her when nearly crushed with sorrow, but she wrote on. I have known her when friend after friend deserted her, but she wrote on. I have seen student after student bring ridicule and reproach upon her, but still she wrote on."

Delays with the book continued. Brown, the printer, made changes in the copy as he went along, altering the meaning, which Mary then had to correct. She, in turn, made further revisions, which slowed him down. At one point, with no explanation, Brown stopped work altogether. Nothing Mary said could get him to continue.

Months passed. Autumn faded to winter, and still the work was at an impasse. Finally, in early 1875, there was a breakthrough. Looking out her boarding room window, Mary noticed that the house across the way was for sale. For many years, she had yearned for a home of her own. Could this be it?

Mary had lived frugally, and her savings were modest. They were adequate for a down payment, however, and she happily bought the house in March. Designed as a two-family home, both floors of 8 Broad Street had to be rented out to tenants to help pay the mortgage, but Mary kept the front parlors and attic for herself. One of the parlors became her classroom; the other, her living room.

Mary finished writing *Science and Health* in this attic room in Lynn

PHOTO MARK THAYER © TMBEL

She set up her study in one of the small attic rooms. Simply furnished, it was hot in summer and cold in winter, but it was all hers. On the wall was a framed copy of her favorite Bible verse: "Thou shalt have no other gods before me." Mary could stand on a chair by the single skylight in the sloping roof and look out across the rooftops of Lynn, or gaze up at the stars. Here, in this humble spot, she finally found the peace she longed for to finish her book.

PHOTO MARK THAYER © CSPS

▲ First edition of *Science and Health*, with some of the original printer's plates

While Mary had been waiting for her printer to resume his work, she found she couldn't get rid of a persistent feeling that she should include more in her book about the nature of evil. She was reluctant to do this, but at the same time felt "the divine purpose that this should be done.... Accordingly, I set to work, contrary to my inclination, to fulfill this painful task."

In her attic sanctuary, Mary drew her rocking chair under the skylight and placed a piece of cardboard across her lap to serve as a desk. Obediently, she added an explanation of what she understood to be wrong mental practice, or "malpractice"—a counterfeit of spiritual healing that seeks to harm rather than heal, and which influences others through hypnotic suggestion and willpower.

At the exact same time that she undertook this addition, her printer resumed his work. Mary had no knowledge of this. On the afternoon that she set out from Lynn to Boston with the new material, Brown set out from Boston to Lynn. The two met at the Lynn train station and were both equally surprised: Mary to learn that Brown had finished his work and come for more copy; the printer to find her on her way to Boston with the closing chapter of the book. No word had passed between them.

On October 30, 1875, a thousand copies of *Science and Health* rolled off the press. Mary was 54. It had been nine years since she started making

USED BY PERMISSION OF LOUISA MAY ALCOTT'S ORCHARD HOUSE

▲ Bronson Alcott went to visit Mary in January 1876, a few months after the publication of *Science and Health.*

notes on the Bible following her fall on the ice, five since she had copyrighted *The Science of Man*. The intervening time had been necessary, though, for as Mary later wrote, she "had learned that this Science must be demonstrated by healing, before a work on the subject could be profitably studied."

Now, after countless healings, she had earned the right to speak and write with authority, and she was ready to put her thoughts before the public.

"This book is indeed wholly original, but it will never be read," wrote one reviewer. "The book is certainly original and contains much that will do good," countered another. Neither writer could know that *Science and Health* would go through more than four hundred printings in Mary's lifetime alone.

So many people would be healed just from reading the book that in later editions Mary expanded it to include a final chapter called "Fruitage." A hundred pages long, it overflows with letters of gratitude for spiritual awakening and uplift, and for the healings that followed — healings not only of physical ills such as tuberculosis, rheumatism, cataracts, heart disease, broken bones, cancer, asthma, and the like, but also of character shortcomings, addictions, business and relationship difficulties, and more.

Mary sent copies of her book to influential thinkers of the day. Most never responded. One exception was philosopher Bronson Alcott, friend of Ralph Waldo Emerson and father of Louisa May Alcott, the well-known author of *Little Women*. Bronson wrote back: "Accept my thanks for your remarkable volume entitled 'Science and Health' which I have read with profound interest...." When clergymen and others mocked Mary's book from the pulpit and in the press, the sympathetic philosopher went to see her in Lynn. His first words were, "I have come to comfort you." Later he wrote: "I hail with joy your voice, speaking an assured word for God and immortality, and my joy is heightened that these words are of woman's divinings." Alcott's words were indeed a comfort, and Mary used them as a testimonial.

After so much labor, what was Mary to do next? Not only was she responsible for writing her book, but also for getting it into the hands of readers. What was the best way to get *Science and Health* the attention she felt it deserved? Mary took the practical step of asking a student to be in charge of book sales. In a letter to Daniel Spofford, she assured him, "Love, meekness, charity or patience with everybody" would increase his success.

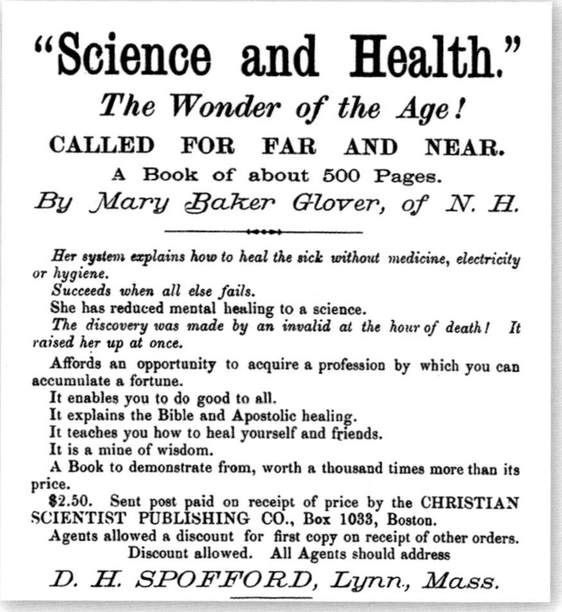

"Science and Health."

The Wonder of the Age!

CALLED FOR FAR AND NEAR.

A Book of about 500 Pages.

By Mary Baker Glover, of N. H.

Her system explains how to heal the sick without medicine, electricity or hygiene.
Succeeds when all else fails.
She has reduced mental healing to a science.
The discovery was made by an invalid at the hour of death! It raised her up at once.
Affords an opportunity to acquire a profession by which you can accumulate a fortune.
It enables you to do good to all.
It explains the Bible and Apostolic healing.
It teaches you how to heal yourself and friends.
It is a mine of wisdom.
A Book to demonstrate from, worth a thousand times more than its price.
$2.50. Sent post paid on receipt of price by the CHRISTIAN SCIENTIST PUBLISHING CO., Box 1033, Boston.
Agents allowed a discount for first copy on receipt of other orders. Discount allowed. All Agents should address

D. H. SPOFFORD, Lynn, Mass.

PHOTO © TMBEL

▲ Newspaper ad for *Science and Health*

Spofford made use of all the normal marketing avenues of the day, taking out ads and printing up promotional flyers that extolled the book's benefits. More important than these efforts, though, Mary realized that just as her own healing had brought *Science and Health* into being, so the practical proof of healing by others would aid in bringing her message to a wider audience.

She wrote to Spofford: "... get students into the field as practitioners, and their healing will sell the book and introduce the science more than aught but my lecturing can do."

Her earnest prayer for more healers had an unexpected result.

11
A Wedding

Excitement swirled around No. 8 Broad Street, Mary's house in Lynn. To the surprise of her friends, on New Year's Day, 1877, Mary Baker Glover married Asa Gilbert Eddy, one of her students. She was 55, he some ten years younger.

A few weeks later, as Mary's friends bustled about arranging gifts and a festive spread of cake and lemonade to celebrate the newlyweds, they still couldn't believe it. Gilbert, as he was called, was such a quiet man. True, he had a "reserve force" as one student put it, but what did they really know about this newcomer?

PHOTO H. F. CURRIER, COURTESY TMBEL

© TMBEL

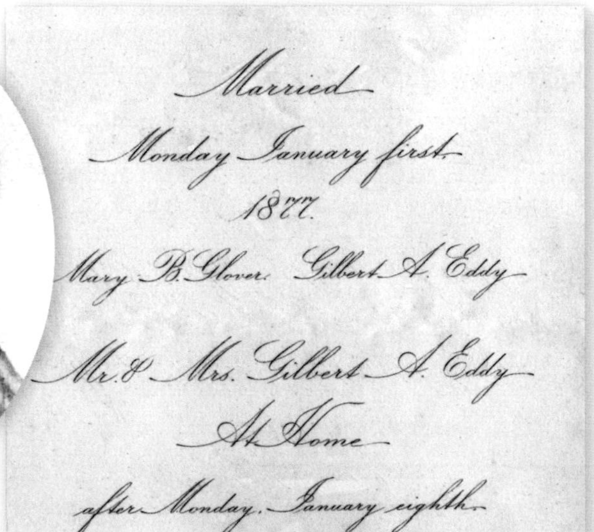

Married
Monday January first
1877.
Mary B. Glover. Gilbert A. Eddy
Mr. & Mrs. Gilbert A. Eddy
At Home
after Monday, January eighth
8 Broad Street
Lynn

➤ Mary Baker Eddy in the 1870s; wedding announcement for Mary and Gilbert. Although the groom's legal name was Asa Gilbert Eddy, Mary and his friends usually called him Gilbert.

Gilbert had first come to see Mary the previous March. He was a traveling salesman who sold sewing machines—at that time considered a wonderful new invention—and Christiana Godfrey, one of his customers, had been cured by Mary almost overnight of an infected finger. When Christiana discovered that Gilbert was often unable to work because of a heart condition, she insisted he go to Lynn and meet her good friend.

© TMBEL

DR. A. G. EDDY,
CHRISTIAN SCIENTIST.

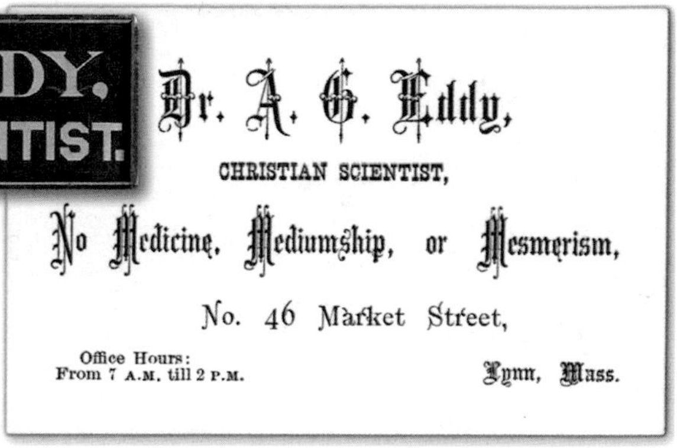
Dr. A. G. Eddy,
CHRISTIAN SCIENTIST,
No Medicine, Mediumship, or Mesmerism,
No. 46 Market Street,
Office Hours:
From 7 A.M. till 2 P.M.
Lynn, Mass.

© TMBEL

▲ Gilbert Eddy's office sign and 1876 business card

After two treatments, Gilbert felt so much better that he joined one of Mary's classes. He liked the idea that Christianity was a Science, provable in daily life, and left his job as a salesman to devote all his time to healing others through prayer. Gilbert Eddy was the first of Mary's students to advertise using the term "Christian Scientist."

It was no surprise then, when Mary came home from a trip one hot July day and fainted, that a friend ran at once for Gilbert. He healed her right away, and Mary told her cousin Hattie about it later. "He was calm, clear and strong and so kind," she confided. "Never before had I seen his real character...."

Before this Mary hadn't paid much attention to Gilbert. Now, she sat up and took notice of this mild-mannered man with the smiling eyes. She saw how he went out of his way to help those who came to him for care and direction, and that he was trustworthy, reliable, and a good listener. When there was an argument among Mary's followers, Gilbert often waited before he weighed in, and he met "any opposition or ridicule of the truth with a gentle reproof rather than a show of anger," noted Arthur Buswell, another of Mary's students and a colleague of Gilbert's.

"He was not easily ruffled," agreed fellow student Clara Choate.

Mary grew fond of this unassuming man.

PEOPLE AND PLACES

GILBERT EDDY

Like Mary, Asa Gilbert Eddy grew up on a farm, the sixth of seven children in a big Vermont family. His busy mother taught them all to cook, sew, and clean house. Gilbert was particularly good at tailoring and could cut and sew his own clothes. He was quick, neat, frugal, and capable. As a boy, he was good-looking, with "red cheeks, and quite a dandy in his dress, too," according to a schoolmate. As an adult, Gilbert was quiet and refined, "a man that everybody liked because he had a very pleasing manner," recalled the same friend. He was a favorite amongst children, who were drawn to him because he played games with them, told stories, and amused them by sketching horses and other animals. It was Gilbert who would later organize the first Christian Science Sunday School and serve as its first superintendent.

Growing up, Gilbert learned to spin and weave, and would eventually leave home to work at a textile mill (and later as a salesman for the Singer Sewing Machine Company). In the meantime, he taught penmanship at the local school while looking after his elderly parents. After their death, Gilbert leased the farm and left it for good.

Mary would later say that her husband had "the sweetest disposition" she had ever known, while her friend and devoted student Julia Bartlett noted, "He was always the kind husband and friend and ready helper in all things pertaining to the Cause of Christian Science...."

Mary saw her life work stretching out before her—the need to reach more people, teach more students, and possibly start her own church (she'd undertaken a brief stint of preaching in the summer of 1875). Quiet Gilbert seemed an unlikely choice for a marriage partner, yet he and Mary were knit together by a common purpose: a steadfast commitment to her Cause. As husband and wife, they gave each other strength and good cheer, and the two shared a close union. Gilbert was a strong supporter, giving Mary aid and comfort any way he could, and his "buoyant hopefulness" gave confidence to the young students in their healing practice.

"He was ever on the alert, quick to note a better way or a more convenient time for doing things," recalled Clara Choate, who was a young wife and mother when she first met Mary's new husband. "He was most reliable both in word and deed."

Gilbert taught his first class in April of 1878 at Clara's home in Salem. During this time, the Choates' young son fell violently ill. Gilbert quickly healed him. As Clara rejoiced, Gilbert

COURTESY TMBEL

▲ This photograph of Gilbert Eddy shows him sporting a high pompadour called a "roach," a hairstyle often adopted for formal portraits at that time. Those who knew him, however, including Christiana Godfrey's daughter Mary, recalled that Gilbert wore his hair more naturally, with bangs that fell over his left eyebrow.

told her, "Why, your child was all right all the time, only you could not see it. Truth never changes: it is only ourselves that change, only the human, mortal consciousness, and when we stop being afraid, God's law is manifested."

Family life and work went hand in hand for the newly-married Eddys. Gilbert spent his time healing patients while Mary worked on revising *Science and Health.* She was lecturing and preaching regularly now, too, addressing audiences first in her own front parlor and then in more public venues.

The couple had very little money, so they rented out the lower floor of their house and lived upstairs. Gilbert did the cooking and other household chores. Mary scrubbed the back stairs. It was "good exercise after sitting at the writing-table so long," she said to a friend, laughing at his surprise when he found her at this task one day.

Not all of Mrs. Eddy's students were happy that she had re-married. Two of them in particular—George Barry and Daniel Spofford—looked on Gilbert as an intruder. For five years Barry had been like a son to Mary, running errands, carrying up coal for the stove, copying her manuscripts. Now he felt cast aside. In anger, he filed a lawsuit claiming she owed him $2,700 (nearly $60,000 in 2013 dollars) for all the favors he had freely given before. A lien was placed on the Eddy's home during the two years that the suit dragged on. In the end, Mary was vindicated. The court awarded Barry only $350 (slightly less than $8,000 in today's dollars), in payment for his services as a copyist.

Daniel Spofford was hit even harder than Barry. He idolized Mary, and after his own marriage failed he had secretly hoped to marry her himself. When he couldn't have her as his wife, Spofford tried instead to take control of her fledgling movement. He told Mrs. Eddy that she was "unworthy to be the standard bearer of Christian Science" and claimed he should be the leader. But only a few of his patients followed him when he left the group of Christian Scientists.

Several months later, Spofford took part in a bizarre plot against Gilbert Eddy. Gilbert and another man were arrested and charged with killing Spofford, but when a key witness admitted he had lied and it was discovered that Spofford wasn't dead but only in hiding, the proceedings fizzled before coming to trial. Still, the negative press from Barry's lawsuit and this incident hurt the Eddys, taking up precious time and money and giving the public a false impression of Christian Science.

© TMBEC

▲ Note the sign above the second story at 8 Broad Street in Lynn: "Christian Scientists' Home," and the cross-and-crown emblem, forerunner to the official seal on Mary's books. Gilbert Eddy can also be seen sitting inside the upper right-hand window. Mary often faced hostility and ridicule from those who opposed Christian Science, and later told a reporter that at one time stones were thrown through her windows.

When Mary bought her house in Lynn, she put up a sign, "Christian Scientists' Home," and her followers began calling themselves "Christian Scientists." Then, on July 4, 1876, she gave her students, who had formed an organization a year earlier, the name "The Christian Scientist Association." Mary was elected President. In the spring of 1879, at one of the meetings of this "little band of earnest seekers after Truth," as she later called them, Mary made a motion: "To organize a church designed to commemorate the word and works of our Master, which should reinstate primitive Christianity and its lost element of healing."

The group got busy, and by late summer obtained a charter to form an official organization called "Church of Christ (Scientist)." There were twenty-six members. Mrs. Eddy was elected president and ordained as pastor. The newly-formed church's first Sunday service was held at Good Templars' Hall, not far from the place Mary had been headed some thirteen years earlier when she slipped on the icy sidewalk.

HYMN OF CHRISTIAN SCIENCE

FOOTSTEPS OF PROGRESS

In December of 1876, Mary published a new poem in the *Lynn Transcript* called "Hymn of Science."

The verses sprang to life just a few months after she gave her students' organization the name "The Christian Scientist Association," and a little over a year after she withdrew her membership from the Congregational Church in Tilton, New Hampshire.

This must have been a big step for Mary. She'd been a member of that church for 37 years, and it held fond memories for her. It was the church she'd joined as a teenager, and where she'd taught Sunday School, and where her son Georgy had been baptized. Throughout her life, Mary would express great affection for this church and its members, and many years later, on the occasion of its 75th anniversary, she would write, "The history that you celebrate is to me one of thrilling interest replete with tender tones of childhood...."

As this poem shows, however, Mary was beginning to move beyond her early religious training, leaving behind a material sense of worship for a more spiritual standpoint, one without ritualism: "Thou the Christ, and not the creed; Thou the Truth, in thought and deed; Thou the water, the bread, and the wine." She had begun to preach and hold Sunday services of her own, and these steps would eventually lead her to found her own church.

Her poem would later be reprinted in the *Christian Science Journal* of March of 1885 under the title "Hymn of Christian Science," and revised a few years later for the *Journal* of February 1889, where she first linked it to the Communion service. Eventually, it would be revised again and retitled "Communion Hymn" for inclusion in her book Miscellaneous Writings. Like a number of Mary's other poems, in time this one, too, would be set to music.

HYMN OF SCIENCE
by Mary Baker G. Eddy

Saw ye my Savior? heard ye the glad sound?
Felt ye the power of the word?
'Twas the Truth which made us free,
And was found by you and me,
In the Life and the Love that are God.

Mourner, it calls thee—come to this Savior;
Love wipes our tears all away,
And will lift the shades of gloom,
And for thee make blessed room
Where the darkness hath yielded to day.

Come to this fountain, all ye who thirsteth;
Drink of its life-giving stream:
'Tis the Spirit that makes pure;
That exhalts thee, and will cure
Every sorrow and sickness and sin.

Strongest deliverer, friend of the friendless,
God of all being divine:
Thou the Christ, and not the creed;
Thou the Truth, in thought and deed;
Thou the water, the bread, and the wine.

Gilbert, who had taken charge of publishing the latest edition of *Science and Health*, aided and supported Mary as she began traveling to Boston regularly to speak and preach in rented churches and halls.

"I have lectured in parlors 14 years," she wrote to her friend

© TMBEL

▲ Chickering Hall, circa 1895. Before her following grew to the point where she was preaching in venues like this one, Mary Baker Eddy often rented halls where she and her students had to tidy beforehand, sweeping up bits of stray trash and orange peels.

Clara Choate. "God calls me now to go before the people in a wider sense."

Mary's sermons, with titles like "The Bible Teaches Us How to Heal the Sick," "How to Be Healthy and Happy," and "The Art of Healing by Divine Power," struck a chord with her listeners. She spoke with eloquence and conviction, turning to the Bible ("the book of books,—the foundation Truth of all things—yea ... the only revelator of what God is and what God does") for her authority, and as always, emphasizing the importance of healing.

"Christian Science is proof not profession," she told her audience at Shawmut Baptist Tabernacle in an 1879 sermon entitled "Christian Healing and Mesmerism Contrasted." "In it we show our faith by our works and consider faith without the works of healing comparatively dead."

Mrs. Eddy peppered her metaphysics with vivid metaphors, examples from her own healing ministry, and other memorable nuggets such as this one recorded by a student: "Christian Scientists should so live that they will not need to tune themselves like a violin when they are called upon to help—they always should be prepared and ready to meet the need."

By all accounts she was a dynamic speaker, but those who heard her often remarked on the warmth and tenderness she brought to her sermons as well. As Arthur Buswell recalled, "instead of serving Christianity on ice and bringing on the chills she made it appear a thing of daily love and devotion to suffering humanity...." And Clara Choate described her teacher's presence in the pulpit as "one of restful serenity," her faith "forcible in her every word."

Mrs. Eddy's audiences grew steadily larger. Christian Science was on the move.

Into this ferment of activity strode George Washington Glover II. Mother and son had not seen each other for 23 years.

12

George Glover Comes to Town

On a chilly November day in 1879, George Glover stepped off the train in Boston. His journey from the Dakota Territory had been a long one, and he still had to make his way through a maze of unfamiliar city streets to his destination: the boardinghouse where his mother and her new husband, Gilbert Eddy, were now staying. George must have felt a mixture of anxiety and excitement as he climbed the stone steps of 133 West Newton Street and knocked on the front door. Would his mother recognize him?

He was eleven the last time they'd seen each other. Now, he was 35, no longer Georgy but George, a married man and the father of two children. He was also a proud Civil War veteran, with battle scars to prove the service he had given to his country.

After recuperating from the wounds he'd received at the Battle of Corinth, George had returned to his regiment to fight on. And when his first three-year tour of duty was finished, he'd re-enlisted right away. Towards the end of the war he was hospitalized with an illness, and that was the end of fighting for him. George didn't leave the infirmary in New Orleans until the war was well over.

His captain had not expected him to live, but George was a survivor. After his release from the hospital, the young soldier made his way back to the Cheney farm in Minnesota. When Mary heard of his discharge, she longed to go and see him, but her own poor health at the time made it impossible. George stayed on with the Cheneys until Mahala, his foster mother and always his champion and friend, passed away in December of 1866. Then he left the farm for good.

For some years George drifted, trying to adapt to civilian life. Finally he settled in Fargo, a frontier city on the border between Minnesota and the Dakota Territory that billed itself as the "Gateway to the West." There, he found work with a family called Roberts. Mrs. Roberts found George "very jolly and a good honest man," but she also felt that his education had been sorely neglected, as he couldn't read or write.

COURTESY TMBEL

▲ Mary's son, George Glover, circa 1868. He loved to tinker, and is shown here with one of his perpetual motion machines.

Tall and strong, George had blue eyes and a smiling face. "When he'd walk, he'd step right out," his son and namesake later recalled. "He always loved a good joke [and] he had many friends."

In April 1874, George married Ellen Bessant, nicknamed "Nellie," a petite English girl who worked for Mrs. Roberts. Nellie was 16, George nearly 30. Two years later, he was able to buy a land claim right next to the Roberts' property. He and Nellie had two children by then, Edward (called Gershom) and Mary. George started farming, but without success. After his adventurous life, the day-to-day routine seemed dull.

He knew that wheat, grown on the plains of the Red River in Wisconsin and ground into flour, sold well in the hungry mining towns of Dakota's Black Hills, where gold had recently been discovered. But the railroad hadn't kept pace with the territory's growth, so goods had to be brought in by horse and wagon. George decided to try his hand at freighting.

An expert horseman, he bought eight massive Percheron draft horses, hitched them up, and headed into the hills. Once his goods were unloaded, George lingered, relishing the bustle and stir of the remote settlements where tents, sawmills, log houses, and saloons had sprung up as prospectors flooded in. Several new towns had burst into life, including Deadwood, home to such colorful characters as Wild Bill Hickok and Calamity Jane, and neighboring Lead (pronounced "leed"), which means lode or vein, and which took its name from the rich mineral seams in the area.

COURTESY OF THE LIBRARY OF CONGRESS, PRINTS AND PHOTOGRAPHS DIVISION

Early Black Hills miners (and their dog!)

The rough mining life must have reminded George of his army days. The rocks doubtless sparked memories of his collection of quartz, amethyst, crystals, and mica he had been forced to leave behind in New Hampshire as a boy. Gold fever struck, and within a year he sold his farm in Fargo and moved his family to Deadwood, where he bought an acre of land overlooking the center of town. George's great hope was to enlist his mother's help in developing his mines. Evidently he had in mind a partnership of benefit to them both, as he proposed providing a home for her and Gilbert. In August of 1879, he got a friend to write his mother a letter, painting a rosy picture of their mutual prospects:

"The [Black] Hills are immensely rich in gold, quartz and in agriculture and timber.... The climate is milder and more pleasant than your New England home."

He continued, "I have been prospecting and opening mines all summer

THE GOLD RUSH OF 1876

SIGNS OF THE TIMES

The Black Hills Gold Rush began in 1874 with the U.S. Army's Custer Expedition. Although the Treaty of Fort Laramie in 1868 guaranteed the Lakota Sioux sovereignty of this region, after hearing reports that the area contained gold, Lieutenant Colonel George Armstrong Custer was sent in with 1,000 men to investigate.

What Custer and his troops discovered prompted a gold rush. The influx of prospectors antagonized the Lakota tribe, who considered the land sacred and were angry over the violation of their rights. Skirmishes erupted, eventually culminating in the Great Sioux War of 1876-77 and the death of Custer at the Battle of Little Big Horn.

Meanwhile, the prospecting continued. Much of what the early miners found was either small deposits or placer gold, loose gold flakes mixed in with the rocks and dirt around streams. But on April 9, 1876, a rich outcropping near Lead (in present-day South Dakota) was discovered by four men who staked a lode claim and named their new mine the Homestake. The Homestake would turn out to be the most significant gold vein in American history, producing 10 percent of the world's gold supply over the next 125 years.

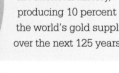

George Armstrong Custer

COURTESY OF THE NATIONAL ARCHIVES

PHOTO © TMBEL

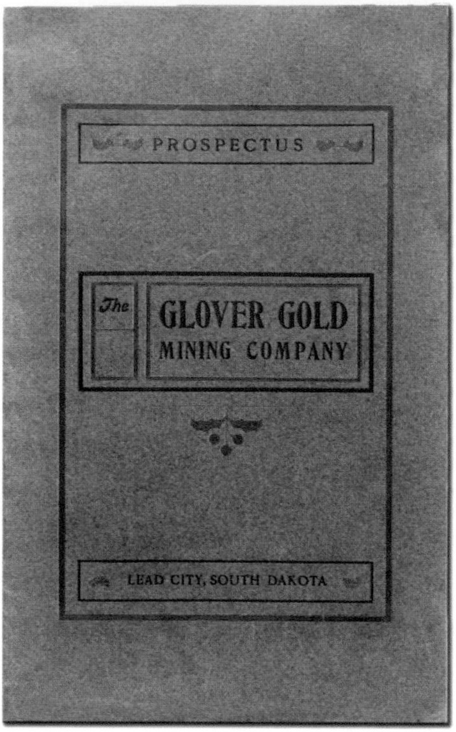

Mining company prospectus belonging to Mary Baker Eddy's son George

and now have six or seven very rich mines. None of them are yet developed sufficient to sell, but in a month or so we expect to have one of them sufficiently opened up to sell at a pretty good figure.... If I had a little more money I could open a large number of very rich mines and make $1,000 [some $23,000 in 2013 dollars] bring a return of $10,000 or a $100,000.

My wife and I would be very glad to have you come and make your home with us as long as you live, and we will endeavor to make everything as pleasant for you as possible."

Absorbed in his own projects, George had little clue as to the currents rippling through his mother's life. She had sent him an inscribed copy of the 1875 edition of *Science and Health*, but he may not have been aware that she'd started a church earlier that spring, one based on the practice of Christian healing, or that one of the reasons she and Gilbert had moved to the city was to be closer to its services.

George had kept his mother's picture with him all during the war. He would have long since memorized every feature—the luminous, deep-set eyes that looked right into your heart, the hair in long ringlets. As he stood there on the doorstep of the boardinghouse, he must have wondered what she would be like now.

When the door at 133 West Newton opened and mother and son finally met again, they were undoubtedly both surprised.

George looked every inch the frontiersman, right down to the long hair and beard, and pants that he wore tucked into high leather boots. He bore a startling resemblance to his father, Mary's first husband Wash, who had been almost exactly George's age when he'd died back in North Carolina. For her part, his mother had the same beautiful face, the same earnest eyes, but what a change had come over her! She no longer struggled with weariness and ill health. The fire of her spirit was burning strong and bright.

George was intrigued. He entered as fully as he could into life with his mother and Gilbert, and stayed in Boston three months. They must have made an unusual trio—the intent mother; the affable, quiet stepfather; and the tall, Wild-West son.

At the time George arrived, the Eddys' lives were in flux. They had left Lynn for Boston, where Mary's fledgling church held services first in nearby Charlestown and then at various locations in downtown Boston. Since they were unsure yet where their home base should be, Mary and Gilbert stayed in boardinghouses. George joined them. As his visit continued, though, one thing puzzled him. Why did they always have to move so often? Inevitably, the friendly smiles that greeted them when they first arrived would quickly change to open hostility and a demand that they leave.

His mother explained these constant upsets as the result of "animal magnetism," or what the Apostle Paul called the "carnal mind" in the Bible. This was Mrs. Eddy's term for mortal mind—the opposite of the divine Mind, God. In this case, it was taking the form of mental malpractice, or wrong practice, which sought to harm rather than help, and which she attributed to Richard Kennedy, the student with whom she had once partnered in the healing practice, but who had been unwilling to give up rubbing his patients' heads. Now, Kennedy directly opposed her, practicing a decidedly un-Christian counterfeit of spiritual healing that mixed in mesmerism and hypnotism and led to personal domination, manipulation, and wrong influence.

ILLUSTRATION BY FRANK A. MUNSEY OF PHOTO BY W. SHAW WARREN COURTESY TMBEL

▲ Mary Baker Eddy at the time of her son George's first visit in 1879

Like the frontiersman and ex-soldier that he was, George took matters into his own hands. As he later described to a newspaper reporter, he marched into Kennedy's office, put a revolver to his head and warned him to back off. If they had to move from one more boardinghouse, George told him, "I will search you out and shoot you like a mad dog." Kennedy "shook like a jellyfish," George recounted, and the threat had its effect. Whatever Kennedy had been doing ceased, and there were no more moves that winter.

Putney Bancroft, who was the same age as George Glover, later wrote that he was a fine-looking young man, and that his mother "loved him dearly, and was very proud of him." She would have liked George to stay back East, Putney noted, but he showed no interest in her work.

A decade later, Mrs. Eddy would corroborate this in a letter to another student, former sea captain Joseph Eastaman, when she told him, "I got the dear child into my class of Christian Science ... but he only took one lesson, I could not induce him to go on."

Perhaps Putney and Captain Eastaman didn't know that the rugged miner couldn't read, and so couldn't follow his mother's teachings on his own.

George politely declined an invitation to membership from the Christian Scientist Association ("home being so far away," he explained), but he went to the Sunday services that his parents held at that time—his mother the earnest pleading preacher, his stepfather the welcoming usher. Their way of thinking was beyond his scope, though, and George's thoughts turned to his wife, Nellie, to his children, and home.

Nellie, in the meantime, who was also illiterate, had a friend write a letter for her, telling her husband of a terrible fire that had swept through the log cabins in town. "We came very near being all burnt up ... it was very windy ... and the sparks flew all over town like snowflakes in a storm.... Little Mary [aged 2] is sitting on her stool singing to herself 'my Papa won't come home and papa will be sorry if he don't come home'... Gerty [Gershom, aged 5] says 'when he gets big he is going to fetch Pa home.'"

Before George left Boston in February, he asked his mother for one thing. He had witnessed her gift for healing and wanted help with his daughter's eyes. Young Mary later noted that a picture taken of her before this time distinctly shows that they were crossed.

"My father expressed much concern about my eyes," she explained. "Grandmother said, 'George you are surely mistaken, Mary's eyes are not crossed.' This evidently made a deep impression on father. When he returned home late at night he … insisted on seeing my eyes, though mother had just succeeded in putting us to sleep. Upon investigation they found my eyes to be straight as grandmother had said."

13
Loss is Gain

"My boy, you will be ruined for life; it is the work of the devil," sputtered Putney Bancroft's uncle, when he heard that his nephew had studied with Mrs. Eddy. Putney's uncle served as deacon of the First Congregational church in Lynn, and his words summed up what many church-goers thought at that time. Putney, however, had the opposite view. He thought of his teacher as "my dear friend … sort of an adopted mother."

By now, Mrs. Eddy was used to strong reactions to her teaching, both pro and con. As interest grew in her book and the ideas it presented, she'd endured ridicule from the pulpits and newspapers, but she found it especially hard when her own family shunned her. Growing up, they had all been so close. In the summer of 1880, Mary was hurt when she went to Tilton, New Hampshire, to see her sister Abi and discovered that her other sister Martha and niece Ellen—the same niece she'd healed years before—had left two days earlier to return home to Illinois. They'd been to visit Abi, too, and hadn't bothered contacting Mary.

She mentioned this in a letter to her son, but he had no words of comfort. He was too caught up in his own concerns. George was hungry for gold—finding it, tracking it, digging it out of the ground. He was busy testing his "attraction"—a device like a divining rod, which he claimed showed him where the precious mineral was. The miner's biggest problem was his shortage of cash.

George wrote back to his mother, enthusing over his latest mining venture and informing her that he'd had to suspend work on the tunnel due to lack of means. "Tell Father [Gilbert Eddy] that my attractions for minerals are perfect and will be the means of producing immense returns by the aid of a little capital ... I have no doubt that from five to eight hundred dollars [some $10,000 to $17,000 today] would do it."

His mother's response was crisp. What happened to the four hundred dollars [$9,000 in 2013] she gave him last time? Did he lose it?

"As your wife says much has gone into those mines but what has come out of them?" she noted. The Eddys had no money to spare. "Try your aunt Abi for a loan. She can well afford to risk losing $800 but you know I have not a hundred to risk.... " She ended more gently: "Your father sends love kiss the children and love to Nellie."

Unable to help George this time, Mrs. Eddy forged ahead with her own work. In a remarkable step for a woman of that era, in January of 1881 she obtained a charter from the state for the Massachusetts Metaphysical College, an institution she formed to teach Christian healing.

"When God called the author to proclaim His Gospel to this age, there came also the charge to plant and water His vineyard," she would write in *Science and Health.* Organizing a church was one step in that process, but hers must be a teaching church. "Jesus mapped out the path for others," she explained in her textbook, and each seeker needed to be given that map. Formalizing an educational structure was the next logical step in doing so.

During the early 1880s, in addition to founding a college, Mary weathered the defection of a handful of students from her fledgling church and published the third edition of *Science and Health.* Through all of these endeavors and trials she had the steady support of her husband, whose admiration, respect, and affection for his wife overflowed in the glowing tribute which prefaced her latest revision:

"Mrs. Eddy's works are the outgrowths of her life," he wrote. "I never knew so unselfish an individual, or one so tireless in what she considers her duty."

Gilbert, who was now Mary's publisher, had a strong desire to protect those works. One of her former students, Edward J. Arens, had printed a pamphlet, copying over thirty pages verbatim from her book and passing it off as his own. Gilbert was outraged.

He felt the best way to protect his wife's writings lay in copyright law. This was of such importance that the Eddys traveled to Washington D.C. in late January of 1882. There, Gilbert's valuable research at the Library of Congress led to a deeper understanding of copyright infringement. While *Science and Health* had been legally protected since its first publication in 1875, Gilbert's new knowledge would enable Mary to deal with plagiarists like Arens through the courts.

While Gilbert was immersed in research, Mary introduced her discovery to the nation's capital through a series of talks. "I have worked harder here than ever," she wrote to a friend, "14 consecutive evenings I have lectured 3 hours.... Go to bed at 12, rise at 6, and work."

Her efforts paid off.

"I have awakened a ripple of interest in this beautiful grand old city," she wrote to Clara Choate, and told another that the reception she received exceeded her expectations.

Mrs. Eddy was invited to the Capitol, and she was also given permission to visit Charles J. Guiteau, who had recently assassinated President Garfield. Very few people had been allowed to speak to Guiteau after his conviction; Mrs. Eddy was one of them. She later wrote, "He had no sense of his crime; but regarded his act as one of simple justice, and himself as the victim. My few words touched him; he sank back in his chair, limp and pale; his flippancy had fled. The jailer thanked me, and said, 'Other visitors have brought to him bouquets, but you have brought what will do him good.'"

There were healings, too, during the Eddys two-month stay in the capitol. A prominent clergymen who had been diagnosed with stomach cancer came to visit and listen to what Mrs. Eddy had to say about the Bible and healing. As suppertime drew near, she invited him to join her and her husband. The minister accepted, but added that it would be just for the company, not the food, as his doctor had prescribed a liquid diet.

"I said to him briefly, that this was an excellent opportunity to put to test our talk of the afternoon," Mary later recalled.

Her prayers brought about quick results. Their guest ate a hearty dinner, "felt no harm and never after was again troubled."

When the Eddys returned from Washington at the end of April 1882, they leased a four-story building at 569 Columbus Avenue in Boston's South End. Here they set up a home for themselves and for the new college. Interest in Mrs. Eddy's classes was growing, and prospects for the institution's future were as bright as the silver plaque on the door that bore its name.

All was not as bright on the home front, however. For nearly six years Gilbert had been a pillar of strength to Mary, standing by her through the storms that raged around them both: the lawsuit with George Barry; the feud with Daniel Spofford that culminated in the bogus murder conspiracy; rebellious students; opposition from the medical establishment and clergy. Now, yet another lawsuit loomed—this one with Edward Arens over the copyright violation. Gilbert seemed disheartened at the prospect, and later that spring his health failed.

Clara Choate recalled that during this difficult time, when Mary prayed for Gilbert he responded and at times appeared to be his old cheerful self, sitting in on her class sessions and going out for occasional carriage rides. He repeatedly assured his wife that he was coping with the illness, and urged her to focus on her work. She reluctantly did so.

COURTESY TMBEL

▲ The Massachusetts Metaphysical College was initially housed at 569 Columbus Avenue, and moved next door to 571 in March of 1884.

On the afternoon of June 2, 1882, Gilbert went out for a drive in a public horse-drawn vehicle and came home saying he felt much better. But before dawn the following morning he passed away quietly while sitting in his chair. The two students who were with him thought he was sleeping.

Mary was desolate. Her world spun to a halt. Home wasn't home without her beloved Gilbert. She had lost her strongest support. Not only was she heartbroken, but her Cause had been dealt a severe blow as well, losing such a stalwart foot soldier.

"I never shall master this point of missing him all the time," she wrote sadly to Clara. Gilbert had championed her with all his heart. As her defender, he had warded off some of the cruelest attacks, coming under direct fire himself. Gilbert was buried in the Baker family plot in New Hampshire, beside the graves of Mary's parents. On his memorial she had inscribed:

A DEVOTED HUSBAND
TRUE PHILANTHROPIST
CHRISTIAN SCIENTIST

After Gilbert's passing, Mary wrote immediately to her son, George, asking him to come to her, but he was busy with his prospecting and couldn't spare the time. Her student Arthur Buswell came instead, and took her and a companion to his home in Vermont. Here she spent some weeks in the countryside, surrounded by close friends.

"It is beautiful here the hills vales and lakes are lovely but this was his native state and he is not here," she wrote to her friend Julia Bartlett.

As always, Mrs. Eddy turned to her Bible for comfort, and spent many long hours in prayer. She drew strength from the assurance in Isaiah 54: "Thou ... shalt not remember the reproach of thy widowhood any more." The quiet, loving attention of her friends helped, too, and in time she found herself able to look to the future. "I would like more than ever to be myself again if only for one short year," she wrote another student. "But I question my ability to walk over all, only as God gives me aid that I never have had before."

God did give her aid, quite literally, in the form of a new aide: Calvin Frye.

Calvin had studied with Mrs. Eddy in the fall of 1881, after his mother was healed of mental illness through Christian Science treatment. The following spring, Gilbert recommended him as a likely candidate for bookkeeper and secretary at the college. Now, Mary acted on her late husband's advice. She telegraphed Calvin, who joined her train as she returned to Boston that August. He proved to be exactly the right choice and would serve her faithfully for the next 28 years.

Mrs. Eddy regained her normal vigor, and before long was teaching and preaching again. In late October, she wrote to a student, "I have on hand the largest class I ever had, and our Sunday services fill all our rooms with interested hearers.... The Ship of Science is again walking the waves, rising above the billows, bidding defiance to the flood-gates of error, for God is at the helm."

Janet Colman, a native of Martha's Vineyard and daughter of the newspaperman who founded the *Vineyard Gazette*, enrolled in one of Mrs. Eddy's classes that winter.

"There were fourteen in my class when I studied in 1883, in our Leader's back parlor on Columbus Avenue," Janet later recalled. She described how their teacher would meet weekly with her students at that time, instructing and encouraging them, and counseling them on how to treat the patients who were coming to them for healing. "We were very fortunate those who lived here in Boston, when I first studied.... She mothered us so kindly."

COURTESY OF LONGYEAR MUSEUM CHESTNUT HILL, MASSACHUSETTS

"The light that shone into my thought has never left me," Janet Colman said of her first meeting with her teacher.

1883 was an eventful year for Mrs. Eddy. At 62, she was at an age when many of her contemporaries were enjoying a quiet retirement. She, on the other hand, was rolling up her sleeves and getting down to business. Not only was she fully engaged as president and teacher at the Massachusetts Metaphysical College, but she also had an active ministry, and continued to lecture and preach (by the end of the year her church's services

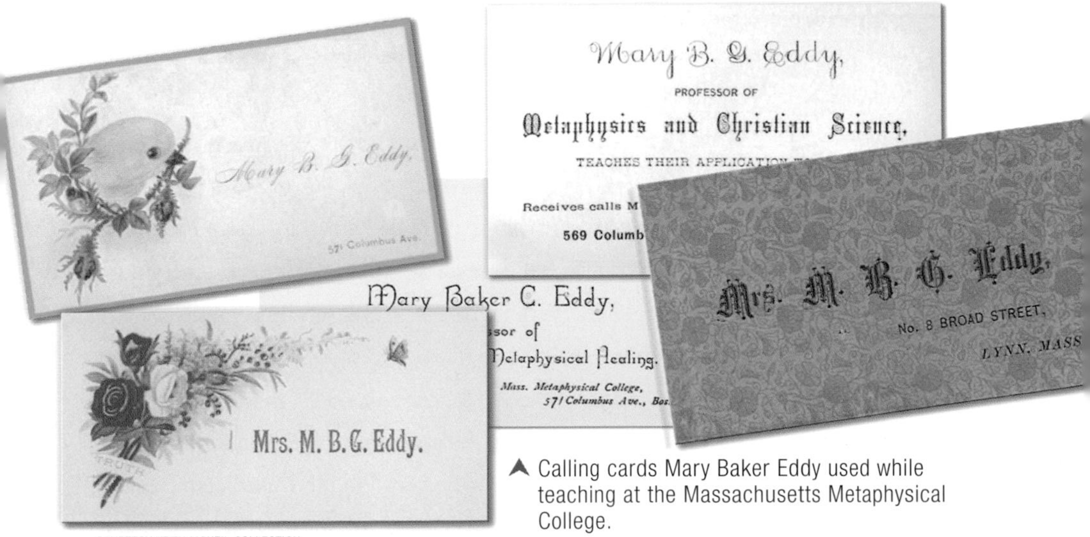

Calling cards Mary Baker Eddy used while teaching at the Massachusetts Metaphysical College.

COURTESY KEITH MCNEIL COLLECTION

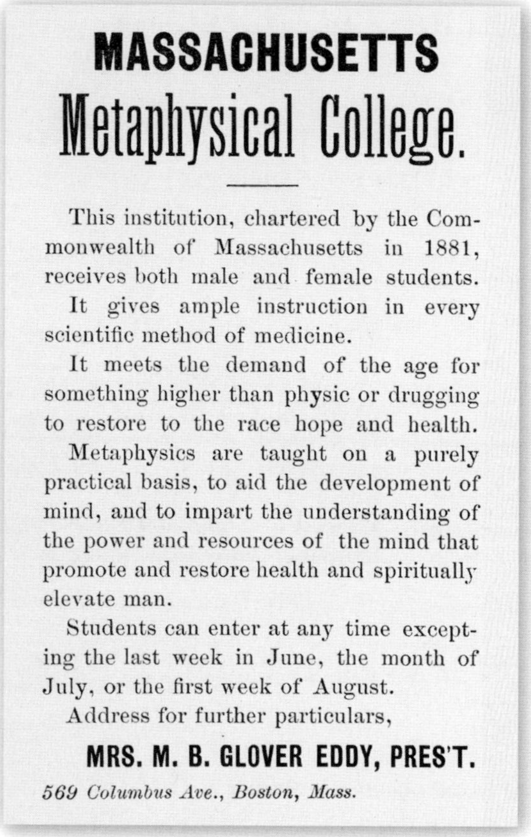

MASSACHUSETTS
Metaphysical College.

This institution, chartered by the Commonwealth of Massachusetts in 1881, receives both male and female students.

It gives ample instruction in every scientific method of medicine.

It meets the demand of the age for something higher than physic or drugging to restore to the race hope and health.

Metaphysics are taught on a purely practical basis, to aid the development of mind, and to impart the understanding of the power and resources of the mind that promote and restore health and spiritually elevate man.

Students can enter at any time excepting the last week in June, the month of July, or the first week of August.

Address for further particulars,

MRS. M. B. GLOVER EDDY, PRES'T.

569 Columbus Ave., Boston, Mass.

Early newspaper ad for the Massachusetts Metaphysical College

would grow to the point where they'd move to fashionable Hawthorne Hall). Plus, she was once again revising her textbook. The sixth edition would be the first to bear the name *Science and Health with Key to the Scriptures.* (The "key" at that time was composed solely of an added glossary, which contained a number of Biblical definitions that could be traced back to the notes she had made on the book of Genesis years before.)

In the early spring of 1883, Mrs. Eddy moved forward to sue Edward Arens for his plagiarism. The copyright infringement case would take about six months to wend its way through the courts, but it was ultimately decided in her favor, and the remaining copies of his pamphlet were destroyed.

Meanwhile, she embarked on a bold new venture—a publication called *Journal of Christian Science.* Mrs. Eddy served as publisher, editor, and writer. For the first year and a half, the magazine came out every other month. After that it was, and still is, a monthly publication, now called *The Christian Science Journal.*

"Dear reader," she wrote in the first issue, "the purpose of our paper is the desire of our heart, namely, to bring to many a household hearth health, happiness and increased power to be good, and to do good."

Mary had high hopes for her new magazine. It could reach well beyond New England, for one thing, bringing her message into far-away homes. First-hand accounts of healing would offer fresh inspiration, and Christian Science practitioners (including her student Janet Colman, who advertised in the very

JOURNAL OF CHRISTIAN SCIENCE.

An Independent Family Paper, to Promote Health and Morals.

"For the weapons of our warfare are not carnal, but mighty through God, to the pulling down of strongholds."

VOL. I. CHRISTIAN SCIENTISTS' PUBLISHING CO. | BOSTON, APRIL 14, 1883. | TERMS: $1.00 PER ANNUM, Postpaid; Single Copies, 17c. | No. 1.

JOURNAL OF CHRISTIAN SCIENCE

MARY B. GLOVER EDDY,
EDITOR.

☞ *Registered at the Post Office in Boston as second-class matter.*

PROSPECTUS.

THE ancient Greek looked longingly for the Olympiad; the Chaldee watched the appearing of a star, to him no higher revelation than the horoscope hung out upon empyrean. But the meek Nazarene, the scoffed of all scoffers, said: "Ye can discern the face of the sky, and how much more should you discern the sign of these times;" and he looked at the ordeal of a perfect Christianity, hated by sinners.

To kindle all minds with a common sentiment of regard the new idea that comes welling up from infinite Truth needs to be understood. The seer of this period should be a sage. Small streams are noisy and rush precipitately in torrents; ... ture of every right idea, and the quiet practice of every duty. After the noise and stir of contending sentiments cease, and the flames fade away on the mount of revelation, we read more clearly the tablets of truth, and write them on the heart.

Humility is the stepping-stone to a higher recognition of Deity, whereby we discern the divine power of Truth and Love to heal the sick. Pride is ignorance, and those assume most who have least wisdom or experience, and they steal from their neighbor because they have so little of their own. The signs of these times portend a long night to the traveler, when we remember that God is just, and the total depravity of mortals, alias mortal mind, must first be seen, and then it must be subdued and recompensed by justice, that eternal attribute of Truth. To-day we behold but the first faint beams of a more spiritual Christianity that embraces a deeper and broader philosophy, and a more rational and divine healing. The time approaches when divine Life, Truth, and Love, shall be found alike the remedy for sin, sickness and death, and man's saving Principle, the Christ, learned through Christian Science.

Man's probation after death is the necessity of his immortality; for good dies not, and evil is self-destructive, therefore evil must be mortal. If man should not progress after death, but should ... he would be inevitable ... elf-annihilated. "They ... whom the second death ... who progress here and ... vil, their mortal element, ... that is immortal — thus ... aterial beliefs that war ... d putting on the spirit- ... goodness, purity and ...

... and *Materia medica* of ... and this divine unit of ... d the sick and cleansed ... only mental method of ... shall vindicate, and en- ... ndard, Christian Science.

While we entertain decided views as to the best method for elevating the race physically, morally and spiritually, and shall express these views as duty demands, we shall claim no especial gift from our divine origin, or any supernatural power; for we hold that good is more natural than evil, and that spiritual understanding, even the true knowledge of God, imparts the only power to heal, and should demonstrate in our lives the power of Truth and Love. The lessons we learn of divine science are applicable to all the needs of man, and Jesus taught them for this very purpose, and his demonstration hath taught us that, "through his stripes" — his bitter experience — and his divine science reduced to the understanding is man healed and saved. No opinions of Gnostic, Pantheist or Spiritualist, enter our line of thought or action. Drugs, inert matter, we never recommend, since mind is more potent than they to govern the body. Hygiene, manipulation, or mesmerism is not our medicine; the Principle of our cure is God, unerring and immortal Mind. And wherefore? Because we have learned that the erring or mortal thought holds in itself all sin, sickness and death, and imparts these states to the body; while the supreme and perfect Mind, as seen in the Truth of being, antidotes and destroys those material elements of error.

Since God is supreme and omnipotent, Materia medica, hygiene and animal magnetism are impotent, and their only efficacy is in deluding reason, denying revelation and dethroning Deity. The tendency of mental healing is to uplift mankind, but when this method is perverted it is "Satan let loose." The silent malpractice of an evil mind working out its own designs of mortal malice, masked in silent mental arguments and the subtle influences of mesmerism, the age has yet to learn that, to certain idiosyncracies, is more fatal to health and morals than the most deadly drugs and the more open enticements to sin. The mind imbued with purity, Truth and

PHOTO © TMBEL

THE CHRISTIAN SCIENCE JOURNAL jsh-online.com
MAY 2013
HEAL THE SICK · RAISE THE DEAD · CLEANSE THE LEPERS · CAST OUT DEMONS
The CHRISTIAN SCIENCE
JOURNAL
"...designed to bear aloft the standard of genuine Christian Science." — MARY BAKER EDDY

© CSPS

⮝ First issue of the *Journal of Christian Science.* Because the editor liked to laugh, she included occasional jokes as fillers, such as this one: "Why is Adam the patron saint of Western pork raisers? Because he had the first spare rib."

⮜ *The Christian Science Journal* today

first issue) could announce their availability to the public. The editor's essays, poems, and articles would offer soul-food to the hungry of heart, and the "Answers to Questions" section would provide a forum to answer the flood of queries that she couldn't possibly respond to on an individual basis.

The first issue included a poignant but resolute poem, one Mary would later revise for a collection of her poetry. Entitled "The Oak on the Summit," she'd written it the previous summer, two months after Gilbert's passing. The final verses read:

> Whate'er thy mission, mountain sentinel,
> O'er my lone heart thou hast a magic spell;
> A lesson grave, of life, thou teachest me—
> I love the Hebrew figure of a tree.
>
> Faithful and patient be my years as thine;
> As strong to wrestle with the storms of time;
> As deeply rooted in a soil of love;
> As grandly rising to the heavens above.

"A great work has already been done, and a great work yet remains to be done," Mary stated elsewhere in that issue's pages. Like the oak tree in her poem, she, too, had wrestled with storms, but her roots stretched deep in the soil of love for her fellow man, and she was looking onward and upward to a brighter future.

14
Sons Old and New

Lead City Oct 23, 1887

Dear Mother,

I beliv [sic] you owe me a letter at any rate I start to Boston the first of November with my family for the peprce [sic — "purpose"] of making you a visit this winter.

we are all quite well from your loving son
George W. Glover

George's cheery note arrived as his mother was swamped with work.

The past four years had brought sturdy growth to the Christian Science movement, and the Metaphysical College (which still doubled as Mary's home) overflowed with students. She continued to serve as pastor of her church, which by now had outgrown Hawthorne Hall and moved to larger Chickering Hall on Tremont Street. By the end of the decade, parlor lectures, held at the college to introduce the public to Christian Science, would eventually evolve into regular Friday evening meetings (later changed to Wednesday evening testimony meetings).

In addition to teaching and preaching—often to standing room only crowds—Mrs. Eddy was juggling writing, editing, and publishing demands, as well as a mountain of mail from those seeking information, counsel, and encouragement.

"I am daft with business," she wrote to a student around this time.

PHOTO © TMBEL

FEED MY SHEEP
(March 1887 version)

Shepherd, show us how to go
O'er the hillside steep,
How to gather, how to sow,
How to feed Thy sheep;
We will listen for Thy voice,
Lest our footsteps stray,
We will follow and rejoice
All the rugged way.

Thou wilt bind the stubborn will,
Wound the callous breast,
Make self righteousness be still,
Break earth's stupid rest;
Strangers on a barren shore
Lab'ring long and lone—
We would enter by the door,
And Thou know'st Thine own;

So when day grows dark and cold
Fear or triumph harms,
Lead Thy lambkins to the fold,
Take us in Thine arms,
Feed the hungry, heal the heart,
Till the morning's beam;
White as wool, ere we depart—
Shepherd, wash us clean.

▲ During her lifetime, Mary Baker Eddy would have several of her poems, including this one, set to music to be used as hymns in Christian Science churches.

In February 1885, she'd published a slim pamphlet entitled *Historical Sketch of Metaphysical Healing*. The following month came *Defence of Christian Science* (written in response to attacks from the clergy and later revised and renamed simply *No and Yes)*, and then in November of 1887, *Rudiments and Rules of Divine Science* (later expanded and renamed *Rudimental Divine Science)*.

In the spring of that year, Mrs. Eddy also published a poem in the *Journal* that would become one of her most beloved. Written while she was shepherding both her Boston flock and her growing movement, it hints at some of her trials, and shows how alone she still felt at times and how humbly she prayed for guidance.

There had been many times in recent years when Mrs. Eddy had seen the day grow "dark and cold," from promising students who rebelled and fell away, to scorn from the press and verbal attacks by clergymen outraged at her challenge to traditional theology. (Outraged, too, perhaps, that some of their own church members were decamping to Christian Science after being healed, helping to fuel the new religion's rapid growth.) But she had seen triumphs as well, including the dedication in Oconto, Wisconsin, in 1886 of the first building constructed for Christian Science church services. She also had the satisfaction of knowing that her book was fulfilling its mission.

"CAPTAIN, WHY DON'T YOU HEAL YOUR WIFE YOURSELF?"

FOOTSTEPS OF PROGRESS

COURTESY TMBEL

Captain Eastaman

Joseph Eastaman was dumbfounded. In the winter of 1884, shortly after returning from a voyage to Peru, he'd come to the Massachusetts Metaphysical College to ask Mary Baker Eddy if she would treat his terminally-ill wife. Instead, she countered with this question.

"Never for one moment had the possibility of my becoming a healer dawned upon me," the sea captain later recalled. "I did not know what to say, or think." Though he was a devout man, and had experienced many instances of God's protection during his decades at sea, he'd only recently heard of Christian Science. Protesting that he'd done everything in his power to help cure his wife, including seeking out the best medical aid for her, he added, "What more can I do?"

"Learn how to heal," Mrs. Eddy told him gently.

Captain Eastaman enrolled on the spot, and three days later found himself in her classroom, being taught how to heal as Jesus did.

Mary Eastaman recovered so rapidly under Joseph's fledgling Christian Science treatments that she was able to sit in on the final class session with him. A few months later she, too, received instruction from Mrs. Eddy. Husband and wife both became Christian Science practitioners and teachers, and Captain Eastaman would later recount his adventures on the high seas and his spiritual voyage in a series of articles entitled "The Travail of My Soul" published in the *Christian Science Journal* in 1892.

Today, just as in the early days of the Christian Science movement, earnest seekers of truth still have the opportunity to sit in a classroom and receive the kind of teaching that Captain Eastaman would have received, through what is called "Primary class instruction."

This inspiring 12-day course digs deeply into the teachings of the Bible and *Science and Health with Key to the Scriptures*, explains more about God and each individual's relationship to Him, and equips students with the principles of Christian healing.

Taught by experienced Christian Science practitioners who have completed a course of instruction called Normal class and earned a teaching degree, Primary class is structured around the chapter in *Science and Health* entitled "Recapitulation," which evolved from Mary Baker Eddy's own class-book. And just as she patiently counseled and mentored her students, so today's Christian Science teachers patiently counsel and mentor theirs. One way in which this life-long mentoring occurs is through an annual association meeting, when pupils of each teacher gather together for a day of continuing instruction.

COURTESY TMBEL

Mary Eastaman

More information about class instruction can be found in the *Church Manual* under the chapter heading "Teaching Christian Science" (Articles XXVI and XXVII). The names of authorized teachers of Christian Science can be found in any copy of *The Christian Science Journal*, or on the church's website, www.christianscience.com.

COURTESY TMBEL

The Glover family circa 1887: Mary, George Washington Glover II, Nellie, Evelyn, and Gershom

"Since 'Science and Health' was published, I have been constantly in receipt of letters informing me that people are healing themselves and others by the knowledge gained from that book," Mrs. Eddy noted in *Historical Sketch of Metaphysical Healing*. "I knew it would be so, and for this I wrote it."

Another triumph occurred in May of 1884, when she traveled to Chicago. There, she taught a class of 25 pupils and gave a public lecture at Hershey Hall. Both were successful, and helped launch Christian Science in the Midwest.

Mrs. Eddy also established a Normal class at her college that year to educate properly trained teachers of Christian Science for the expanding field. This new course was open to those who had been instructed in a Primary class, and who had practiced Christian healing for one to two years.

Janet Colman enrolled in the Normal class of 1885, and almost immediately after becoming an authorized teacher offered to go to Nebraska in response to a request for instruction there. Janet taught the first class west of the Missouri River, and her healing and teaching work throughout the Midwest would help blaze a trail for the expansion of the Christian Science movement.

Other of Mrs. Eddy's students did likewise, and through their work as well as through the outreach of *Science and Health* and the *Journal*, the seed of Christian Science spread.

As it did, people flocked from all corners of the country to attend the Massachusetts Metaphysical College. Male and female, young and old, wealthy and poor, from the city and from the country they came. Mrs. Eddy's students were farmers and homemakers, merchants and mechanics, bankers and businessmen. Distinguished lawyers, doctors, judges, and ministers shared classroom space with those of more humble background, all of them wanting to learn how to heal like Jesus did and understand more about God and their relationship to Him.

When George's letter arrived that fall of 1887 announcing his plans to come East, his mother was in the middle of teaching a class, with another scheduled close on its heels. It was hardly the perfect time for a family visit.

It had been eight years since George's last unexpected trip to Boston. He'd recently inherited $10,000 (over $200,000 in today's dollars) from his Aunt Abi, who had passed away the previous year. Perhaps this influx of cash spurred his desire to bring his wife, Nellie, and their three children—Gershom (12), Mary (10), and newest-arrival Evelyn (7)—to see his mother.

PHOTO MARK THAYER © TMBEL

➤ Mary Baker Eddy bought this brownstone townhouse at 385 Commonwealth Avenue in December of 1887. She had the tower added in 1895, and would later deed the property to her church to be used as the First Reader's residence.

Mrs. Eddy wrote back, urging them to postpone their journey. She had nowhere to put them, she explained. George and his family came anyway.

Mrs. Eddy graciously found lodging for them in nearby Chelsea, and put them in the care of her old friend Captain Eastaman. She did her best to include her family in her busy life, inviting them for meals and Thanksgiving festivities. The three children immediately charmed their grandmother. She called them "sweet" Gershom, "bright" Evelyn, and "my dear little namesake" Mary. Her heart leapt at their promise. Like many a grandmother, she wanted to show off her grandchildren, so before she preached one Sunday she took them up on the platform with her and introduced them to the congregation.

The longer the Glovers stayed back East, though, the more it became clear to them all how little they had in common. Mrs. Eddy felt keenly the whole family's lack of schooling, for one thing. Here she was, head of a flourishing college, and her son and his wife either couldn't or wouldn't learn to read! She was particularly concerned for her grandchildren's future, and dashed off a note to George:

"I want your children educated. No greater disgrace rests on my family name than the ignorance of the parents of these darling children.... For the sake of your dear children you should both of you learn to read and write. It would be a great help to them."

Between visits with each other, lessons for the children, and sightseeing, six months passed swiftly for the Glovers. Finally, it was time in everyone's estimate for them to go home.

There were very likely disappointments on both sides. George's yet-to-be-born son and namesake would later quote his father as forever yearning for "a regular mother"—someone who would have cooked, kept house, supported his mining ventures, and visited his family. Mrs. Eddy would have liked an educated son, one who understood the breadth and importance of her work and the difficulties of her task, yet who loved her for herself. Their differences didn't diminish their mutual affection, however. Soon after they left she wrote warmly: "Hope you are happy and safe at home and doing lots of business and growing wiser and better as life wears away. Kiss the 'wee' ones for me love to the wife and more than all others love for you."

Mary turned again to the many tasks at hand, including settling into the new house on elegant Commonwealth Avenue that she'd moved into in late December. Classes were still held at the Metaphysical College, but now, at 66, she had a home entirely of her own for the very first time, one that didn't have to be shared with lodgers or students.

The new home was a visible symbol of just how far Mrs. Eddy had come. It wasn't that long ago that she'd been teetering on the brink of poverty, forced to move from boardinghouse to boardinghouse. Now, she was financially stable—no small accomplishment for a woman at that time, especially since she'd achieved it under her own steam. She was a successful author and lecturer, founder and pastor of a church, president of a college, and the chief executive officer of a movement with national scope.

The same year that George came to visit, the National Christian Scientist Association held its convention in Boston. Some 150 representatives came from 15 states, and it must have been encouraging to Mrs. Eddy to see this tangible evidence of progress.

Shortly before George and his family left to return to South Dakota, a new student enrolled at the Massachusetts Metaphysical College. His name was Ebenezer J. Foster. Mrs. Eddy called him Benny.

Short, plump, and balding, Benny was 40 when he attended one of her classes. He was a graduate of Hahnemann Medical College in Philadelphia, and had practiced homeopathy in Pennsylvania and Vermont, where the healing of an old army buddy through Christian Science caught his interest.

CSA & NCSA

FOOTSTEPS OF PROGRESS

The Christian Scientist Association (CSA), formed by Mary in 1876, was an organization of students who had taken one or more classes with her. It differed from the National Christian Scientist Association (NCSA), which was open not only to her own students, but also to students of those students. The NCSA was formed in 1886, as Mrs. Eddy later wrote, "to meet the broader wants of humanity, and provide folds for the sheep that were without shepherds...." It thrived until May of 1890, when it was dissolved at her request. The CSA was formally disbanded in 1889, although it continued to meet occasionally on an informal basis.

He wrote to Mrs. Eddy's student Julia Bartlett, detailing his professional background, then added, "but if Christian Science is better, I want it."

Three years younger than George and unmarried, Benny was all that Mrs. Eddy's son was not—educated, polished, attentive. He sang and played the piano, and he struck a chord in his teacher's life, adding lightness to her moments of relaxation. They could laugh together. They could watch the sunset from her bay window, touched by the same beauty. Benny gave her his devoted attention.

His first letter to her began with "My Dear Spiritual Mother," and ended by wondering how he'd been admitted into her class, "which is so far in advance of anything else." Had she seen anything in him that "promised good results?" Mrs. Eddy did see promise in Benny and soon invited him to join her household. That July, Benny jotted down a note: "Sunday the 8th ... was a most glorious day to me because it had been spent with my dear Mama—for such she seemed to me—Mrs. MBG Eddy."

Mrs. MBG (Mary Baker Glover) Eddy—or Mary Baker Eddy, as she would soon come to be called—quickly promoted Benny, and three months later the doctor was teaching a course at the Massachusetts Metaphysical College. Mrs. Eddy felt convinced that here was a true son, and saw in him a possible champion for her Cause. Despite the misgivings of such trusted old friends as Christiana Godfrey, at the end of 1888 she adopted him. Benny was now associated with her "in business, home life, and life work," she told the court, "and she needs such interested care and relationship."

Her close students were dumbstruck. They knew that their teacher had felt abandoned by George after Gilbert passed on and he'd refused to come and help comfort her in her grief. They'd seen for themselves how different the two of them were, and how hopelessly ill-suited George would be to assisting Mrs. Eddy in her work. But why had she taken the legal step of adopting Benny?

It's certain that she was fond of him, but it's likely there was more to it than that. For one thing, her own family was dwindling. Her brothers Samuel and Sullivan were long gone by now, and both of her sisters had passed on as well—Martha in 1884 and Abigail in 1886. George had put down roots half a continent away, clearly disinterested in sharing her life in Boston. Perhaps she missed the close-knit family circle she had enjoyed growing up, and hoped to recreate this with Benny.

The adoption may also simply have been a move to protect her church. By this point in her life, Mrs. Eddy's once-threadbare finances were flourishing. George was always in need of money, and he liked to litigate. In fact, suing people was how he made a living much of the time. His mother was well aware of this. She would later write to a student, "my son in Dakota is a victor at law," and in a reply to George about one of his legal triumphs, she remarked drily, "I should think you would be the terror of the West in such matters."

NOTMAN PHOTOGRAPHY CO. LTD. COURTESY TMBEL

▲ Mary Baker Eddy's adopted son Ebenezer J. Foster, whom she called "Benny."

It was around the time of Benny's adoption that Mrs. Eddy began looking into the possibility of writing a will that would allow her to leave all of her property to her church. Under Massachusetts law, an adopted child had the same rights and privileges as a birth child. If George were ever to contest her will, Benny, who seemed to hold her and her teaching in such high regard, might be able to see that her wishes were upheld.

In June of 1888, five months before Benny's adoption was formalized, Mrs. Eddy brought him along when she went to Chicago for a meeting of the National Christian Scientist Association. She herself only decided to go a few days beforehand. Imagine her surprise when she walked into the hall and discovered that she was the featured speaker!

About 800 Christian Scientists had gathered at Central Music Hall, but the public had also been invited, and the crowd had grown to some 4,000 people. Not only that, but the press was out in force to cover the event, too. With no time to make a single note, Mrs. Eddy gave a spontaneous address that left her audience wild with excitement.

"Science and the senses are at war," she warned. "It is a revolutionary struggle. We have had two already in this nation, and they began and ended in a contest for the true idea, for human liberty and rights. Now cometh a third struggle for the freedom of health, holiness, and Heaven."

How many, she asked, were "ready to suffer for a righteous cause, to stand a long siege, take the front rank, face the foe, and be in the battle every day?"

Quite a few, apparently. According to the *Chicago Times*: "When the speaker concluded the audience arose en masse and made a rush for the platform. There were no steps provided for getting on the rostrum, but that did not deter [the crowd]. They mounted the reporters' table and vaulted to the rostrum like acrobats. They crowded about the little woman and hugged and kissed her until she was exhausted and a man had to come to her rescue and lead her away."

Among the audience was Susan B. Anthony, the well-known advocate for women's rights. She had been taught in a Primary class held in Washington, D. C., the previous year by Laura Lathrop, one of Mrs. Eddy's students. Although she never publicly espoused Christian Science, Susan kept the copy of *Science and Health* given to her by her teacher as a gift at the close of that class for many years, after which she passed it along to a close friend, adding her own inscription.

PHOTO © TMBEL

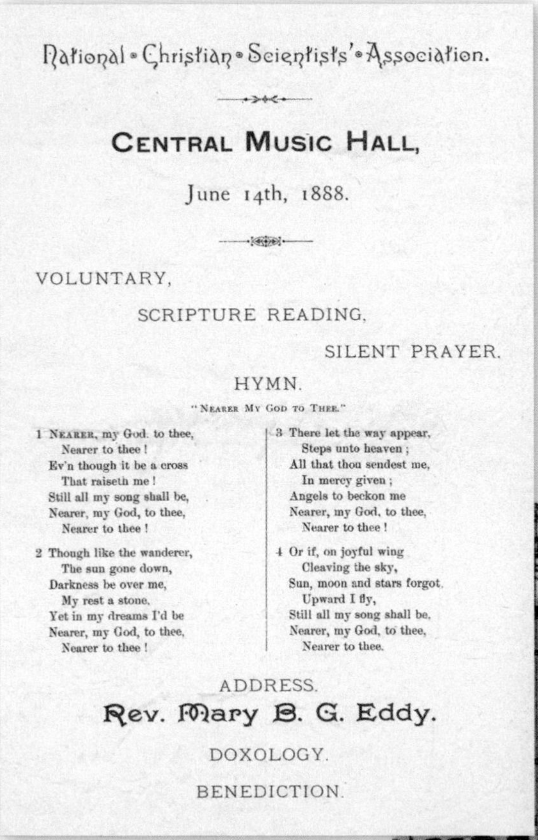

National • Christian • Scientists' • Association.

CENTRAL MUSIC HALL,

June 14th, 1888.

VOLUNTARY,

SCRIPTURE READING,

SILENT PRAYER.

HYMN.

"NEARER MY GOD TO THEE."

1 NEARER, my God, to thee,
Nearer to thee!
Ev'n though it be a cross
That raiseth me!
Still all my song shall be,
Nearer, my God, to thee,
Nearer to thee!

2 Though like the wanderer,
The sun gone down,
Darkness be over me,
My rest a stone,
Yet in my dreams I'd be
Nearer, my God, to thee,
Nearer to thee!

3 There let the way appear,
Steps unto heaven;
All that thou sendest me,
In mercy given;
Angels to beckon me
Nearer, my God, to thee,
Nearer to thee!

4 Or if, on joyful wing
Cleaving the sky,
Sun, moon and stars forgot,
Upward I fly,
Still all my song shall be,
Nearer, my God, to thee,
Nearer to thee.

ADDRESS.

Rev. Mary B. G. Eddy.

DOXOLOGY.

BENEDICTION.

Mrs. Eddy didn't know she was on the program for this event!

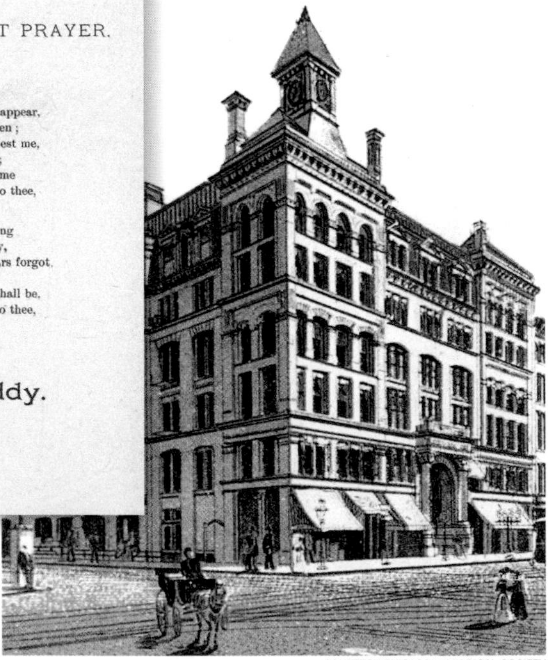

Mary Baker Eddy addressed a crowd of 4,000 here at Central Music Hall in 1888.

COURTESY CHICAGO HISTORICAL SOCIETY

In 1902, Susan would send Mrs. Eddy an autographed copy of Vol. IV of the *History of Woman Suffrage*, signing it "yours for justice to women," and commenting in the accompanying letter: "I remember of hearing you speak in the Chicago Music Hall a good many years ago." She also asked: "If you do not wish [the book] yourself, will you put it in some high school, normal school or public library?"

Mrs. Eddy kept the book.

COURTESY OF THE LIBRARY OF CONGRESS, PRINTS AND PHOTOGRAPHS DIVISION

▲ Susan B. Anthony heard Mary Baker Eddy speak in Chicago in 1888.

15
General-in-Chief

A "huge conspiracy in our midst!" blurted the normally unflappable Calvin Frye. There had been a revolt in Boston while Mrs. Eddy was away in Chicago that June of 1888. The storm had been brewing beforehand, but it wasn't until she was out of town that it broke.

At a special meeting of the Christian Scientist Association, held to resolve a disagreement that a handful of students had with a course of action their teacher had taken, nearly a third of the membership walked out. Mrs. Eddy returned home to find her organization in disarray.

It was a disheartening development, and one more blow in a decade that had brought more than its fair share of them. Mrs. Eddy was grateful to those of her followers who continued to stand by her. "I bless Him for the faithful ones who remain true to Christ and love me much, and more than perhaps I deserve," she wrote to one of them.

She, too, continued to love, including those who opposed her: "I never felt my Father so near," she told two of the students who had spearheaded the defection, inviting them to return to church. "I shall preach next Sunday, and I hope you will be there to learn more of the way to heaven, the joys that are imperishable. May God bless you and save you from sin is the prayer of your Pastor and Teacher."

PHOTO W. S. WARREN © TMBEL

▲ Reverend Mary Baker Eddy in the 1880s, at the height of her teaching and preaching activities

If she found these events discouraging, she was also cheered by the rush of applicants to her college that autumn. In November of 1888, she wrote to a student: "Our Cause has had a great propulsion from my late large classes. Over fifty members have gone into our C. S. Association since the stampede out of it."

Clara Shannon, a 30-year-old Englishwoman from Montreal who was a trained concert singer, enrolled in the September class. As Mrs. Eddy was finishing up a lesson one day, a man arrived with his sister, who was suffering from mental illness. Right in front of them, she fell to the floor screaming. Recalling how her teacher prayed for the raving woman, Clara later recounted, "O, the love that was expressed in our Leader's face as she looked down on her, stretched out both arms and lifted her up saying, 'Get up, darling.'" The woman was healed on the spot, and never suffered from delusions again.

All this time, Mrs. Eddy continued to pray about the split amongst her followers. At the November meeting of the Christian Scientist Association, she told them, "Love will meet and destroy every claim of error."

She was thinking long and hard about the future, "examining the situation prayerfully and carefully," as she would put it. Though Boston would always remain what she termed "the headquarters of Christian Science," the movement was growing, and with students like Clara and others from outside the United States now enrolling in her classes, it was increasingly clear that its reach would not be just national but international. What was the best way to nurture this growth? Should she continue the various organizations she had started to strengthen her students, or should she regroup and rethink things? She also felt a strong desire to once again revise her textbook, *Science and Health.* Mrs. Eddy yearned for time and space for the kind of quiet listening to God she needed while the storms of everyday life brewed and whirled around her.

In February of 1889, she traveled to New York City where she gave a successful address at Steinway Hall. Then in March, she taught her largest class yet, with some 70 students. It would be her last at the college, however, for she had decided on her course of action.

As always, once Mrs. Eddy felt her steps to be directed by God, she acted swiftly. In May of 1889 she resigned as pastor of her church in Boston, and in June turned over editorial supervision of her much-loved *Journal* to the National Christian Scientist Association. And then she made a surprising move—she left

COURTESY LONGYEAR MUSEUM CHESTNUT HILL, MASSACHUSETTS

▲ Mary Baker Eddy lived in this house at 62 North State Street from June 1889 to June 1892.

Boston to return to her native state of New Hampshire.

Settling into a rental house in Concord, she continued to make sweeping changes, dissolving the Christian Scientist Association in September and, to the shock of her followers, closing the doors of the Massachusetts Metaphysical College in October.

"I was simply astounded," wrote Frank Mason, one of her students, who had just conducted a class of his own in Iowa. "I supposed the College like the gate to Heaven would always be ajar. The West and in fact the whole country is dazed at the apparent sudden termination of the original source of Christian Science teaching."

Concerned about this decision, a trio of Mrs. Eddy's prominent students—Reverend Lanson P. Norcross, the Boston church's pastor; Edward Bates, a successful businessman from Syracuse, New York; and a distinguished Civil War general (likely Gen. Erastus Bates, who had recently been appointed president of the college)—felt it their duty to travel to Concord to advise her to change her mind.

"They said as far as spiritual things were concerned there was no question as to our teacher's judgment and ability," Julia Bartlett later recalled, "but in matters of business it was not expected she would understand and to close the College when a large number were only waiting the opportunity to enter was to them a great mistake...."

Mrs. Eddy was busy when the men arrived, but soon came to the room where they were waiting. Before they could bring up their concerns, she talked to them for a few minutes about how she had been led to make this move. The conversation completely took the wind out of her visitors' sails.

"Oh, nothing in particular," mumbled one of them in reply, when she finally asked what it was they had come to see her about. The others did likewise, equally mortified by their presumption. Afterwards, the men told Julia that they'd wished the floor would have opened up and swallowed them.

In the end, the board of officers of the college gave Mrs. Eddy their full support.

Her unexpected decisions may have startled her followers, and were not made lightly—in early November, Mrs. Eddy would write to a student, "I have had little else this year but loss and cross"—but she kept to her course. In late November, she dissolved the formal organization of her Boston church, requesting its members to continue to conduct services, but as a voluntary group rather than an official one.

To clarify, she placed this announcement in the December *Journal*: "Be it understood that I do not require Christian Scientists to stop teaching, to dissolve their organizations, or to desist from organizing churches and associations."

Looking back on these decisive moves, one of Mrs. Eddy's followers later noted that they marked a shift in her role. "She had previously been the Teacher," he wrote. Now, "she became the General-in-chief, and *the* Leader."

16

The 50th Edition and a "Sweet Home"

Peace was what Mary longed for, peace to think and work on her book. She looked for it in the quiet, tree-lined city of Concord, New Hampshire, near where she had grown up. The capital city was close enough to Boston to allow her to keep an eye on things and easily communicate with many of her students, but far enough away to provide a bit of a buffer.

It was clear to her at this point that she needed to devote all her time and energies to revising her book, and to praying for an answer as to how best to re-organize her church. She settled down to work.

There were the usual distractions, of course—people still beat a path to her door, both literally and via their letters that poured in. Mrs. Eddy assured her students that she hadn't retired and wasn't abandoning them, but that she had a higher work to do at the moment.

"God has given me new lessons, and I too must 'be about my Father's business,'" she wrote to one. "Do not think it is for lack of love, but only a conviction of duty that makes me desire to be isolated from society."

The biggest distraction of all arrived in the form of Josephine Woodbury, a student who had become a prominent Christian Science practitioner and teacher. Her teaching and dealings with students had come into question over the past few years, and now her morals had, too. She continued to make peculiar statements to fellow Christian Scientists and was also beginning to make them to the press. This would culminate in a magazine article a few years later in which she claimed Mrs. Eddy taught that "women may become mothers by a supreme effort of their own minds."

Mrs. Eddy taught nothing of the kind. In spite of Josephine's bizarre

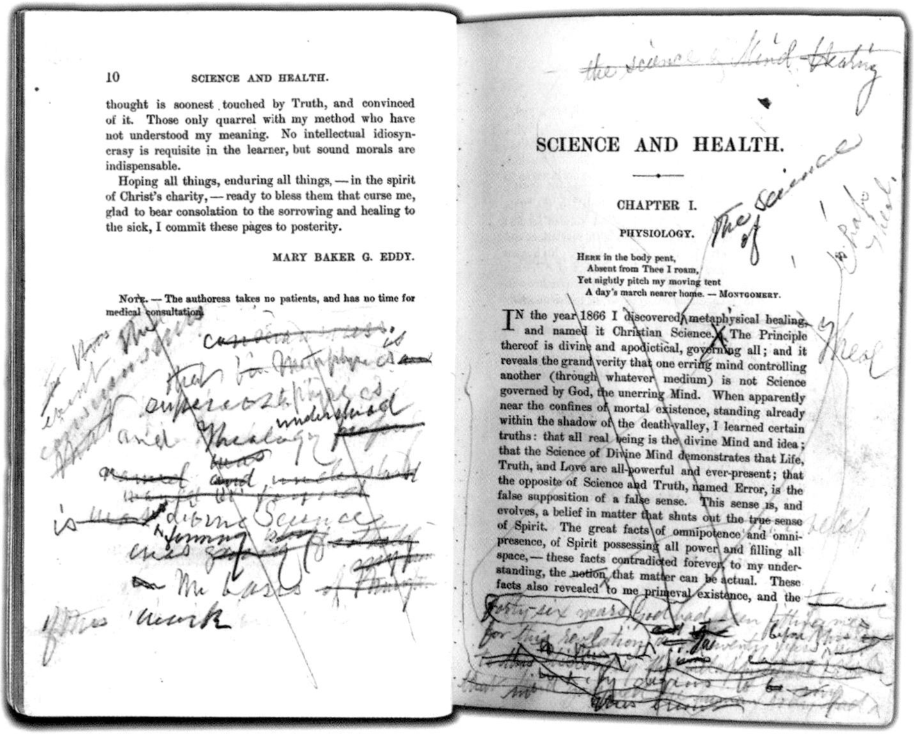
10 SCIENCE AND HEALTH.

thought is soonest touched by Truth, and convinced of it. Those only quarrel with my method who have not understood my meaning. No intellectual idiosyncrasy is requisite in the learner, but sound morals are indispensable.

Hoping all things, enduring all things, — in the spirit of Christ's charity, — ready to bless them that curse me, glad to bear consolation to the sorrowing and healing to the sick, I commit these pages to posterity.

MARY BAKER G. EDDY.

NOTE. — The authoress takes no patients, and has no time for medical consultation.

SCIENCE AND HEALTH.

CHAPTER I.

PHYSIOLOGY.

HERE in the body pent,
Absent from Thee I roam,
Yet nightly pitch my moving tent
A day's march nearer home. — MONTGOMERY.

IN the year 1866 I discovered metaphysical healing, and named it Christian Science. The Principle thereof is divine and apodictical, governing all; and it reveals the grand verity that one erring mind controlling another (through whatever medium) is not Science governed by God, the unerring Mind. When apparently near the confines of mortal existence, standing already within the shadow of the death-valley, I learned certain truths: that all real being is the divine Mind and idea; that the Science of Divine Mind demonstrates that Life, Truth, and Love are all-powerful and ever-present; that the opposite of Science and Truth, named Error, is the false supposition of a false sense. This sense is, and evolves, a belief in matter that shuts out the true sense of Spirit. The great facts of omnipotence and omnipresence, of Spirit possessing all power and filling all space, — these facts contradicted forever, to my understanding, the notion that matter can be actual. These facts also revealed to me primeval existence, and the

PHOTO © TMBEL

▲ An example of Mary Baker Eddy's editing work (36th edition of *Science and Health* shown here)

behavior, and the ridicule it brought down on Christian Science in the public arena, she didn't cut her off completely, however. As was always the case with wayward students, Mrs. Eddy worked hard—often over many years—to love and forgive them, and try to win them back to the truth.

"Be patient as you can with her shortcomings," she wrote to Clara Shannon, who had returned to her home in Montreal, where Josephine had recently spent a number of months. "She has her good points as well."

As distressing as was a flap like this one, Mrs. Eddy couldn't allow it to keep her from her work. Her revision was paramount. She had caught the vision of the shape her new edition would take. Now that she was stepping back from teaching, *Science and Health* must become the instructor. Her book must be crystal clear as it continued to unlock the healing power of the Scriptures, answer the questions of newcomers, and comfort, strengthen, and guide all of its readers.

At the end of April 1890, she asked Rev. James Henry Wiggin, a former Unitarian minister her printer had previously recommended to help proofread her work, to again lend a hand. "I and my students greatly desire the first chapter of S & H to be introductory to the whole work," she wrote him, explaining that she wanted to convey her meaning "gently but perfectly and systematically" to the minds of her readers. The book should have "consistency beauty, strength and honesty."

A flurry of paperwork soon flew between Boston and Concord as copy and proofs traveled back and forth between Mrs. Eddy and Wiggin and the printer and publisher.

The book underwent significant restructuring. Chapters were rearranged, many were given new titles, and new ones were added, including "Teaching Christian Science." Mrs. Eddy removed the literary quotations from the chapter headings, replacing them with quotes from the Bible. Marginal headings were inserted to help guide readers. Nearly every page was revised in some way. It was a massive undertaking.

When the 50th edition finally came out in January 1891, Reverend Norcross, pastor of the Christian Science congregation in Boston, was happy to report that "the new volume seems to take us back to the College, to gather up its fresh methods and inspired sayings, so that little stretch of the imagination is required to convince us that the teacher herself again is before us, though this time in impersonal form."

Mrs. Eddy was thoroughly pleased with the result as well.

"It gives me joy unspeakable to think of the good that I know it will accomplish," she wrote to Captain Eastaman. "The old editions did their work and did it well. But the new has a new task, it takes into its office

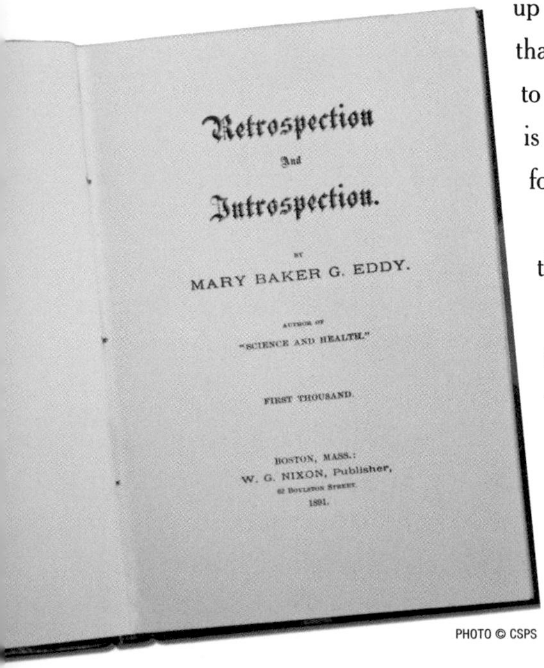

PHOTO © CSPS

While living on North State Street, Mrs. Eddy also revised and expanded her *Historical Sketch of Metaphysical Healing* into *Retrospection and Introspection*, which she published in November 1891.

that of teacher as well as healer; it becomes a living power to uplift the whole human race. I have done for this edition what the lapidary does,—brought out the gems and placed them well burnished, in sight."

With her work on this landmark edition of *Science and Health* complete, she could write cheerily to George: "Many happy New years to you all," and thank him for the ring he had sent her, made from gold he had mined himself. "I shall keep it so long as I live on this earth in loving memory of my son."

COURTESY OF LONGYEAR MUSEUM
CHESTNUT HILL, MASSACHUSETTS

▲ This ring that George gave to his mother is made of several colors of gold from Dakota's Black Hills.

There'd been triumphs for George as well, including another addition to his family. Mrs. Eddy's granddaughter Evelyn had written the previous year to tell her of the arrival of George Washington Glover III:

> *My Dear Grandmother, … it makes me quite happy to be able to write to you these few lines. Oh Dear I must tell you we have a darling baby boy he has eight teeth and can say lots of words real plain he is fat and strong he is very handsome.*
>
> *I only wish you could see him you would laugh to here [sic] him call papa to the top of his voice … From your little Granddaughter*
>
> *Evelyn Tilton Glover.*
> *God bless you.*
> *God bless you fore ever [sic].*

George had also recently won a sizable sum in yet another lawsuit, this one over property rights. His mother was quick to urge him: "Now dear one, I have a request to make, namely that you proceed at once to invest in a suitable house for your children. Do not wait one week, nor until you spend the good sum of money you have been paid, but buy a lot large enough for a home and build on it. Will you do this?"

Mrs. Eddy was in the market for a suitable home for herself as well. The house she had rented in Concord was on a noisy street and in need of repair. She asked Ira Knapp, a trusted student, to help her in her search.

HOME SWEET HOME

PEOPLE AND PLACES

"The strongest tie I have ever felt, next to my love of God, has been my love for home," Mary Baker Eddy once wrote to a student.

Of all the homes she would own in her lifetime, Pleasant View was her favorite. "Oh! The singing birds and glorious view from my 'sweet home' is so lovely I cannot be sufficiently thankful for it," she wrote to friends shortly after moving in.

From her study window Mrs. Eddy could see the distant hills of Bow, where the old Baker homestead of her girlhood still stood. The house itself, which a reporter would later describe as a "well-ordered, well-kept country residence," was a typical New England frame-built structure, gracious but not luxurious. Renovations added an attractive tower and a covered porch along the back where she could walk when the weather was unpleasant. Some of her students contributed funds for a pond and a rowboat, and there would eventually be a boathouse, a greenhouse, a gazebo, ornamental gardens lush with flowers, and a fountain with resident goldfish that she enjoyed feeding. Everything inside and out was kept as neat as a pin, just as Mrs. Eddy liked it, and she took a keen interest in every detail of her estate.

Pleasant View was a working farm as well as a peaceful refuge, and its bounty helped supply food for the table. Dinner was at noon, served family-style around the big dining room table. Household members would later fondly recall hearing the grinding of the ice cream freezer each day starting at 11 a.m., as Mrs. Eddy's favorite dessert was prepared.

"You seem to know just what I want," she wrote him in August of 1891. "Stillness and nature and God."

In the end, though, it was Mary herself who found the perfect spot. While on a carriage ride that fall, she saw a 36-acre farm for sale on the outskirts of the city. She purchased the property in December and set about remodeling the house, which she named "Pleasant View." She moved in on June 20, 1892, just a few weeks shy of her 71st birthday. It would be her home for nearly 16 years.

Well over a hundred people worked in the Pleasant View household at different times over the years—as secretaries and handymen, gardeners and groundskeepers, coachmen, cooks and companions, dressmakers and maids. Many of those who served were there

PHOTO MINNIE B. WEYGANDT © TMBEL

▲ Household worker Laura Sargent with one of Pleasant View's sweet-tempered Jersey dairy cows (a reporter noted that they came when called, "as though they were great pets").

PHOTO THOMAS E MARR COURTESY TMBEL

▲ Pleasant View, Mary Baker Eddy's home in Concord, New Hampshire

➤ Laura Sargent at her desk

COURTESY TMBEL

because their lives had been transformed by Christian Science, and in gratitude they gave up family and church obligations for up to a year at a time (later three years) in order to assist Mrs. Eddy.

Laura Sargent was one such worker. After being healed of an illness through Christian Science treatment, she studied with Mrs. Eddy in her Chicago class, then entered the public practice of healing back in her hometown of Oconto, Wisconsin. In 1886, Laura went through Normal Class at the Massachusetts Metaphysical College, returning to teach in Wisconsin and Minnesota. Mrs. Eddy asked her to join her staff in 1890, while she was still living on State Street. Laura did, and remained with the household for the next 20 years.

Always willing to help her teacher in whatever way she could, Laura served as Mrs. Eddy's personal assistant and companion. On several occasions

PHOTO MARK THAYER © TMBEL

▲ Mary Baker Eddy gave Laura Sargent this carving as a thank you for her work as a courier.

after arriving in Concord she also worked as a courier, ferrying manuscripts and page proofs back and forth between Pleasant View and Mrs. Eddy's publisher.

Mrs. Eddy nicknamed her "my pigeon" and called her "a bright bearer of messages." As a thank you, she gave her an exquisite little ivory carving of a carrier pigeon, which Laura treasured for the rest of her life.

Each day at Pleasant View brought a steady stream of decisions to be made, correspondence to be answered, and visitors to be seen. Mary Baker Eddy may have been living in rural New Hampshire, but she was still the leader of the growing Christian Science movement, and Pleasant View was its vibrant headquarters. Although she might not have known it at the time, she was a pioneer in telecommuting, making good use of the technology of her day, from telegrams to mail service that picked up and delivered several times a day, to the trains that ran frequently, taking couriers from Concord to Boston and back.

Mrs. Eddy kept to a regular schedule, rising early and often working far into the night. She looked forward to her afternoon drive—often the only respite in her busy day.

As always during these years, Mrs. Eddy was hard at work writing. In addition to dozens of articles, essays, and poems, in November of 1891 she published an account of her own history entitled *Retrospection and Introspection*; in December of 1893 came *Christ and Christmas*, an illustrated poem; and *Pulpit and Press* in April of 1895.

For a while now, she no longer officially saw patients. To a reader of the *Journal* who'd asked a decade earlier, "Has Mrs. Eddy lost her power to heal?" she responded, perhaps with a twinkle of good humor, "Has the sun forgotten to shine, and the planets to revolve around it?"

Healing was as natural to her as breathing, and she continued to help people in need—including her student David Easton, a former Congregational minister who came to see her in the fall of 1891 when he was in the last stages of consumption. A week after their visit, Mrs. Eddy received a letter from him:

"I am healed. I realized it the next day after I saw you.... When I called

COURTESY TMBEL

▲ Mary Baker Eddy on her daily drive. Calvin Frye is at the reins.

on you, I seemed to be in a swift current of mortal thought, that I could not resist and that was carrying me down, down. Your few but vigorous words seemed to lift me out of that current. I feel like a new man."

Mrs. Eddy wished she had more time to see visitors. Increasingly, though, she found she had to limit her social activity in order to stay focused on what she would call in a *Journal* article the following summer "my life-purpose, namely: to impress humanity with the genuine recognition of practical, operative Christian Science."

She continued to keep in touch through letters, though, including those she exchanged with her son George. In December of 1891, he had written to her about the arrival of his "fourth of July boy" Andrew Jackson Glover. Young George by this time was almost three; Andrew was five months and as "fat as a pig," according to his proud parent. George also sent his mother a Christmas present of a heart-shaped glass locket filled with gold dust from his latest mine.

"Accept my more than thanks for your heart, filled with gold dust!" Mary wrote back, adding "But dear son, I wish it was full of love for God, and I hope that it is." She closed by sending love to her grandchildren, to George's

"ALWAYS SPEAK TO THE HORSES"

EVERYDAY LIFE

It was while living in Concord that Mary Baker Eddy began the custom of her daily drive. Away from the demands of her desk, away from the bustle of her household, her carriage ride was an oasis in the day, taking her into the countryside for a little fresh air, a change of scene, and the opportunity to greet (and on numerous occasions heal) her neighbors and fellow townspeople. She often took bags of peanuts and candies to pass out to the children she'd see along her way. This daily drive wasn't just a mini-vacation, though.

"This is my time for communion with God," she wrote to Maurine Campbell, one of her followers. And to another she said, "I have uttered some of my best prayers in a carriage."

Though Mrs. Eddy would eventually purchase several automobiles for her household, she only rode in one once, much preferring horse-drawn vehicles. From her girlhood she had loved horses, and she owned a number of them over the years. Some worked in the fields; others pulled carriages and sleighs; all were loved and cared for. In addition to Duke and Prince there were Dolly and Princess, Jerry and Jean, Eckersall and Tattersall (who proved too skittish to pull her carriage), and Nellie and Major.

Mrs. Eddy would occasionally walk down to the stables to visit her horses, and enjoyed feeding them handfuls of hay grown right at Pleasant View. Above the stable door hung a sign, "Always speak to the horses before entering the stalls," and she did just that—and not only when they were in their stalls, either.

"When she returned from her drive and got out of her carriage she would often go to the end of the verandah nearest to the horses' heads, and speak to each one," recalled Clara Shannon, who lived and worked at Pleasant View for a number of years. (And yes, Mrs. Eddy would pat them, too.)

"dear wife" and told him to "take a good share for yourself, with a Mother's tender wish for the welfare and happiness of you all this New Year."

Mrs. Eddy had sent her granddaughters special copies of her newly-revised *Science and Health*, and in a P.S. George added: "Except [sic] my thanks for the beautifull [sic] books you sent to the girls. Gold is of no value compared."

Next, in April of 1892, Mrs. Eddy heard from her granddaughter Evelyn, who wrote to "tell you we are all well." Evelyn ended her letter with a heartfelt (if somewhat misspelled) ditty:

Roses are red
And vailets [sic] are blew [sic]
And sugar is sweet and
so are you
And if you love me
you will ancer [sic] this letter

Mary Baker Eddy's horse, Major, lived to the ripe old age of thirty in pampered retirement.

COURTESY TMBEL

To Mrs. Eddy's surprise, her son George arrived in the spring of the following year, bringing his four-year-old namesake with him. The "little chubby darling" delighted his grandmother. He trundled his small wheeled toy with her down to the pond, where they fed the ducks together; he rang the electric bell she used to summon her staff; he went for rides with her in her carriage and waved proudly at everyone they passed. Little George fixed himself firmly in Mrs. Eddy's affections, and from that point on, his education and future were close to her heart.

COURTESY OF LONGYEAR MUSEUM CHESTNUT HILL, MASSACHUSETTS

Four-year-old George Washington Glover III—whom Mary Baker Eddy called the "little chubby darling"—quickly won his grandmother's heart.

Though Mary would have loved to see all of her grandchildren more often, she didn't have the leisure to travel, and her son's out-of-the-blue visits were difficult, given her busy schedule and the many demands on her time. Their reunions were always bittersweet for them both, as George still yearned for a "regular mother," while she was keenly aware of how far apart their interests in life were. Once, when she walked in on her son as he was explaining one of his mining inventions to some visitors, she noted drily, "That was always the difference between George and myself. George was always looking down and I was always looking up."

Plus, it was sadly evident that her son was as much interested in her growing prosperity as he was in her life and work. By the following year, George was in debt again. This time his attorney, James P. Wilson, decided to write to Mrs. Eddy himself:

"If you can help him at this time I know it will be thankfully received and save him many thousand dollars. Will you do it? He needs $2,000 [some $50,000 in today's dollars] badly.... You know as well as I there are times if a person can get help when it is needed it is worth ten times the amount later on."

George's mother did know what it was like to be in need, and so she helped him out of his immediate predicament. Her own need, however, was of a different nature. Mrs. Eddy was hard at work rebuilding her church.

17
A "Prayer in Stone"

Ever since her move to Concord, Mrs. Eddy had been praying for God's guidance as she pondered what form her church should take in the future.

By the summer of 1892, she was ready to move forward. She asked 12 tried and true students to meet and incorporate as The First Church of Christ, Scientist. From that number, she appointed a four-person administrative Board of Directors (later expanded to five), who were duly voted on and accepted by the others. This constitutional government was a step away from the congregational structure that Mrs. Eddy had known from her youth, and after which she had patterned her earlier church. As early as the mid-1880s, she'd envisioned a church that was no longer just a local one, with members involved in the day-to-day running of things—making it susceptible to the kind of quarrels and disputes that had caused trouble in the past. Now was the time to implement this vision. Her reorganized church would be open to Christian Scientists everywhere, and its government would rest on divinely inspired laws.

The following winter, Mrs. Eddy asked the newly-formed board to appoint Rev. Easton, the student she had healed of consumption, to succeed Lanson Norcross as pastor of her church in Boston. Before long, it would come to be known as The Mother Church, the home church for Christian Scientists worldwide. But first, it needed a permanent location.

Mrs. Eddy already had the land for it. Back in the summer of 1886, a triangular plot in Boston's Back Bay had been bought by the church. Mrs. Eddy purchased the mortgage at one point, and eventually deeded this land over to the Board of Directors in September of 1892. Six months later, Joseph Armstrong was elected to the Board. A former lumberman and bank owner from Kansas, he had taken up the study of Christian Science after his wife was healed of an illness her doctor had said was incurable. It was to Armstrong that Mrs. Eddy wrote in October of 1893, after several delays in moving the project forward, urging him to act right away to lay the foundations for the church building before the frost set in. He followed her instructions, and within two days contracts were signed for the work of excavation, pile driving, and the laying of a stone foundation.

When more money was needed, Mrs. Eddy wrote to a select number of her students, asking each one to contribute $1,000 ($25,000 in 2013 dollars) to the building fund. This was a large sum, considering her household staff earned about $800 ($20,000 today) a year (most also received room and board in addition to their salary), and that the country was suffering through another major economic depression. Happy to show their gratitude for all that Christian Science had done for them, though, donors stepped up to the plate. Within three months, $40,000 (just under $1 million today) had been received, allowing the Directors to put out bids for further contracts. By the fall of 1894, though, funds were again low. How could the project's deadline possibly be met?

As far back as March of 1893 Mrs. Eddy had urged: "The church must be built in 1894 Deo volente [God willing]." Nine months later, she issued a "Word to the Wise" in the December 1893 *Christian Science Journal:*

"Our church edifice must be built in 1894.... No doubt must intervene between the promise and event; faith and resolve are friends to Truth, seize them, trust the Divine providence, push upward our prayer in stone and God will give the benediction."

By April of 1894, things had ground to a halt once more, and Mrs. Eddy wrote to the board again, asking them to move forward. Finally, on May 21st the cornerstone was laid. Then in the fall, she issued a directive to finish the church in time to hold the first service on December 30th, the last Sunday of the year, and a special dedication service the following Sunday, January 6th, 1895.

That hardly seemed possible. As the work inched forward, the earliest snow in years blanketed Boston. It piled up inside the unfinished church, which was still open to the elements.

On November 5th, the day before the snowstorm, Edward and Caroline Bates had come to town. A businessman from Syracuse, New York, Edward had been given the contract for the church's heating and ventilation systems.

His wife Caroline was donating a stained glass window to the new church — a circular or "rose" window depicting Jesus raising Jairus' daughter — and had come along to check on its progress.

An architect friend accompanied the Bateses to the art glass studio, and he happened to see a copy of the church plans. He spotted a problem: the ceiling trusses were too low. Anyone trying to go into the balcony of the church would have to stoop to enter, and the rear seats would be useless. When the Board of Directors heard this, they immediately hired the architect to take charge of correcting the design flaw and asked Edward Bates to oversee the necessary work.

A little over a week later, this work complete, Edward was on the train home when he found himself nagged by the feeling that his church needed him. Setting his own business concerns aside, he turned right around and went back to Boston to offer his services as on-site manager. The Directors gratefully accepted.

With seven weeks left to go until the day Mrs. Eddy had chosen for the first service to be held, things looked discouraging. Ice and snow still covered the

THE MOTHER'S EVENING PRAYER

(August 1893 version)

Oh gentle presence, peace and joy and power;
Oh Life divine, that owns each waiting hour,
Thou Love that guards the nestling's faltering flight
Keep Thou my child on upward wing to-night.

Love is our refuge, only with mine eye
Can I behold the snare, the pit, the fall;
His habitation high is here, and nigh,
His arm encircles me, and mine, and all.

Oh make me glad for every scalding tear,
For hope deferred, ingratitude, disdain!
Wait, and love more for every hate, and fear
No ill — since God is good, and loss is gain.

Beneath the shadow of His mighty wing;
In that sweet secret of the narrow way,
Seeking and finding, with the angels, sing:
"Lo! I am with you always," — watch and pray.

No snare, no fowler, pestilence or pain;
No night drops down upon the troubled breast,
When heaven's aftersmile, earth's teardrops gain,
And mother finds her home and far-off rest.

▲ In the August 1893 *Journal*, Mrs. Eddy published a poem entitled "The Mother's Evening Prayer." Perhaps one way of looking at the verses is as a prayer for the progress and safety of her church. In December 1909 she would change the final line to read: "And mother finds her home and heavenly rest."

building site, and there was little visible activity.

Why the continued delay? Edward and Caroline, along with Mrs. Eddy's other faithful students, recognized that the work that lay before them was just as much metaphysical as physical. This was an opportunity for them to put Christian Science into practice, and to demonstrate through prayer that "all things are possible" with God, as the Bible promises.

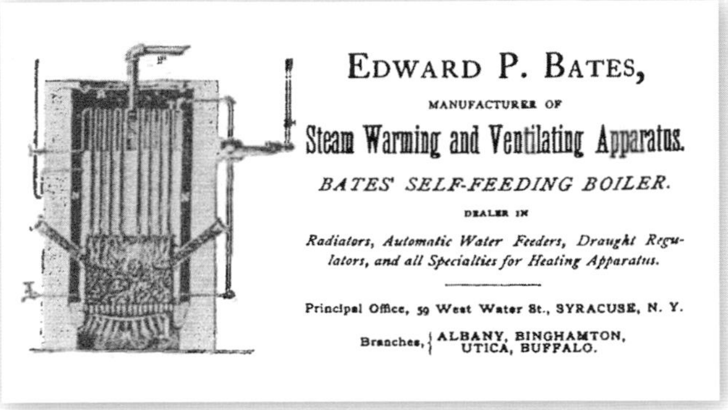

▲ An advertisement for Edward Bates' heating system

The first few days that Edward was in charge, there were only a few laborers. When he went home for lunch, work stopped. After two days, he no longer took a lunch hour, but stayed on the job from 8 a.m. until 5 p.m., or later if the men worked overtime. The project finally kicked into high gear. Edward increased the number of workmen until 20 contractors and over 200 men were hard at work, racing to meet the deadline.

On Friday, December 7th, Caroline Bates received a letter from Mrs. Eddy: "Finish the tower and plaster the church." She was astounded, and so was her husband. Out of all the tasks that needed doing, Mrs. Eddy had put her finger on the two most daunting. But why had the letter been sent to Caroline, and not to Edward or the Directors?

Perhaps Mrs. Eddy sensed a kindred spirit in Caroline. A practical-minded physician's daughter from New Haven, Connecticut, Caroline had a can-do attitude and resourcefulness that her teacher appreciated. At the building site, it was Caroline who'd found a solution to a troublesome chandelier. Meant to hang in the church's auditorium, it obstructed the view of the platform from the balcony. Caroline designed a sunburst skylight for the ceiling instead, which was wired with 144 light bulbs for added illumination during the services.

Still, Caroline was surprised to receive this message from her teacher. Shortly after its arrival, however, the reason behind it became clear. Her ingenuity was once again needed! The stonemasons, bricklayers, and steel men couldn't agree how to finish the church's tower, and it was Caroline who told them, "We will go up and find a way to do it."

As she later recalled, the men began to laugh. "You can never go up there," they told her. The tower was 120 feet high, and to reach it meant climbing two long ladders that had been lashed together without any stay or support.

Undaunted, Caroline picked up her long skirts and away she went, the ladders swaying in the icy wind with every step. "I entertained no fear whatever," she later wrote. "There was but one thing to do, which was to carry out Mrs. Eddy's instructions to finish the tower."

When she reached the top, Caroline "saw at once it was a very difficult piece of work." A large stone had to be moved in order for a roof rafter to be set in place. The danger was that in the process, the brick lining of the smoke flue might fall in. Caroline came up with a plan which surprised the men, but they agreed to follow her instructions. She remained with them for the next four hours, until the rafter was in place and bolted securely.

The workers "all thanked me for coming up and directing them how to do the work," she noted. "Mr. Bates did not know where I was or what was being worked out. He had over two hundred men to keep busy."

Mrs. Eddy delighted in Caroline's prowess: "Woman, true to her instinct, came to the rescue as sunshine from the clouds," she would write in the church's dedicatory sermon, "so, when man quibbled over an architectural exigency, a woman climbed with feet and hands to the top of the tower, and helped settle the subject."

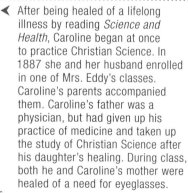

COURTESY OF LONGYEAR MUSEUM CHESTNUT HILL, MASSACHUSETTS

After being healed of a lifelong illness by reading *Science and Health*, Caroline began at once to practice Christian Science. In 1887 she and her husband enrolled in one of Mrs. Eddy's classes. Caroline's parents accompanied them. Caroline's father was a physician, but had given up his practice of medicine and taken up the study of Christian Science after his daughter's healing. During class, both he and Caroline's mother were healed of a need for eyeglasses.

After the problem with the tower was solved, the Bateses prayed all night for guidance as to how best to carry out the remainder of Mrs. Eddy's request concerning the plaster. The next morning, December 8th, found Boston under a foot of snow and a northeast gale dumping torrents of rain. Edward asked the contractor to plaster the vaulted ceiling in the church auditorium that night. It took two hours standing in the freezing cold to convince him. Finally, the plasterer agreed to order 24 tons of plaster to be delivered that afternoon.

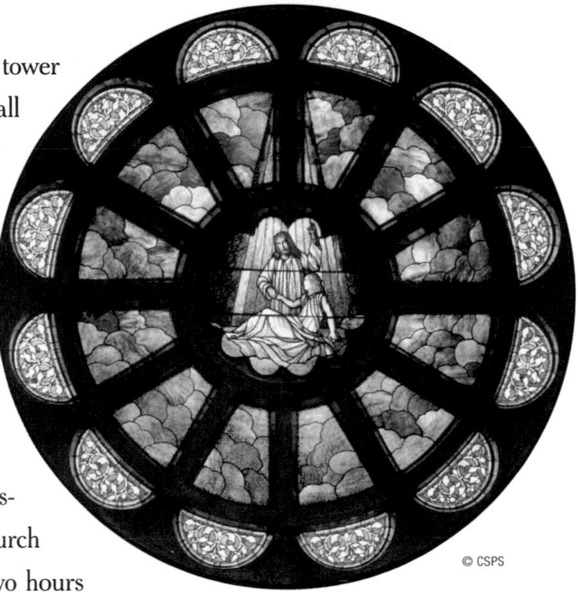

© CSPS

▲ Stained glass window donated by Caroline Bates

At 2:00 p.m., one load of four tons arrived. But where were the other 20? The delivery driver told Edward that was all he'd been told to bring, and refused to go back for more. Edward spent the afternoon on the phone and finally managed to locate the additional plaster, along with someone willing to deliver it in the storm. By now it was almost 5:00 p.m. When he returned to the church, he found it plunged into total darkness. The gale had blown down the wires and there was no electricity.

The contractor was furious. "I have all this force of men to put this plaster on, and all we have in the church is four tons," he told Edward in disgust.

➤ Mary Baker Eddy once called Edward Bates the most helpful student she ever had. After Christian Science healed his wife, Edward turned to it and was healed of an illness as well. He eventually devoted his life to serving the church as a practitioner and teacher, and in a number of other capacities, including president of The Mother Church.

PHOTO E. C. DINTURFF & CO. COURTESY TMBEL

"We will have more soon," Edward promised.

"Where are the lights? My men can't work without lights."

"The lights will be on." Edward had complete confidence that this delay, too, would yield to prayer.

The workers remained, and at five o'clock the electric lights came back on.

"Boys, to the scaffold!" Edward called out, and the men hurried to start the work.

The lathers tackled the unfinished ceiling ahead of the plasterers, affixing the wire "lath" backing that would give the plaster something to cling to. By 9 p.m., the remaining plaster had arrived, and by midnight, the first coat had been applied. The men took a break and ate the meal provided for them by Caroline, then returned to the scaffold.

Plastering is hard, wet, messy work. But that night, it proceeded like clockwork. "I was on the scaffold part of the time and on the floor part of

▼ The First Church of Christ, Scientist, in Boston under construction

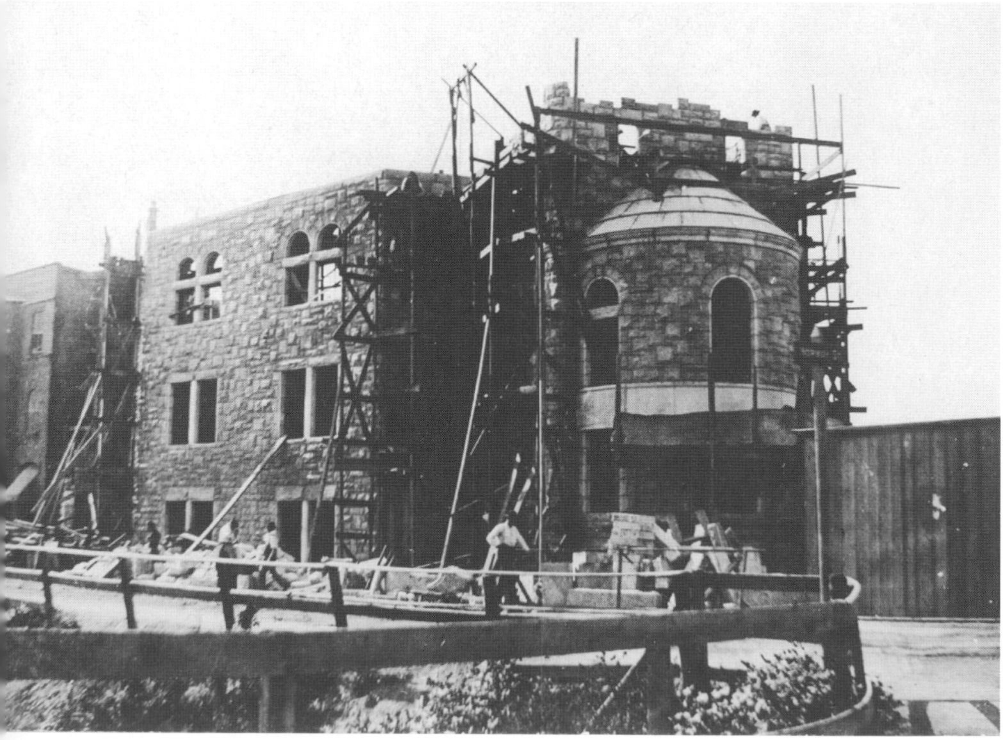

▲ "Sunburst" skylight window designed by Caroline Bates

the time and I don't think a piece of plaster as large as a ten-cent piece fell on my coat," Edward later commented. At five o'clock the next morning, the work was finished.

The contractor was dazzled. "I have never seen nor heard anything like it," he said. "It is wonderful." All the plasterers agreed. The contractor had predicted it would take 12 weeks to apply both coats to the inside of the church. It had taken 12 hours. For Edward, there was nothing miraculous about this—it was clearly Mrs. Eddy's vision that had opened the way. He saw that "she would not have issued that order if she had not known what could have been accomplished; we did not comprehend it until it was finished."

Communication from Concord to the workers in Boston went on almost daily, as Mrs. Eddy inquired about the church's progress, "and gave instructions as to particular points on which to concentrate our energy," according to Caroline. "To obey was the great lesson," she noted, "then all would go well."

Obstacles arose constantly, but each time, "I would lift my thought and know that God governed and I could witness Mrs. Eddy's work."

When they did so, Edward explained, "the work progressed rapidly. So rapidly that it seemed as though when we commenced a piece of work, it was done. And so, little by little, we learned to do what seemed to be impossible...."

As the deadline for the church's completion drew closer, work continued at a rapid pace. Painters labored all night to finish. William Johnson, one of the Directors, slept on a pile of burlap bags and dropcloths in a corner of the

A CHURCH OF HER OWN

FOOTSTEPS OF PROGRESS

Back when she was living in Lynn, Mrs. Eddy said to several of her students, "I shall have a church of my own some day!" With the building of The First Church of Christ, Scientist, in Boston, she finally did.

Fitting the edifice to its site—a triangle of land in Boston's Back Bay—posed an architectural challenge. Several designs were submitted, and the one selected (the work of Franklin I. Welch of Malden, Massachusetts) envisioned a modest, wedge-shaped structure that fanned out from a circular front. The building material was originally meant to be brick, but this was changed at Mrs. Eddy's request to pink and gray granite from her native state of New Hampshire.

Romanesque in style, the church has stone porticos, doors of carved antique oak, and a turreted 120-foot bell tower (the bells are played before every church service). Inside, there is seating for about 900, and details include marble floors and richly-colored stained glass windows.

Many familiar Bible scenes are depicted, including Jesus raising Lazarus; the heavenly city; and Mary, the mother of Jesus. Among the windows specifically requested by Mrs. Eddy are the two flanking the Readers' platform: on the left, below a smaller window showing an open Bible, Jesus is pictured on resurrection morning; on the right, below a smaller window showing a copy of *Science and Health*, is the woman crowned with stars, from the book of Revelation.

vestry, in order to be on-site in case there was a need to pay overtime or hire extra help.

The roof and windows, the finish coat of plaster, the paint, the seating in the auditorium and balcony, the doors and lighting fixtures and marble and sidewalk and trim—everything right down to the smallest detail—were all completed in record time.

The day before the first church service was scheduled to be held, there was still much work

The original edifice of The First Church of Christ, Scientist, in Boston, Massachusetts. Mary Baker Eddy called it "our prayer in stone."

COURTESY TMBEC

to be done, "but we were not the army of retreat," Edward stated firmly. At 4:00 in the afternoon, the keystone of the arch over the entrance to the lower vestibule was placed, completing the exterior of the building.

Meanwhile, Christian Scientists who had come from many different parts of the country to celebrate the dedication pitched in to help clean up the church's interior. While the workmen put the final touches in place, brooms, dusters, buckets, and mops were distributed.

© CSPS

Called the "Window of the Open Book," this was a gift from the Board of Directors and has as its theme New Jerusalem, the city foursquare described in the book of Revelation.

"The work went on quietly but rapidly," Edward reported. As the clock struck midnight, he looked around the church and noticed people streaming toward the vestibule. "I was surprised. Every person in that room finished his work at the same moment. There were cleaners, masons, carpenters, brick layers, electricians, and so on,—all manner of work going on, and all finished and went to the stairways to place their tools in the lower vestry at the same moment."

The work was done; the church was ready.

Noted Edward, "Mrs. Eddy's demonstration was complete to the minute."

18

The *Church Manual* as Guide

On a shiny April morning three months later, Joseph Armstrong swung open the oak doors of the new Mother Church. To his surprise, there stood Mary Baker Eddy! She had written to tell him that some friends would be visiting, but he had no idea that she would be joining them. Mrs. Eddy and two of her household, Clara Shannon and Calvin Frye, had come by train in a private compartment from New Hampshire that day. She wanted to see the new church without fanfare.

Climbing the marble stairs from the vestibule, Mrs. Eddy stepped into the rosy glow of the auditorium. The oval sunburst in the ceiling sent out a soft, shimmering light. The others stayed back as she walked slowly, silently all around the church, looking at the many beautiful stained glass windows. Then she knelt in reverent prayer on the first step of the Readers' platform.

She spent the night in the "Mother's Room," a small apartment in the church that had been designed for her use. Christian Science Sunday School pupils under the age of 12 had raised money to furnish it. Their nickname? The Busy Bees. In appreciation of their efforts, Mrs. Eddy dedicated her book *Pulpit and Press* to "The Dear Two Thousand and Six Hundred Children" who had raised $5,568.51 ($150,000 in 2013 dollars) by their own efforts. "Ah, children," she told them, "you are the bulwarks of freedom, the cement of society, the hope of our race!"

COURTESY OF LONGYEAR MUSEUM CHESTNUT HILL, MASSACHUSETTS

➤ Janet Colman's daughter Ruth was one of the early Busy Bees.

Touched by their generosity and always practical, Mrs. Eddy later invested $4,000 (over $100,000 today) in municipal bonds for these children. As each contributor turned 21, he or she received an equal share of the dividend with interest, along with a thank you letter from her.

Mrs. Eddy visited her church only twice more: once in May 1895, and again in January 1896. Both times she came to Boston on Saturday, spent the night in the Mother's Room, and addressed the congregation the next day. Her topic on that May morning was sin and the need for repentance, yet a teenager who attended the service described Mrs. Eddy afterwards in a letter home as "all love. You simply feel as if she was your best friend."

A man visiting Boston that day also heard Mrs. Eddy preach. He could hardly walk, and found life difficult to bear. Hearing the chimes of the new church, he decided on the spur of the moment to attend the service. He later told how he felt a change come over his body and his thought as he listened to the sermon. He left the church able to walk again, completely forgetting his canes until he returned to where he was staying.

This kind of healing was exactly what Mrs. Eddy expected from her church's services. She viewed her church as much more than just a physical structure. In the glossary to *Science and Health,* she defined church as "the structure of Truth and Love; whatever rests upon and proceeds from divine Principle." She called for it to be an institution that "affords proof of its utility"—as always, zeroing in on the practicality of her religion, whose healing works were at the core of its theology.

Her church, she explained, "is designed to be built on the Rock, Christ; even the understanding and demonstration of divine Truth, Life, and Love, healing and saving the world...." She yearned for this spiritual idea of church and its practical proof in daily life—demonstration—to flower in the hearts and minds of her followers.

And it did. Christian Science congregations by this time had begun springing up all over the United States and Canada, impelled in large part by the healings their members experienced. All of these young congregations needed direction and guidance, and the questions came pouring into Boston. How should they run their services? Who could be a member? Were there

FOOTSTEPS OF PROGRESS

THE BUSY BEES

"I love children more than pen can tell," Mrs. Eddy wrote to Maurine Campbell on February 14, 1895. Six weeks earlier, at the dedication of The Mother Church, a special second service was held for the Busy Bees, who were the first ones allowed to see the room they had built and furnished. Maurine Campbell was the one responsible for bringing most of them there.

As a young woman, Maurine had been healed of a serious eye injury through Christian Science, and in August of 1889 she moved to Boston to work for the newly formed Christian Science Publishing Society. She also taught Sunday School, and would eventually serve on the Bible Lesson Committee, and practice and teach Christian Science in Pasadena, California, for many years.

PHOTO MARK THAYER © TMBEL

▲ This miniature gold charm was a gift to Mrs. Eddy "from her loving bees."

As the building of the church began to move forward, Maurine was eager to do her part.

"I asked God to direct my steps," she later recalled, and the answer that came was to start a Children's Fund for the purpose of creating a special room for Mrs. Eddy.

On March 1, 1891, a dozen students in the Boston Sunday School formed the nucleus of what would shortly be dubbed the Busy Bees. Maurine gave them each a new silver dime as seed money. "Each was to make use of his 'talent' and see how much it would gain in three months," she explained.

The children came up with a number of creative fund-raising schemes. One girl went into partnership with her twin brother, using their combined funds to purchase materials to make paper dolls to sell. (A doll was later sent to

any rules to govern the early steps these groups were taking?

Yes, there were. Back in 1879 when she first organized a church, Mrs. Eddy drafted three religious tenets which those uniting with it were asked to sign. When that church was reorganized as The Mother Church, The First Church of Christ, Scientist, in Boston in 1892, these tenets were revised, with further revisions continuing until their final form in 1908.

Mrs. Eddy also wrote some rules, or By-laws, to govern the church. By 1895, the original By-laws had changed and grown. In their new form, they provided ready-made answers for the budding churches. All that was needed was to gather them together in one place. She envisioned a small book or manual, much like the one she had seen in the Congregational church in which she had grown up.

In short order, the *Church Manual of The First Church of Christ, Scientist,*

Mrs. Eddy, who wrote back in thanks, calling it a "rare gift.") Another enterprising fellow started a popcorn business, spending seven cents on popcorn, two cents on paper bags, and a penny for butter and salt. His first batch sold out quickly, and he soon had regular customers. Other Bees sewed aprons, ran errands, sold rose bushes, painted fences, shoveled snow, picked strawberries, and made soap, among other things. A 14-month-old baby even got in on the action with the contribution of a dollar "earned by kisses."

By the time of their first meeting (a party called a "swarming"), the Busy Bees, who now numbered 52, had raised $135.64 (a little over $3,000 in today's dollars). Each was given a hive-shaped bank in which to store their future earnings. As word spread about this activity, more children joined, and before long Busy Bees were "buzzing from every quarter of the globe," as Maurine Campbell put it. In the end, the group numbered nearly 3,000 and raised over $5,500 ($140,000 in 2013 dollars) for the building and furnishing of what would be called "Mother's Room."

▼ Beehive banks

PHOTO MARK THAYER © TMBEL

In recognition of their efforts, a little onyx beehive was placed in the room, containing all of their names. Over 200 Busy Bees were present at the Dedication Service on January 6, 1875. Each child received a special white badge, along with a commemorative mosaic tile, both of which were sent to the Bees who couldn't attend. The children were all given a tour of the room that their fund-raising efforts had built and furnished, and afterwards they wrote their names in an autograph book, which was sent to Mary Baker Eddy in Concord. The group disbanded at Mrs. Eddy's request in 1898.

in Boston, Mass., was published in 1895. The rules it contained "were not arbitrary opinions nor dictatorial demands, such as one person might impose on another," Mrs. Eddy wrote. "They were impelled by a power not one's own, were written at different dates, and as the occasion required. They sprang from necessity, the logic of events,—from the immediate demand for them as a help that must be supplied to maintain the

➤ Maurine Campbell (who called herself the "Queen Bee") at home in Pasadena in her later years

COURTESY OF LONGYEAR MUSEUM CHESTNUT HILL, MASSACHUSETTS

FOOTSTEPS OF PROGRESS

MARY BAKER EDDY'S DEFINITION OF CHURCH

CHURCH. The structure of Truth and Love; whatever rests upon and proceeds from divine Principle.

The Church is that institution, which affords proof of its utility and is found elevating the race, rousing the dormant understanding from material beliefs to the apprehension of spiritual ideas and the demonstration of divine Science, thereby casting out devils, or error, and healing the sick." (*Science and Health*)

dignity and defense of our Cause...."

She wanted to help keep her flock from straying, or falling into the kind of quarrelsome disputes they had in the past. The new *Manual* would serve as an enclosure, or sheepfold, to keep them safe. As she would explain to a student in August of 1896, "I was compelled by a sense of responsibility to put up the bars for my flock."

In addition to guiding principles, the new "branch" churches needed preachers, but good preachers were hard to come by. Many of Mrs. Eddy's students were too new, spiritually, to lead their congregations. Their sermons mixed in old theological ideas of God and their own opinions with the fresh teachings of Christian Science.

"My students were preaching and were sending me copies of their sermons," Mrs. Eddy told her student Daisette McKenzie. "They grew worse and worse. Finally one came which was so great a mixture that if I had not known the fact, I should not have been able to tell whether

FOOTSTEPS OF PROGRESS

THE CROSS AND CROWN

Long associated with Christianity, the cross and crown would have been a familiar symbol to Mary Baker Eddy, who likely first encountered it when she was growing up (it was printed on the cover of the book of church rules used in the Congregational Church in Concord, New Hampshire).

In the mid 1870s, she would use a cross and crown on the sign on her home in Lynn (see photo on p. 92), and in 1881 she chose a different version (pictured here), encircled with Jesus' words, for the mark that she placed on the cover of the third edition of *Science and Health*.

In 1908, the trademark was again redesigned, and among other changes, the princely coronet was replaced with a celestial or Christian's crown. Slightly modernized in 1971, the design is a registered trademark of The First Church of Christ, Scientist.

COURTESY TMBEC

▲ The Cross and Crown seal as it appeared in 1881.

EVOLUTION OF THE TENETS OF THE MOTHER CHURCH

FOOTSTEPS OF PROGRESS

These religious tenets or "important points," as Mary Baker Eddy called them, are read in Christian Science branch churches twice a year, at the communion services held in January and July.

Here's how they originally appeared in 1879, in the minute book of The Church of Christ (Scientist):

Tenets and Covenant

To be signed by those uniting with this church.

1st As adherents to Truth, we take the Scriptures for our guide to Life eternal.

2nd We rest our hope and faith on God, the only Life, Truth and Love, depending for salvation not on the person of God, but on the understanding of the Principle or Spirit that is God, and the demonstration of this Spirit or Principle according to those commands of our Master, "Go ye into all the world, preach the gospel, heal the sick, and these signs shall follow them that believe" (understand). "They shall lay their hands on the sick and they shall recover."

3rd And we solemnly covenant to faithfully obey the ten commandments to walk worthy [of] our high calling, to deal justly, love mercy, and walk humbly with our God; to abhor a lie, to love Truth, to do good to man, to have but one God, and to strive habitually to reach that higher understanding of Christian Science contained in the Sermon on the Mount, whereby to cast out error and heal the sick.

Here's how they appear in the *Church Manual* today:

Tenets of The Mother Church
The First Church of Christ, Scientist

To be signed by those uniting with
The First Church of Christ, Scientist,
in Boston, Massachusetts

1. As adherents of Truth, we take the inspired Word of the Bible as our sufficient guide to eternal Life.
2. We acknowledge and adore one supreme and infinite God. We acknowledge His Son, one Christ; the Holy Ghost or divine Comforter; and man in God's image and likeness.
3. We acknowledge God's forgiveness of sin in the destruction of sin and the spiritual understanding that casts out evil as unreal. But the belief in sin is punished so long as the belief lasts.
4. We acknowledge Jesus' atonement as the evidence of divine, efficacious Love, unfolding man's unity with God through Christ Jesus the Way-shower; and we acknowledge that man is saved through Christ, through Truth, Life, and Love as demonstrated by the Galilean Prophet in healing the sick and overcoming sin and death.
5. We acknowledge that the crucifixion of Jesus and his resurrection served to uplift faith to understand eternal Life, even the allness of Soul, Spirit, and the nothingness of matter.
6. And we solemnly promise to watch, and pray for that Mind to be in us which was also in Christ Jesus; to do unto others as we would have them do unto us; and to be merciful, just, and pure.

THE BIBLE LESSON-SERMON

FOOTSTEPS OF PROGRESS

Originally, the fledgling Christian Science churches relied on the International Series of Bible lessons written for use by Protestant Sunday Schools (which included both adults and children at that time). In 1888, notes on these lessons written from a Christian Science standpoint began appearing in the *Journal*. Then in December 1889, a Bible Lesson Committee was formed at Mrs. Eddy's request, in order to provide weekly Lesson-Sermons geared specifically for her young church.

In a move away from personal sermons, these lessons, which first appeared the following April, paired Bible references with passages from *Science and Health with Key to the Scriptures*, the two books that Mrs. Eddy would ordain as pastor of her church in April 1895.

Three years later, Mrs. Eddy provided 26 subjects designed to be repeated twice each year. Using these as their guide, the Bible Lesson Committee would choose (and continues to choose) fresh, inspiring selections for each week's Lesson-Sermon, to be studied by students of Christian Science throughout the week, then read aloud as the Sunday sermon. According to William McKenzie, a former Presbyterian minister and English professor whom Mrs. Eddy appointed to the committee and who served on it for 21 years, "It was understood that these topics covered the course of instruction given by [Mrs. Eddy] in class teaching."

Underscoring the significance of these Bible Lesson-Sermons, Mary Baker Eddy noted in her *Church Manual,* "The Readers of The Mother Church and of all its branch churches must devote a suitable portion of their time to preparation for the reading of the Sunday lesson,—a lesson on which the prosperity of Christian Science largely depends."

the writer were a Christian Scientist, a spiritualist, or a theosophist. I said to myself, 'Something must be done and at once.' I withdrew from all other work, and in solitude and almost ceaseless prayer, I sought and found God's will. At the end of three weeks, I received the answer, and it came to me as naturally as dawns the morning light: 'Why, of course, the Bible and *Science and Health.*'"

In December 1894, Mrs. Eddy stopped all personal preaching in The Mother Church, replacing sermons by individuals with Lesson-Sermons drawn from the Bible and the Christian Science textbook.

"This will tend to spiritualize thought," she explained in a letter to the Board of Directors that month. "Personal preaching has more or less of human views grafted onto it. Whereas the pure Word contains only the living health giving Truth."

An announcement in the *Journal* of April 1895 expanded this directive to apply to all branch churches: "Humbly, and as I believe, Divinely directed," Mrs. Eddy wrote, "I hereby ordain, that the Bible, and Science and Health with Key to the Scriptures, shall hereafter be the only pastor of the Church of Christ, Scientist, throughout our land, and in other lands."

It was a startling move, and caused quite a stir amongst her followers, among them Irving Tomlinson. "Could a church replace an eloquent preacher with two

Readers and still continue to grow and prosper?" he wondered. "These questions disturbed many, including myself, who having but recently left the ranks of the clergy was accustomed to a personal preacher. But they did not disturb the Founder of the Christian Science movement. She asked only: What is God's direction? And as true as the needle to the pole, so true was she to the divine voice."

In the end, the young Christian Science churches were quick to accept this revolutionary change and adopt it into their own By-laws. From that point on, Sunday sermons consisted of selections from the Bible and the Christian Science textbook. Two Readers, elected from each church's membership, read the Bible Lesson-Sermon aloud to the congregation each Sunday.

By abolishing personal preaching, Mrs. Eddy lifted her church from dependency on person, freeing congregations to progress by relying on God, and not on the opinions or personality of a minister or featured speaker.

The following summer, in June 1896, she published a poem in the *Journal*, a prayer which speaks of "brother birds," asks to be freed "from human strife," and "fed by Thy love divine"—perhaps

PHOTO © TMBEL

◄ The first issue of the *Christian Science Quarterly*

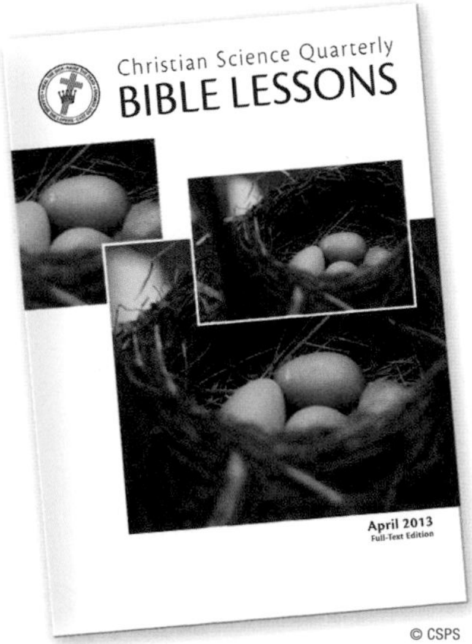

© CSPS

➤ The *Christian Science Quarterly* today

an indication of the kind of loving fellowship and true nourishment that she expected to be the hallmark of her young church.

Over the next 15 years, the *Manual* would grow and change with the needs of the expanding church. Practically every By-law was edited; many were dropped and many more were added. The first edition was 39 pages long. The final edition, the 89th, has 138 pages.

As the *Manual* developed, Mrs. Eddy referred to it more and more. When the Board of Directors asked for advice, she often turned them to its pages, reminding them that the *Manual* was their source of authority now in church government. By weaning her followers from personal dependence upon her, she was setting her church on a firm foundation for the future.

The *Church Manual* would be both sheepfold and guide.

LOVE
(June 1896 version)

Brood o'er us with Thy shelt'ring wing
 'Neath which our spirits blend
Like brother birds that soar and sing,
 And on the same branch bend.
The arrow that doth wound the dove
Darts not from those who watch and love.

If thou the bending reed wouldst break
 By thought or word unkind,
Pray that His spirit all partake
 Who loved and healed mankind.
Seek holy thoughts and heavenly strain,
That make men one in love remain.

Learn, too, that wisdom's rod is given
 For faith to kiss and know;
That greetings glorious from high Heaven
 Whence joys supernal flow,
Come from that Love divinely near
Which chastens pride and earth-born fear.

Through God who gave that word of might
 Which swelled creation's lay—
"Let there be light, and there was light."
 What chased the clouds away?
'Twas Love whose finger traced aloud
A bow of promise on the cloud.

Thou to whose power our hope we give,
 Free us from human strife.
Fed by Thy love divine we live,
 For Love alone is Life;
And life most sweet, as heart to heart
Speaks kindly when we meet and part.

▲ Mary Baker Eddy would later amend the third line of the second stanza to read "Pray that His spirit you partake."

19

The Center But Not the Boundary

The next decade found the Christian Science movement expanding rapidly, a period of growth easily seen in the number of people who came to Pleasant View for two out of a handful of occasions when Mrs. Eddy invited her followers to visit.

In July of 1897, some 2,500 church members showed up. By June of 1903, that number swelled to at least 10,000 as Christian Scientists from across the country jammed onto the special trains for Concord added by the railroad to accommodate them. Reporters covered the scene as the crowds flocked to hear Mrs. Eddy address them from the balcony of her home.

Twelve-year-old Alice Noble was among them. She wanted to go "like everything," she confided to her diary, but didn't have the $1.60 ($42 in 2013 dollars) train fare. Somehow she managed to scrape up the funds, and off she went with her Aunt Eva.

"Mrs. Eddy is lovely," she recorded afterward in her journal. "She has the loveliest, purest face."

Not all who joined the throngs making their way to Pleasant View that particular summer day were Christian Scientists like Alice. Many local folks went, too, including a boy whose grandmother dressed up for the occasion in a big straw hat festooned with red roses.

➤ Mary Baker Eddy on the day Alice Noble saw her

PHOTO W. G. C. KIMBALL COURTESY TMBEL

"We must hear Mrs. Eddy," she told him, "because even though we do not agree on religion, she is a great woman, and we should be proud to have her living in our city."

The Boston Journal

A Newspaper for All the People. Good Easy Reading

Fair and Warm Today and Tomorrow; Light Southwesterly Winds

NO. 22,867—ESTABLISHED 1833 BOSTON, TUESDAY, JUNE 30, 1903. PRICE ONE CENT

MRS. EDDY GREETS TWELVE THOUSAND CHRISTIAN SCIENTISTS

THE MOST REMARKABLE RELIGIOUS PILGRIMAGE IN THE HISTORY OF AMERICA

TRUSTEES MAKE DR. COX ACTING ALMSHOUSE HEAD

Man Whom Mayor Collins Refused to Appoint.

BOARD MEETING STORMY

Possibility That Mayor May Have a Word to Say About It.

SENSE OF GUILT DRIVES SERVIANS TO COURT DEATH

Reported Suicides of Those Who Helped in Royal Murders.

ARMY SPLIT IN TWAIN

Officers of Provincial Garrisons Send Challenges to Conspirators.

JOURNAL FINDS FIRST TRACE OF JOSEPH LAMOTHE

He Took a Horse and Buggy From Stable at Pelham.

POLICE TAKE UP TRAIL

Girl Victim of Lowell Shooting Is Not Expected to Live.

CONCORD THRONGED BY MRS. EDDY'S FOLLOWERS

Founder of Faith Extends Affectionate Greeting.

DELIVERS SHORT ADDRESS

Chorus of 12,000 Voices Lifts Up Spontaneously as She Finishes.

JOURNAL ARTIST CATCHES TWO REMARKABLE PHOTOGRAPHS

▲ Mrs. Eddy's address to her followers in June of 1903 was front-page news.

Concord *was* proud of its most famous resident, and grateful for her support, too. Mrs. Eddy was always on the lookout for ways in which she could bless others, and her philanthropy extended far beyond her adopted hometown. She donated generously to a variety of worthy causes, including disaster relief in far-flung spots. But she was a good civic neighbor as well, and she supported many local causes. On several occasions she donated new shoes to Concord's needy children, and she patronized local merchants and businesses, including the quarry that provided granite for the churches in Boston and Concord. She helped the city develop the State Fair Grounds that adjoined her property, and made a gift of a pair of swans to grace the pond in White's Park. The road that ran from Pleasant View into town was the first street in Concord to be paved, thanks to Mrs. Eddy's generosity — a deed that sparked an upgrade for many of the city's roadways.

Years later, in 1908, a group of local businessmen would estimate the financial boon that Mrs. Eddy had brought to their city at over $1.5 million (some $35 million in 2013 dollars).

No price tag could have been put on the healing work she did while living in Concord, though. Henry Morrison, the manager of the local Western Union telegraph station, certainly valued what she did for him. He suffered from a chronic stomach problem, as well as severe colds, and told her so when she stopped by his office one day while on her carriage ride to send a telegram to Boston. She healed him on the spot, and he never suffered from either condition again.

There were countless other similar incidents over the years, including the neighbor girl healed of tuberculosis and the worried dairy farmer whose dry well filled overnight during a drought, after Mrs. Eddy was informed. ("Oh! if he only knew, Love fills that well," was her response when she heard of his predicament.) Mrs. Eddy's understanding of God as infinite, ever-present divine Love also healed Reverend E. N. Larmour, a young Methodist minister who came to call, of extreme nearsightedness, as well as a lineman who was helping install telephone wires in front of Pleasant View. When the man was accidentally hit in the eye by a wire, one of his co-workers ran into the house and asked that a doctor be sent for. Instead, Mrs. Eddy talked with the lineman, and witnesses saw him back on the job the next day, completely well.

The Pleasant View years were productive ones for Mrs. Eddy, who kept to an orderly routine.

▼ Mary Baker Eddy hard at work in her study at Pleasant View

PHOTO CALVIN A. FRYE © TMBEC

"I rise at about 6 o'clock A.M. eat my breakfast at about 7 A.M," she wrote. "Open my Bible and read whatever I open to with a mental invocation that the divine Lord give me grace, meekness, understanding and wisdom for each hour of the day.... I daily look into the rooms of my house to see that neatness and order are preserved and afternoons I take my daily drive."

The Christian Science Weekly

Published Thursday By The Christian Science Publishing Society

VOL. 1 BOSTON, MASS., U.S.A., SEPTEMBER 1, 1898. NO. 1

SALUTATORY.

We herewith launch a new publication in connection with our movement. The growing necessities of the situation seem to demand, at times, a speedier means of communication with the Field than our monthly *Journal* affords.

New or amended By-Laws and Church Rules, which, from time to time, are passed to meet accruing needs and emergencies, should sometimes reach the Field more promptly than is possible with only a monthly messenger. The *Weekly* is projected, in part at least, to meet this need. Then, too, our files contain many communications in the nature of experiences, testimonies, and dissertations which, for want of space in the *Journal*, must often be indefinitely laid aside or entirely withheld from publication, and which are too valuable and helpful to meet such a fate. The *Weekly* will tend to remedy this difficulty and afford an additional means of spreading the good Word.

Let it not be inferred, however, that the *Weekly* is to take the place of the *Journal*. Not so. The *Journal* occupies, and shall ever occupy, a necessary and distinctive place in the history and literature of Christian Science. It can never, by the logic of events, sink lower in the scale of its mission and existence, but by the necessity of growth and progress, must continue in an ascending scale to perform the important function which gave it birth. Its establishment was fraught with far too much of sacrifice, struggle, and hardship,—its place in the rise and progress of the Cause has been, is, and shall continue to be, much too important, to admit of its losing one jot or tittle of its proverbial value. The *Weekly* will be but a convenient, and, we trust and believe, an invaluable adjunct to the *Journal*; a friend and co-laborer, as it were.

It is likely we shall hear from our beloved Leader, the Rev. Mary Baker Eddy, through its columns, from time to time. It will not, however, we feel warranted in saying, become, by any means, an exclusive avenue of communication from her to the Field. She will regard the *Journal*—her first born—as the more important and regular channel for the impartation of her words of loving counsel, admonition, and rebuke to her large and rapidly increasing family of children. The *Journal* will be the mother publication; the *Weekly* its child.

It will be a feature of the *Weekly* to supply, in each issue, a brief synopsis of the current events of the world, sufficient, perhaps, to keep the busy workers fairly well informed as to the more important facts of general interest.

For prices and terms see the advertisement on the fourth page.

CURRENT EVENTS.

Saturday, August 20, witnessed a grand parade of battleships on North River, New York. Sampson and Schley and their men came home in six steel ships, and their coming was the occasion of a most enthusiastic demonstration by the citizens of New York.

The President sent his Cabinet officers to meet them. The mayor of New York and a committee of distinguished citizens told them of the country's pride and gratitude, and gave them the keys of the city at its gate.

It was a glorious morning when the victorious
steamed up the harbor in majestic sin
saluting, and accompanied by a floti
steamboats, yachts, and launches, dens
ing from shore to shore. New York
tacle before.

From throats of a million or more of
countrywomen on two shores rose the
the returning heroes. The heart of a
in the cry.

Steadily through the crowded waters
ers and battleships—seven in all, whi
them—keeping the signalled distance a
signalled speed of eight knots, guided by
which had made them irresistible.

Thus they moved up and reached th
said, "Let us have peace," set on a bill, t
was hidden by a cheering, flag-waving m

A general revival of business is certain
ing in of peace. If the administration
including the members of the Senate an
sentatives at Washington, will now add
the building up of the country's vast resou
energy and in the same non-partisan s
acterized their action in relation to the
a prosperity will ensue sufficiently general
some of the oppressions and inequalities
More genuine patriotism and less politics a
piping times of peace, would tend greatly t
the present inequitable conditions.

The conclusion of the war is signalized b
out of a part of our volunteer troops. It
from seventy-five to one hundred thousand
tered out and returned to their homes.
who volunteered in defence of their nation'
the right, although released from their servi
than might have been anticipated, will recei
welcome at the hands of their dear home f
other good people, that their unselfish devoti
and principle deserves.

Admiral Cervera was given a rousing ov
arrival at the Union Station in Boston recently
through on his way to New York. A great cro
him at the station and a still greater saw hi
Fall River boat train. "Three cheers for Ce
proposed and given with a will. The Spanish
his acknowledgments with uncovered head. In
presence of policemen, the admiral's hand wa
shaking hands with his enthusiastic admirers, u
finally safely landed aboard the train.

Copyrighted, 1898, by Mary Baker G. Eddy.

PHOTO © TMBEL

◀ First issue of the *Christian Science Sentinel*, originally called the *Weekly*. Mary Baker Eddy said that it was "intended to hold guard over Truth, Life, and Love."

▼ The *Christian Science Sentinel* today

© CSPS

As had been her practice since childhood, Mrs. Eddy set aside regular time for prayer and spiritual refreshment. "Three times a day, I retire to seek the divine blessing on the sick and sorrowing," she said at one point to a clergyman who accused her of being "prayerless."

The porch outside her study was one favorite spot to "talk with God," as she put it. Staying close to God was important to Mrs. Eddy, and she guarded those hours in prayer carefully, encouraging her students to do the same.

Just as a mother watches over the growth of her child, so Mrs. Eddy kept careful watch over every aspect of the Christian Science movement. Those quiet moments alone with God helped her accomplish all that she did, for Pleasant View was not just her home but also the busy hub of her church, one that by now had international reach, with nearly a dozen branch churches in Canada, regular services in London and Hannover, Germany, and practitioners and informal services scattered elsewhere in the British Isles and Europe.

"Home is the dearest spot on earth, and it should be the centre, though not the boundary, of the affections," Mrs. Eddy had written in *Science and Health*, and nowhere was that more true than at Pleasant View, for Christian Science was proving itself to be a religion without borders.

Letters and inquiries poured in from around the globe. "To-day I have entertained letters from Congo Free State, from several European countries, and answered a letter from the wife of our minister to China," Mrs. Eddy told a reporter from the *Boston Journal* in 1899.

Keenly interested in the world, Mrs. Eddy read widely and was well-informed, keeping up with current affairs through newspapers and magazines. She would later astound another reporter, who may have made the mistake of thinking her simply an elderly woman living in quiet retirement in a sleepy New Hampshire town, when after telling her about his recent trip to China, she talked to him for over an hour in great detail about that country's social, political, and economic conditions.

"Just one more surprise," the reporter remarked to a fellow journalist as he left Pleasant View, clearly wowed by Mrs. Eddy's grasp of the subject, "one more instance of where we came to preach, and remained to pray."

Mrs. Eddy generated enough work to keep two to three secretaries employed full time. She spent her days dictating letters, attending to church business, counseling students, writing books and articles, editing her periodicals, and responding to magazines and newspapers that asked for her views on matters of national and international importance. She was every inch the Leader of her church and movement, its commander-in-chief.

In February of 1897, Mrs. Eddy published *Miscellaneous Writings*, a compilation of articles, essays, poems, letters, sermons, and more written between 1883 and 1896.

© TMBEL

Mary Baker Eddy around the time she taught her final class

So important did she consider this book that she requested via the next month's *Journal* that all teaching of Christian Science be suspended for a year. Her students and followers were to focus instead on this new volume and allow it to instruct them, for as Mrs. Eddy noted in its dedication, the book contained "practical teachings indispensable to the culture and achievements which constitute the success of a student and demonstrate the ethics of Christian Science."

More growth was ahead for the movement, as 1898 would bring a bumper crop of advances. In January, Mrs. Eddy created the Board of Lectureship to oversee the men and women who travel to give talks on Christian Science, and she also established The Christian Science Publishing Society. In the following months, she gave the Directors the 26 subjects for the weekly *Bible Lessons;* created the Board of Education, to train and authorize teachers of Christian Science; moved testimony meetings from Friday to Wednesday evenings in all Christian Science churches; and started a new weekly magazine, the *Christian Science Sentinel.*

"I have wrought day and night this year to make way for our church and a systematic order of action in all the departments of Christian Science," she wrote to one of her students.

Mrs. Eddy wasn't done yet. Before the year was through she would create the Committee on Publication, an office whose purpose was and still is to correct misinformation and false impressions about Christian Science in the press, and, in a move aimed squarely at the future, she taught one final class.

In mid-November, 70 hand-picked students received confidential telegrams from Mrs. Eddy, asking them to be at Christian Science Hall in Concord, New Hampshire at 4 p.m. on November 20th. All but three came, some from very far away—England and Scotland, as well as all across the United States and Canada. Those chosen were not just seasoned students, but also promising newcomers.

"We were all very happy to be called, but distinctly human in our speculation as to the reason for the call," noted Emma Easton (later Newman), one of those to receive a telegram.

She and the others who gathered in Concord as requested soon discovered that they'd been invited to attend a class with Mrs. Eddy, a gift designed "to spiritualize the Field," as their teacher later explained to Irving Tomlinson, one of the attendees.

The class met for two hours that Sunday afternoon, and for four hours the following day. It was by all accounts an invigorating, inspiring time.

"Only two lessons!" wrote Judge Septimus Hanna, summarizing the event for the next month's issue of the *Journal*, "but such lessons! It were futile to attempt a description or review.... To say that this teaching lifted one Heavenward — Godward, — that it sank deep into the consciousness of all present, is only feebly to hint at the actual fact."

Their teacher was "perfectly natural. She was ever alert, with a keen sense of wit and humor, and at the same time, her listening attitude to hear what God would give her to say was apparent," noted Emma Shipman, another student who was present. "She spoke to us with deepest reverence and understanding of Christ Jesus, the Way-shower, and pointed out the vital necessity of following him."

Mrs. Eddy wasn't just giving a "fresh impulse" to her students with this class, as she put it in some introductory remarks, she was also planting seeds for the future of her movement. When asked why she had included so many young people, she

Later retitled "Christmas Morn," this poem would eventually be revised and included in the *Christian Science Hymnal*.

CHRISTMAS HYMN
(December 1898 version)

BLEST Christmas morn, could murky clouds
Pursue thy way
Or light be born? no storm enshrouds
Thy dawn or day!

Dear Christ, forever here and near,
No cradle song,
Nor natal hour and mother's tear,
To thee belong.

Thou God-idea, Life-encrowned,
The Bethlehem babe
Beloved, adored, replete, renowned,
Was but thy shade.

Thou living gleam of deathless Love,
O little Life!
So infinite — so far above
All mortal strife,

Or creed, or earth-born taint,
Fill us to-day
With all thou art — be thou our saint —
Our stay, alway.

replied, "Because I want my teaching carried on."

There would be one final gift from Mrs. Eddy that year—a Christmas poem. Published in the December 1898 *Journal*, it, too, would later be revised and set to music for use as a hymn. Years earlier, her healing in Lynn had given her a glimpse of "a world more bright," as an earlier poem expressed it—a spiritual reality whose light was now shining ever more brilliantly.

In her new poem, later titled *Christmas Morn*, she writes of the living Christ whom Jesus embodied as "forever here and near," a radiant, present reality whose dawning in thought nothing could obscure.

20
Sons Near and Far

Mrs. Eddy continued to keep up with her son George and his family out in South Dakota. She urged her namesake Mary to learn to type, so that she could write her father's letters in a professional way, and sent her money to buy the latest model typewriter.

Mary typed a letter back: "I have got the machine and it is a very fine one, which I am very thankful to you for. I am trying my best to learn to use it."

COURTESY TMBEL

Mary Baker Eddy's granddaughters Mary (l.) and Evelyn (r.). Mary typed letters to her grandmother on the typewriter that she bought for her.

She included the latest news on the family, including her little brother, who like his father and grandfather before him had been named for America's first president:

"Georgie speaks a patriotic peice [sic] on Gen. Washington's birthday, and he is to appear in full dress like Gen. Washington with Martha Washington by his side. Father has dressed him with sword and everything compleate [sic] you would laugh to see him with his velvet coat tails, gold braid and stars hanging to his knees."

For years, Mrs. Eddy had asked her son to build a proper house for his family, one near good schools. But he couldn't seem to bring himself to spend that much money on anything above ground. Finally, in 1899, she decided to give George a house as a surprise Christmas present. She asked two of her students who lived in the area to tell him they needed land to build a church, and inquire if he could spare some of his property for it.

George gave them a spot at the corner of a lot he owned on Main Street

COURTESY TMBEC

Mary Baker Eddy gave her son George and his family this home as a Christmas present in 1899

in Lead, and building began. The large brick structure was unusual among all the log cabins in town, and George watched its progress with interest. When he found that it was going to be a house and not a church, he thought he'd been hoodwinked. The angry miner pitched such a fit that the only way Mrs. Eddy's students could quiet him was to tell him the truth.

A surprise present from his mother? George was dumbfounded. Why hadn't she told him? He kept the secret for the sake of his children, though, who were thrilled when the family moved in on Christmas Eve.

"I was only ten years old and that Christmas I don't believe I'll ever forget," Mrs. Eddy's grandson George recalled later in life. "To move into a big house like that … was something for a youngster."

Nellie Glover and the children enjoyed their new home, which with all its furniture and fittings was more costly than Pleasant View. At first, George wished he was back in his familiar old log cabin, but he eventually grew to be proud of the house. It was a mansion by Lead standards, with five large rooms on the first floor, all but the kitchen having their own fireplaces. A winding staircase led to five more rooms upstairs. George set up a fine workshop in the basement, and the attic, which covered the entire third floor, served as a playroom for the children, who rode their tricycles and bicycles around in it during the winter months. The attic had a water tank, too (this was before the town had running water), and the house was fully electrified, although the Glovers couldn't afford to pay for electricity until many years later. The local newspaper called their new home a "handsome" residence, "one of the most elegant and beautiful gifts ever made in this city." George wrote a gushing letter of thanks to his mother, but in his heart he had better uses for that money.

In the meantime, she had written to him: "I am alone in the world, more lone than a solitary star… my home is simply a house and a beautiful landscape. There is not one in it that I love only as I love everybody."

Ebenezer Foster Eddy—Benny—had been Mrs. Eddy's bright star. When she adopted him, her hopes were high. He carried her directives to the Board and her other students. She made him publisher of her books. But, most of all, she loved his visits. If she felt lonely, she had only to pick up her pen, write him a note, and Benny would be at her side. Not since Gilbert had she had the luxury of such a close relationship.

Why then after almost eight years had it ended, as she wrote to a student, "sharper than vinegar to the teeth?"

In business, as in all her dealings, Mrs. Eddy liked to be exact. Back in January of 1893 she had entrusted Benny with publishing her works, with the admonition "… see that you start rightly in publishing this year (for much depends on right beginnings)." The following year, she gave him the copyright to *Science and Health*. The royalties provided a handsome salary, and he also received a share of the profits of her new book, *Christ and Christmas*. But Benny did very little work, and his accounts were bungled.

Mrs. Eddy tried to correct this: "Your books

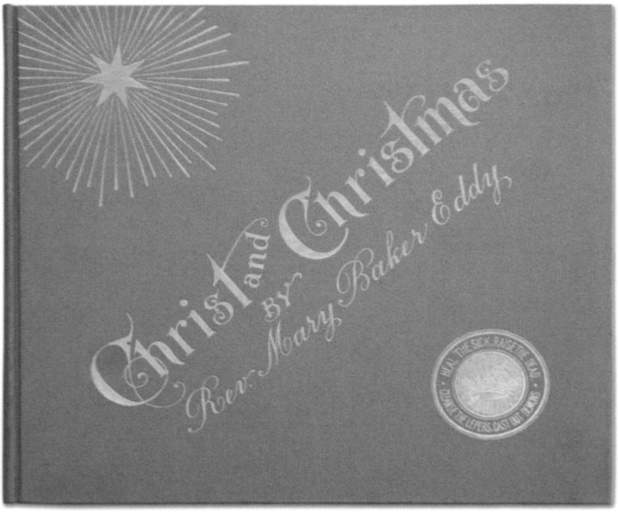

A collaboration between Mrs. Eddy and artist James F. Gilman, this illustrated poem was first published in December 1893. Shown here is the 1906 edition.

PHOTO © CSPS

could not be audited, they were kept in such a manner, and it can be shown that in the list you sent to Mr. Frye from the binder's bills, you made a mistake of over 500 books! Now dear, this was not intentional, but is not safe," she wrote, adding with a burst, "you must never guess at accounts!"

As publisher, Benny was equally unsuitable.

"We found in him an agreeable personality with a gratifying willingness to accept suggestions and make promises to cooperate; but there it stopped," noted William Dana Orcutt, who as head of the University Press in Cambridge, Massachusetts (Mrs. Eddy's printer), worked closely with Benny. "Over and over again we had to refer details direct to Mrs. Eddy because Dr. Foster-Eddy was not at his office and could not be located for days at a time ... the responsibility which Mrs. Eddy still had to assume personally was unfortunate."

Orcutt also remarked on Benny's extravagance—he traveled by more expensive hired cab, as opposed to the public transportation that Mrs. Eddy and her staff normally used—as well as his penchant for flashy clothing, including a fur-lined coat, matching fur cap, and a "stunning" diamond tie-pin.

Benny clearly liked the perks that came with being Mary Baker Eddy's adopted son, including living at her elegant home on Commonwealth Avenue, but according to Orcutt he was disorganized and lacked discipline, and he appeared to have little interest in shouldering his responsibilities. In short, Benny was all show and no substance. When more experienced students rejected him, he complained that they were trying to drive him out of Boston.

As was her custom, Mrs. Eddy tried valiantly to keep him in the fold, alternately admonishing and encouraging him for the better part of a decade. Benny would promise to do better, then promptly backslide. By this time, even Mrs. Eddy's patience was wearing thin.

"If ever I wear out serving students, it shall be in the effort to help them to obey the Ten Commandments and imbibe the spirit of Christ's Beatitudes," she'd written in the *Journal* in 1891. Perhaps she was thinking of Benny.

When Benny and his married secretary's morals were called into question, this proved the last straw. In the summer of 1896, Mrs. Eddy finally took the publisher's work away from him. In a last-ditch effort to see if he could redeem himself, she sent him off to Philadelphia to form a new branch church there.

Benny failed at this task, too, joining an existing branch church instead, and by 1897 had managed to get himself expelled from its Readership and all other offices by his exasperated fellow members. He claimed that his "persistent unswerving fidelity" to his adopted mother caused others to hate him, and he assured Mrs. Eddy that he would be ready to come to her whenever she called him.

But would Benny keep his promise?

Others hadn't, including Josephine Woodbury. Mrs. Eddy's wayward student had continued to waffle between remorse for her misdeeds and further deceit, and in 1896 had been dropped from membership in The Mother Church. Her teacher's upright life and patient shepherding only served to expose Josephine's own shortcomings, the way a GPS device, pointing out the correct route, shows a traveler he or she is off course. This sparked resentment in Josephine which, when coupled with her boundless ambition, proved a deadly combination.

In the summer of 1899, after Mrs. Eddy gave an address which Josephine interpreted as a personal attack on her character, Josephine struck back.

"I will have Mrs. Eddy's place or pull the whole thing down upon their heads," she told her brother.

Enlisting the help of Frederick Peabody, a Boston lawyer who quickly developed a dislike for Mrs. Eddy as sharp as her own, Josephine sued for libel. Eventually, she was soundly defeated in court, but not without cost to Mrs. Eddy, who felt keenly the toll of this bid for revenge. The court case and the sensation it caused in the press endured for two long years, and it was an unpleasant and exhausting experience for Mrs. Eddy to have Christian Science and her own good name wrongly dragged through the mud.

SATISFIED
(January 1900 version)

It matters not,
What be thy lot,
So Love doth guide;
For storm or shine—
Pure peace is thine—
Whate'er betide.

And of these stones;
Or tyrant's thrones,
God able is,
To raise up seed—
In thought and deed—
To faithful His.

Aye, darkling sense
Arise, go hence,—
Our God is good:
False fears are foes,—
Truth tatters those,
When understood.

Love looseth thee,
And lifteth me,
Ayont hate's thrall:
There Life is light,
And wisdom might,
And God is all.

The centuries break!
The earth-bound wake!
God's glorified;
Who doth His will,
His likeness still,
Is satisfied.

▲ Mary poured her heart out in poems like this one, which like a number of her others would be revised and set to music for use as a hymn in Christian Science churches.

Once again, Mrs. Eddy poured her heart out on paper. Like a diamond forged from carbon under great pressure, a poem she wrote during this trying time ("Satisfied") shines with the unwavering trust she continued to place in God, ever-present divine Love, to sustain her.

Around this time, she would also write to a student, "Forgive, be unselfish, meek and Christlike or you cannot be a Christian Scientist."

In June of 1901, not long after the trial began, Frederick Peabody unexpectedly rested his case, and the judge directed the jury to return a verdict in favor of the defendant. It was a victory for Mrs. Eddy.

Among her loyal followers who stood shoulder to shoulder with her through this ordeal was Calvin Frye. Mrs. Eddy counted two sons, George and Benny. Close in age to them both, though, and more trustworthy, dependable, and dedicated than either of them was Calvin. Night and day he was at her service, two worn spots in the carpet by his bed showing where his feet had rested as he sat up at the ready when it was his turn to "watch"—to pray vigilantly—for the household, the Christian Science movement, and the world. Calvin gained few presents or privileges; he had no airs and grac-

PEOPLE AND PLACES

CALVIN FRYE

"I don't know how he does as much as he does," Mrs. Eddy once said of Calvin Frye.

For 28 years, Calvin was her right-hand man, serving in whatever capacity she needed him, from bookkeeper and secretary to metaphysician, copyist, coachman, and confidante. During all the time he worked for Mrs. Eddy, Calvin only took one vacation—for three hours, when he went to see an air show. Born August 24, 1845, in Andover, Massachusetts, Calvin never went to college, although his father had been a classmate of Ralph Waldo Emerson's at Harvard. Mr. Frye senior suffered from a crippling lameness that limited his options for work, and due to the family's reduced financial circumstances, young Calvin had to leave school and get a job to help make ends meet.

He apprenticed to a machinist, working at a woolen mill in Lawrence and later at a sewing machine factory. He eventually married, but his wife Ada died in 1872, just a year after their wedding, and Calvin moved back home. His widowed sister Lydia was there as well, caring for their mentally-ill mother. When a relative was healed by one of Mrs. Eddy's students, Calvin and Lydia turned to Christian Science for their mother and were overjoyed when her sanity was restored. In 1881, Calvin and his sister went to Lynn to study with Mrs. Eddy.

Calvin left his old life behind when Mrs. Eddy sent for him in the summer of 1882 after es; he was too direct to curry favor. He was every inch the dignified—some said dour—New Englander, but his eyes had a smile lurking in them, for he looked at the world with a dry sense of humor.

Calvin's greatest asset was that he could be trusted one hundred percent. His greatest reward was that Mrs. Eddy so trusted him. One time when she went for her daily drive in Concord, her horses shied and the coachman lost control. Mrs. Eddy was helped to the sidewalk by a passer-by, while the driver struggled to calm the panicked animals. After that, Calvin, wearing a uniform, sat next to the coachman each day on her drive. By doing this, he sacrificed an hour of his own precious free time, but he did it without question.

Was there rivalry between George, Benny, and Calvin?

Yes.

Calvin was the only one constantly at Mrs. Eddy's side, and he saw his role as protector against all intruders. Among these he counted George, with his continual demands for money, and Benny, with his emotional outbursts

▼ Calvin Frye in the 1880s, around the time he went to work for Mrs. Eddy

COURTESY TMBEL

Gilbert's passing. It must have taken a lot of humility for Calvin to answer that call, for it was unusual in the 19th century for women to take leadership roles, and to have a woman for a boss was definitely an oddity. Calvin's love for Christian Science spurred him to obey, however, and his scrupulous integrity and Yankee work ethic proved just the qualities that Mrs. Eddy needed in a steadfast aide-de-camp. Described by a reporter in 1907 as "a quiet, earnest man with a clear and placid countenance," Calvin's "honest devotion to Mrs. Eddy made him bend every effort to do whatever she expected him to do," recalled Minnie Weygandt, who for many years served side by side with him in Mrs. Eddy's household as maid and cook.

Calvin had an artistic bent, and in addition to playing the piano and the auto-harp, he was a photography buff, and took many candid photographs of Mrs. Eddy and her household.

In his later years, he served as First Reader at the Christian Science church in Concord, New Hampshire, and as president of The Mother Church. Calvin also finally took some vacations, too, visiting Florida and Europe.

COURTESY TMBEL

"He has done more practical work in my behalf to aid our Cause than any other Student," Mary Baker Eddy wrote to the Board of Directors about Calvin Frye in August 1903. She asked them to send him a gift of appreciation, which they did — a fine roll-top desk and chair, very likely the ones pictured here.

which upset Mrs. Eddy's peace. While Benny had direct access to his mother, George Glover never did. George visited his mother on five different occasions in his adult life. The first three visits were casual and relaxed; the last two — in 1903 and 1907 — were tense and strained. In the 28 years these visits spanned, their only other mode of communication was by letter. The question uppermost in George's mind early in the first decade of the 20th century was, did his mother receive all of his letters? He suspected not. But who would prevent them reaching her?

Could it be Calvin Frye?

The year 1903 was a terrible one for George Glover. A partner he had taken on cheated him out of a large sum of money made by selling stocks in Glover's mine. When the mine failed and George tried to pay back the stockholders, he fell heavily into debt. In March, he traveled East to see his mother. While he was there, he made derogatory comments about her and her household to Hermann Hering, who was serving as First Reader of The Mother Church. Mary was indignant when she found out ("Your remarks about me are so unjust they would justify me in disinheriting you," she wrote him bluntly). Nevertheless, she wrote him a check for $5,000 ($125,000 in today's dollars) to cover his debts. Then in August of that year, George's dearly loved second daughter, Evelyn, by now a married woman, died. George was desolate.

Eva Thompson, a friend of his two daughters, came to visit the Glovers in Lead, and George poured out his tale of woe. He was in tears. His family was nearly penniless. Sympathetic Eva wrote a long letter describing this visit to Irving Tomlinson, who was First Reader of the Christian Science church in Concord, New Hampshire. Irving claimed to have shown the letter to Calvin Frye, but no word of it reached Mrs. Eddy.

Was Calvin the roadblock?

Possibly. Calvin's reputation for playing "mother bear" was legendary. As William Rathvon, who would later work side by side with him in Mrs. Eddy's household, noted, "We have two aims in our work here: first, to protect our Leader; and second, to protect the Cause." Calvin on the other hand, he noted with a twinge of exasperation, had only one: "first, to protect our Leader, and second, to protect our Leader."

So George Glover's suspicions weren't unfounded. As Calvin himself explained, writing in the third person, "Glover naturally believed he was shut out from his mother and that probably Frye was the one who stood in his way between him and his mother and prevented her from giving him assistance." He continued, "Knowing as he does that she was abundantly able to relieve his family from suffering from hunger and cold and believing that Frye prevented his getting this help, he naturally conceived a strong prejudice against Frye and probably does to this day and believes that if Frye were away from Pleasant View his mother would feel differently towards her son and render him more help financially."

That was exactly how George Glover did feel, and a few years later it would drive him to take action, with momentous results.

21
The "House of Mystery"

On Sunday October 14, 1906, there was a sharp knock on the front door of Pleasant View. Two reporters from the *New York World* asked to see Calvin Frye, whom they suspected controlled the house and its main occupant—Mary Baker Eddy.

Calvin duly appeared and talked with them for a few minutes. Mr. Slaght and Mr. Lithchild claimed they had just one simple question: Was Mrs. Eddy dead or alive? Calvin told them that they couldn't possibly see his employer right away, but that he might be able to arrange a visit tomorrow. He would have to check and let them know later. He shut the door.

Reluctantly, like hounds called off a strong scent, the reporters turned to leave. They hadn't been honest with Calvin; they were actually after a story for their paper.

Slaght and Lithchild were journalists of the lowest sort, muckrakers adept at digging up scandal, fraud, and other skullduggery. If they didn't find a story, they'd simply make one up. The two men had not taken the long train ride from New York City to Concord only to be turned away. They were determined to penetrate the "House of Mystery," as the media had dubbed Pleasant View.

Besides, there was the competition to consider. *McClure's* magazine was about to run a 14-part series on Mrs. Eddy. Their paper planned to "scoop" that story.

At one time, Calvin Frye would have automatically said no to the two reporters, but much as he wished to protect Mrs. Eddy's peace and quiet, he had found that refusing to grant interviews with the press did not always pay off.

Three years earlier, Georgine Milmine, an unknown journalist, claimed she was turned away from the very same door. She had planned to write a series on a dozen famous American women, and Mrs. Eddy, who by this time had become a national figure, was on her list. When she was bluntly refused an interview at Pleasant View, Georgine became suspicious. Could there be something wrong with Mrs. Eddy? Was she ill, perhaps? She decided to inquire further.

The young woman spoke to several people who were unfriendly toward Mrs. Eddy. Payments were made in exchange for some of these negative accounts. Georgine took her material to *McClure's*, and the result was one-sided and inaccurate. The first installment of the story even mixed up the photographs, running one of an elderly lady from Brooklyn instead.

"Of all the history of lies ever written I believe this article is the most in excess," Mrs. Eddy wrote to a student about it in disgust.

Would Georgine have been less hostile, perhaps, if she'd been granted an interview?

The *World* reporters had no way of knowing that Mary Baker Eddy, now 85, still maintained the same busy schedule she had for decades, rising early and keeping her household on their toes throughout the day and often into the night. The extent and scope of her work was far-reaching—much more than most people imagined.

What aggravated the press was Mrs. Eddy's refusal to meet with them. While most public figures sought the limelight, she shunned it. She kept away not just from journalists, but also from casual visitors and curiosity seekers, including her own followers. She couldn't afford idle interruptions and still carry on her work. The press, however, didn't understand. They felt seclusion meant secrecy, and that secrecy suggested there was something to hide. This point of view Mrs. Eddy was beginning to grasp.

So when Calvin Frye told her that two *World* reporters wanted an interview, Mrs. Eddy took immediate action. She asked her neighbor, Professor Kent, to come and vouch for her identity. She sent her carriage to the Eagle Hotel, where Slaght and Lithchild were staying, to bring them to Pleasant View. As they left the house after the interview, one of Mrs. Eddy's secretaries heard Lithchild comment, "She is certainly a well-preserved woman for

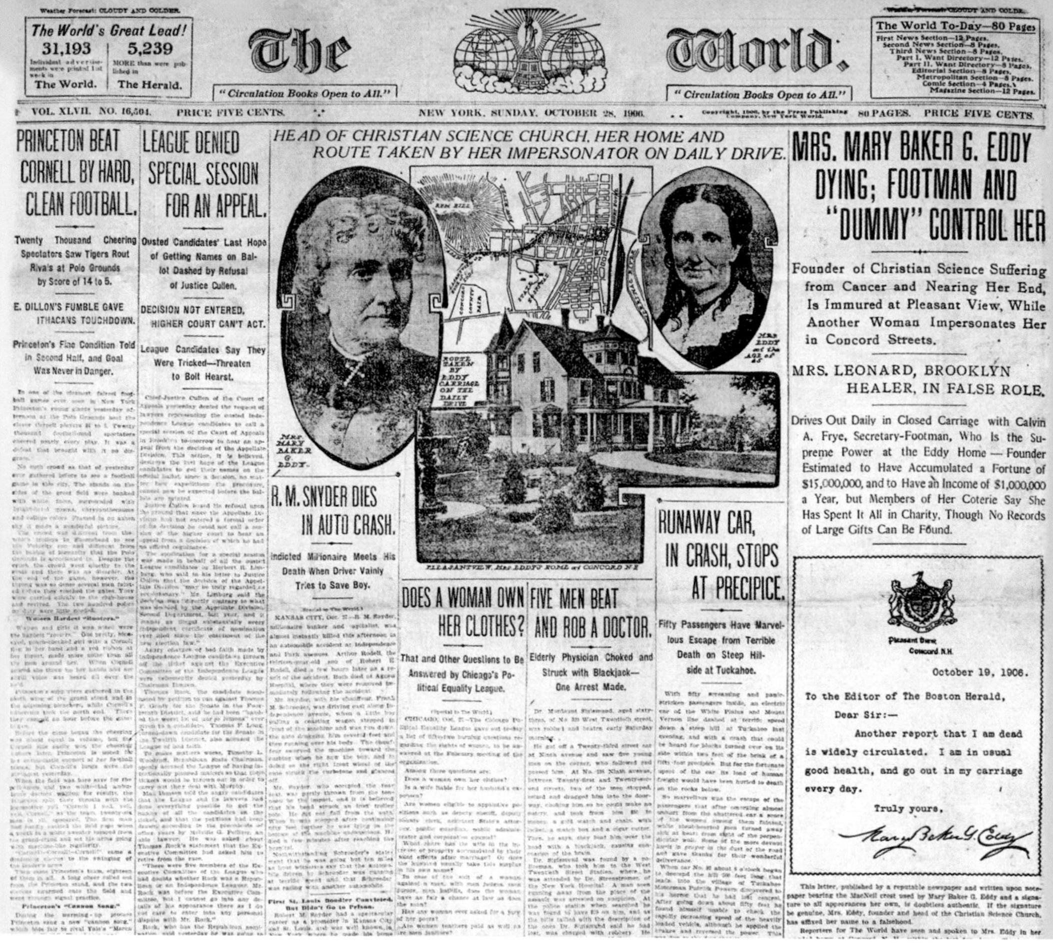

Weather Forecast: CLOUDY AND COLDER.

The World's Great Lead! 31,193 Individual advertisements were printed last week in The World. 5,239 MORE than were published in The Herald.

The World. "Circulation Books Open to All."

The World To-Day—80 Pages

VOL. XLVII. NO. 16,504. PRICE FIVE CENTS. NEW YORK, SUNDAY, OCTOBER 28, 1906. 80 PAGES. PRICE FIVE CENTS.

PRINCETON BEAT CORNELL BY HARD, CLEAN FOOTBALL.

Twenty Thousand Cheering Spectators Saw Tigers Rout Riva's at Polo Grounds by Score of 14 to 5.

E. DILLON'S FUMBLE GAVE ITHACANS TOUCHDOWN.

Princeton's Fine Condition Told in Second Half, and Goal Was Never in Danger.

LEAGUE DENIED SPECIAL SESSION FOR AN APPEAL.

Ousted Candidates' Last Hope of Getting Names on Ballot Dashed by Refusal of Justice Cullen.

DECISION NOT ENTERED, HIGHER COURT CAN'T ACT.

League Candidates Say They Were Tricked—Threaten to Bolt Hearst.

HEAD OF CHRISTIAN SCIENCE CHURCH, HER HOME AND ROUTE TAKEN BY HER IMPERSONATOR ON DAILY DRIVE.

R. M. SNYDER DIES IN AUTO CRASH.

Indicted Millionaire Meets His Death When Driver Vainly Tries to Save Boy.

DOES A WOMAN OWN HER CLOTHES?

That and Other Questions to Be Answered by Chicago's Political Equality League.

FIVE MEN BEAT AND ROB A DOCTOR.

Elderly Physician Choked and Struck with Blackjack—One Arrest Made.

RUNAWAY CAR, IN CRASH, STOPS AT PRECIPICE.

Fifty Passengers Have Marvellous Escape from Terrible Death on Steep Hillside at Tuckahoe.

MRS. MARY BAKER G. EDDY DYING; FOOTMAN AND "DUMMY" CONTROL HER

Founder of Christian Science Suffering from Cancer and Nearing Her End, Is Immured at Pleasant View, While Another Woman Impersonates Her in Concord Streets.

MRS. LEONARD, BROOKLYN HEALER, IN FALSE ROLE.

Drives Out Daily in Closed Carriage with Calvin A. Frye, Secretary-Footman, Who Is the Supreme Power at the Eddy Home — Founder Estimated to Have Accumulated a Fortune of $15,000,000, and to Have an Income of $1,000,000 a Year, but Members of Her Coterie Say She Has Spent It All in Charity, Though No Records of Large Gifts Can Be Found.

Pleasant View
Concord, N.H.

October 19, 1906.

To the Editor of The Boston Herald,

Dear Sir:—

Another report that I am dead is widely circulated. I am in usual good health, and go out in my carriage every day.

Truly yours,

Mary Baker G. Eddy

COURTESY TMBEL

▲ Mary Baker Eddy was front-page news, and for unscrupulous journalists, fabricated stories like this one were better than no stories at all.

her years." Slaght agreed on the soundness of her physical and mental condition. And yet, on October 28, 1906, the *World* ran this sensational headline:

MRS. MARY BAKER G. EDDY DYING;
FOOTMAN AND "DUMMY" CONTROL HER

This was not the first time a celebrity had been reported dead, or dying. American humorist Mark Twain, a contemporary of Mrs. Eddy's, once noted wryly, "The report of my death was an exaggeration."

Mrs. Eddy herself was no slouch when it came to snappy comebacks. With a flash of the wit for which she was well known, she greeted a carpenter at Pleasant View the following day with, "Good morning, Mr. Frost; I am so glad we are not all dead this morning."

But the *World's* account showed a deliberate lie in the making. The reporters even tried to bribe Ernest Gosselin, a local chauffeur, to say that he had driven a physician to Pleasant View in order to perform an operation on Mrs. Eddy. Gosselin turned them down flat.

Shocked by the *World's* headline, the citizens of Concord rallied to Mrs. Eddy's defense. The same day the paper was published, her lawyer, General Frank Streeter, drove out to see her with the mayor of Concord, Charles R. Corning.

This popular cartoon sparked a clash between rival news organizations that resulted in a new trend in journalism.

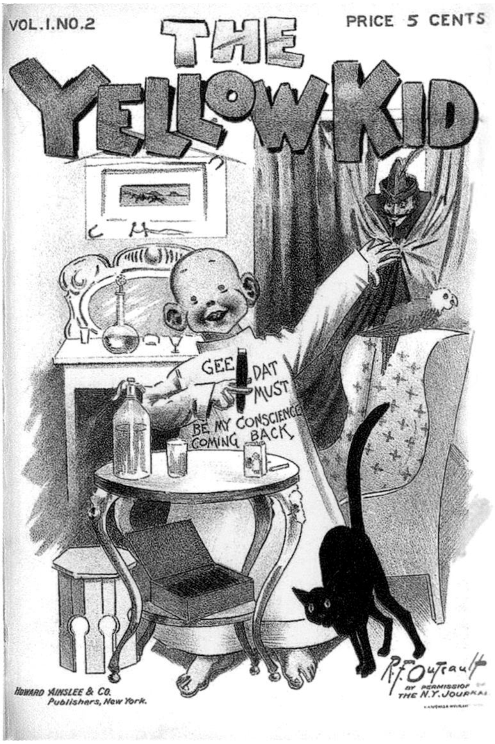

VOL.I.NO.2
PRICE 5 CENTS
THE YELLOW KID
GEE DAT MUST BE MY CONSCIENCE COMING BACK
R.F. Outcault
BY PERMISSION OF THE N.Y. JOURNAL
HOWARD AINSLEE & CO. Publishers, New York.

EXTRA! EXTRA! READ ALL ABOUT IT!

SIGNS OF THE TIMES

It started with a cartoon.

"Hogan's Alley," a popular cartoon in Joseph Pulitzer's *New York World* in the 1890s, featured a character dressed in yellow and named "the yellow kid." When rival publisher William Randolph Hearst, who owned the *New York Journal* along with a number of other newspapers, lured away artist R. F. Outcault, Pulitzer struck back by commissioning another cartoonist to create a second "yellow kid." Soon, the two papers were competing fiercely for readers, not just through cartoons, but also through flamboyant, melodramatic stories, scandal-mongering, and headlines that grew more and more exaggerated and sensational.

For instance, in reporting on a hotel fire in California, another Hearst-owned paper ran this headline: "HUNGRY, FRANTIC FLAMES. They Leap Madly Upon the Splendid Pleasure Palace by the Bay of Monterey, Encircling Del Monte in Their Ravenous Embrace . . . Rushing in Upon the Trembling Guests with Savage Fury."

Tactics like this came to be called "yellow journalism," and gave the newsboys on street corners plenty to shout about as they battled to boost sales. The term is still used today to describe unethical tabloid fiction and any news media that acts in an irresponsible or unprofessional manner, misleading readers, listeners, or viewers with distorted coverage and opinions masquerading as fact.

The mayor hadn't met Mrs. Eddy in person before, and in an interview afterwards with the *Boston Herald* he said:

"I had gone expecting to find a tottering old woman, perhaps incoherent, almost senile. Instead when she rose to greet me her carriage was erect, her walk that of a woman of forty.... To say that she is mentally vigorous is inside the mark. She is wonderful for an octogenarian. Her face is not full, her figure is slight, but she looks commanding, her eyes are bright, her handclasp is firm ... when she rose to bid us good-by, Mrs. Eddy showed no signs of fatigue."

After this rebuttal of the *World* by the *Boston Herald*, more reporters flocked to Concord, wanting to know firsthand what was really going on. With Mrs. Eddy's consent, eleven of them waited in her living room to catch a quick glimpse of her on her way out for her carriage ride. She paused long enough to answer three short questions:

"Are you in perfect bodily health?"

"Indeed I am."

"Have you any other physician than God?"

With a sweeping gesture she replied, "No physician but God. His everlasting arms are around me, and that is enough."

"Do you take a daily drive?"

"Yes."

And with that, Mrs. Eddy stepped into her carriage.

Even still, confusion reigned. According to one reporter's account of this brief visit, "she stood before them shaking with palsy, a physical wreck, tottering, pallid like a vision from beyond the grave"; while another countered: "she stood before them erect and upright, nerved for the ordeal." The reporters couldn't even agree on what she was wearing: "she wore a black cloak"; "she wore a cape of white ermine...."

Meanwhile the *World* mounted a fresh attack. Promoting its own fiction—that Mrs. Eddy couldn't manage her own affairs and was being held hostage in her own house—it pretended to have found a way to "rescue" her, proposing a lawsuit against Calvin Frye and nine other of Mrs. Eddy's faithful workers—the "gang" said to be keeping her captive.

Two figures at the *World* were at work behind the scenes: Ralph Pulitzer, who had taken the reins as editor from his famous father, Joseph Pulitzer, and Bradford Merrill, the paper's managing editor. They hired William Chandler, a former senator from New Hampshire and owner of one of Concord's two newspapers, to prosecute the case.

Chandler framed the case in a way that was particularly humiliating to Mrs. Eddy. The lawsuit was to be filed in her name, *Eddy vs. Frye*, by her "next friends." Legally, "next friends" sue on behalf of a minor, or someone who is unable to act for himself—someone dependent and helpless. Chandler was thus implying that this was Mrs. Eddy's condition. But in order to sue, he needed a genuine relative to be a "next friend." Who would that be?

George Glover, of course.

"If the son is willing to make a move all is plain sailing," Chandler wrote to Bradford Merrill.

Losing no time, Slaght, the *World* reporter, took the next train out to Lead, South Dakota. In his pocket he carried a letter from Chandler—bait for the hook for George. The letter described Mrs. Eddy as "worn out, a confirmed invalid, restrained, incapable," painting the picture of a doddering woman surrounded by "designing men" who wanted control of her large property—his inheritance.

George hadn't seen his mother for several years. Chandler's letter troubled him. On the one hand, it confirmed what he already feared—that his mother was at the mercy of those around her, especially Calvin Frye. On the other, he found it hard to believe that she was incapable of thinking for herself. Aggravating matters was the fact that he had hit rock bottom financially, and was likely tormented by the suggestion that his inheritance was threatened.

George Glover at the time of the Next Friends lawsuit

COURTESY TMBEL

Now, with Chandler's letter in hand, George's first move was to ask Hermann Hering, who was by this time serving as First Reader at the Christian Science church in Concord, to give him an update on his mother's health. Hermann responded by sending George a copy of the *Concord Monitor* with its October 29, 1906, headline: "Cruel Falsehoods Promptly Refuted."

He also wrote: "You can rest assured that the statements in the *Monitor* are correct. I have seen Mrs. Eddy several times lately and can vouch for her good health and spirits."

On the basis of this, George wrote to a friend in Denver: "I know that [what] the *New York World* made is all a lie in reference to mother. I have authentic news direct from Concord that she is alright and in her usual good health. It will be printed in a Lead City paper in a few days. I will send you one."

In spite of these brave words, George had lingering doubts. He ended up asking Chandler if he could go and see her for himself, and take along his daughter Mary, now 25. "Should I discover that my mother is infeebled [sic] in mind and body as represented and that she is helpless in the power of Calvin A. Frye and his associates," George told Chandler, "I will gladly avail myself of your legal services in the protection of her rights and my own."

Certain that he had hooked his fish, Slaght returned to New York and wrote jauntily to Chandler: "Mission to Lead entirely successful." He went on to paint a vivid picture of how heavily in debt George was, and consequently how ready he was to do anything Chandler advised.

Chandler arranged for George and his daughter to meet him in New York in December at the newspaper's expense. After such a long stretch

PHOTO © TMBEL

CONCORD, N. H., MONDAY, OCTOBER 29, 1906.

CRUEL FALSEHOODS PROMPTLY REFUTED.

Concord Citizens Come Forward With Alacrity to Speak for Mrs. Eddy.

Mayor Corning Tells of Interview With Christian Science Leader Sunday Afternoon—General Streeter Was Present Also—Both Say That Mrs. Eddy Was in Good Health and Fine Spirits—New York Newspaper's Sensationalism Fervently Condemned by Concord People Who Know the Facts.

Mrs. Eddy is keen of intellect and strong in memory. She is a surprising illustration of longevity; bright eyes, emphatic expression, and an alertness rarely to be encountered in so venerable a person.—Mayor Charles R. Corning.

Mrs. Eddy's mind is not only unimpaired, but she exhibits the same clearness, strength, alertness and vigor which have so long distinguished her.—General Frank S. Streeter.

Mrs. Eddy has no cancer, or any chronic or organic or functional disease.—Calvin A. Frye.

Mrs. Eddy herself has driven in her carriage daily, with the exception of one day in the early spring, when the roads were so bad that she did not go out.—Lewis C. Strang.

I have seen Mrs. Eddy's carriage on State street almost daily. The occupant has always been Mrs. Eddy herself.—Hermann S. Hering.

I most emphatically say that Mrs. Eddy is in every way capable of conducting her business affairs.—Fred N. Ladd, Treasurer Loan and Trust Savings Bank.

I can state from personal knowledge that it is Mrs. Eddy, and no other person, whom I see riding in her carriage.—Josiah E. Fernald, President National State Capital Bank.

▲ The day after the *World's* opening salvo, the *Concord Monitor* sprang to Mrs. Eddy's defense.

of poverty and hardship, how comforting to be pampered and paid for! A strong bond grew between the Glovers and their lawyer, whose judgment they trusted implicitly.

George and young Mary enjoyed a lengthy stay, then proceeded on to Concord. It had been four years since George had last seen his mother, and he arrived at Pleasant View on January 2, 1907, primed by Chandler to expect signs of infirmity and weakness. He and his daughter overlooked Mrs. Eddy's probing questions about mining. They were too busy straining to hear the sound of the "galvanic battery" — the device that the *World* had fabricated in one of its reports and said was keeping Mrs. Eddy alive — and they interpreted various ordinary household noises to be just that.

George reported that his mother was wistful when it came time to leave. They kissed one another affectionately, and then she said, "You will come and see me again, both of you, won't you?"

"Yes, mother, we will," he told her.

George and his daughter went straight to Washington, D.C., to report to Chandler. Mrs. Eddy, unaware that her son was being courted by her opponents, wrote to him the following day, January 3, 1907:

"It is sweet to me to recall my little visit from you and my dear grandchild Miss Mary. God bless you and guide you in all your ways."

22
Turning the Tide

William Chandler was flabbergasted. The *World* had decided to drop the case.

In early February of 1907, he fired off a letter to Ralph Pulitzer reminding him of the injury the paper had done to the Glovers "by seeking them out and taking them up and buoying them into hope during long weeks of thought and preparation and then dumping them into the depths of despair." A large contribution was in order, he suggested, "to enable them to get out of the hopeless predicament in which I have them in charge."

COURTESY OF THE LIBRARY OF CONGRESS, PRINTS AND PHOTOGRAPHS DIVISION, HARRIS & EWIG COLLECTION

Shown here in 1914, Ralph Pulitzer, son of newspaper magnate Joseph Pulitzer (who endowed the Pulitzer prize), was in charge of the *New York World* at the time of the Next Friends suit.

Ralph sent a check for $5,000 ($125,000 in today's dollars), along with a note instructing Chandler to disburse the funds as he saw fit in order to meet the "moral obligation ... that may have been incurred, resulting from any steps that may have been taken" by the *World* and its representatives. He added, "We are sure you will appreciate that we regard this as a generous payment to all parties and we wish it to entirely terminate the matter."

Actually, as far as the *World* was concerned, its mission was accomplished. The paper had stirred up a hornet's nest and their readers were abuzz. The *World* could keep attacking with stinging articles at regular intervals, but if it were discovered that they had initiated this lawsuit, it would reflect on them badly. Their own lawyer had advised dropping the case, saying they had no facts to support it.

Surprisingly, Chandler decided to press on alone. What made him continue the suit without his original backers and without any financial support? One reason may have been his own commitment to the Glovers—he had taken a liking to George and his daughter, and didn't want to abandon them. Additionally, he felt a deep-seated antagonism towards Christian Science, one shared by Frederick Peabody, one of the lawyers Chandler had chosen to work with him.

Peabody was the Boston-based lawyer who had prosecuted the *Woodbury vs. Eddy* libel suit in 1901 and been soundly defeated. Humiliated by the loss, he afterwards mounted a vitriolic public campaign against Mrs. Eddy on his own, speaking out against her at Tremont Temple and afterward publishing his scathing lecture, in which he called her a fraud and a humbug, in pamphlet form. When he was approached by Slaght to work for Chandler, Peabody purred: "Nothing could give me greater professional satisfaction than to participate in such a proceeding."

On March 1st, Chandler made his move, filing suit in Concord on behalf of George Glover and "Next Friends": George's daughter Mary and Mrs. Eddy's nephew George W. Baker. The following day, the *World* pretended to report the case it had initiated, claiming that Mrs. Eddy was being "controlled" and her income mismanaged by Calvin Frye, Alfred Farlow, and other prominent members of the church.

To bolster their position, Chandler tried to enlist as many of Mrs. Eddy's relatives as possible as "next friends." One of those relatives was Foster Eddy. On March 4th, Benny wrote a gushing letter to Laura Sargent, Mrs. Eddy's personal assistant at Pleasant View, pledging his loyalty and support:

> *I want the dear little Mother, and the older members of 'the household,' to know that I am not at all in sympathy with these diabolical actions against her. I believe her perfect demonstration will be of more value to the world than all the money in it....*

I send you this because of what I saw in the paper yesterday.

With a whole lot of love to our dearest Mother, and kindest regards to you all,

I am, as ever,

E.J. Foster Eddy.

A week later, Benny was in Chandler's pocket. Along with Mrs. Eddy's cousin Fred W. Baker (who withdrew from the suit two months later), he, too, signed on as a "next friend."

COURTESY TMBEL

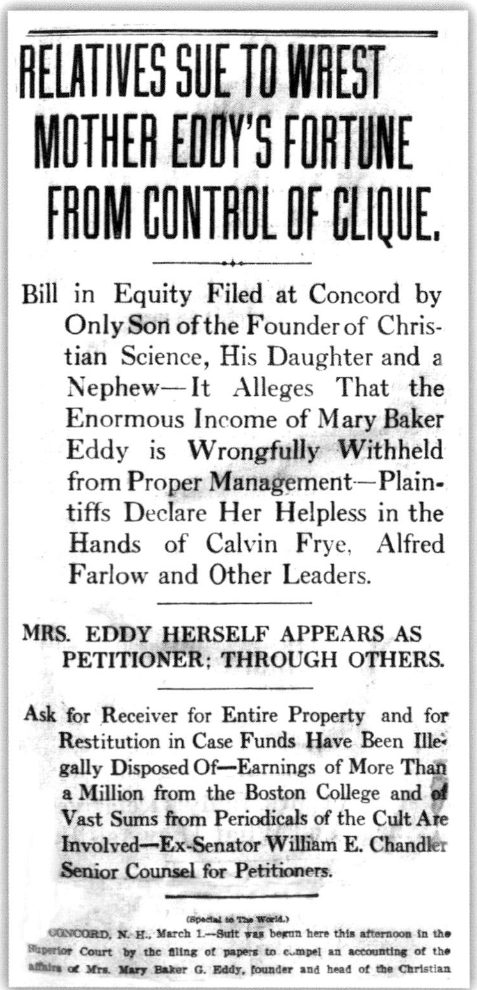

RELATIVES SUE TO WREST MOTHER EDDY'S FORTUNE FROM CONTROL OF CLIQUE.

Bill in Equity Filed at Concord by Only Son of the Founder of Christian Science, His Daughter and a Nephew—It Alleges That the Enormous Income of Mary Baker Eddy is Wrongfully Withheld from Proper Management—Plaintiffs Declare Her Helpless in the Hands of Calvin Frye, Alfred Farlow and Other Leaders.

MRS. EDDY HERSELF APPEARS AS PETITIONER; THROUGH OTHERS.

Ask for Receiver for Entire Property and for Restitution in Case Funds Have Been Illegally Disposed Of—Earnings of More Than a Million from the Boston College and of Vast Sums from Periodicals of the Cult Are Involved—Ex-Senator William E. Chandler Senior Counsel for Petitioners.

(Special to The World.)

CONCORD, N. H., March 1.—Suit was begun here this afternoon in the Superior Court by the filing of papers to compel an accounting of the affairs of Mrs. Mary Baker G. Eddy, founder and head of the Christian

On March 2, 1907, the *World* pretended to report on the lawsuit it had initiated.

One of the central issues of the lawsuit was financial mismanagement. As Mrs. Eddy's bookkeeper, Calvin had supposedly cheated his employer out of vast sums of money. But when a well-known accounting firm checked 14 years of his accounts, they discovered that, in fact, Mrs. Eddy owed Calvin $677.41 ($16,522.20 in 2013 dollars)!

In spite of the persecution and injustice, Calvin Frye stood firm. And he wasn't the only one who stayed true to his post. Mrs. Eddy's whole household was at the ready. While *McClure's* and the *World* battered away each month with fresh shot from their lie-making cannons, the Pleasant View household held the fort and "kept watch," as they called it, with vigorous prayer.

How did Mrs. Eddy deal with these betrayals and attacks? What was her first line of defense?

"I live with the Bible," she told her student and household worker Lida

Fitzpatrick in April of 1907.

In a more widespread message that month she wrote, "My beloved Church: As is my wont, I opened up the Bible this morning to take from its sacred pages a thought that enables me to meet 'the cares that infest the day' and I first looked at 2nd Samuel, 22nd chapter." Included in that chapter is this verse: "The Lord is my rock, and my fortress, and my deliverer; the God of my rock; in him will I trust."

Trusting in God was what Mrs. Eddy knew how to do best. "Come and hear what God said to me this morning," she would often tell her household workers, before sharing what she had read in the Scriptures. Frequently, she'd call them into her study to give them a spiritual lesson that they could apply to their tasks, and everyone at Pleasant View was expected to pray his or her way through the day. "Lift your thought to God as you go about your work," Mrs. Eddy told them. Whether they were preparing a meal, cutting the grass, writing a letter, healing sickness, or facing an unjust lawsuit, the spiritual basis was the same.

Mrs. Eddy practiced what she preached, no more so than during that trying summer. In response to Jesus' command to "Love your enemies, bless them that curse you, do good to them that hate you, and pray for them which despitefully use you, and persecute you," she had previously written, "Each day I pray: 'God bless my enemies; make them Thy friends; give them to know the joy and the peace of love.'"

And in a letter she sent at this time to Annie Knott, a stalwart Scot who was the first woman authorized to lecture on Christian Science and later the first female member of the Board of Directors, she noted: "Returning good for evil makes good real and evil unreal."

Living these Christian ideals gave strength to the Pleasant View staff. All of them were called upon to be fearless and persistent. Yet at times the tide of hate appeared so great that even Mrs. Eddy grew troubled. If this lawsuit succeeded, not only was her life's work at stake, but also her own person and where and how she lived were threatened.

"This hour is going to test Christian Scientists and the fate of our Cause, and they must not be found wanting," Mrs. Eddy wrote to her student Calvin Hill, asking him to come to Pleasant View. "I see this clearly that the

ALLIES IN THE PRESS

PEOPLE AND PLACES

Just as a healing led one reporter to decamp from Concord, so another healing would be instrumental in winning Mrs. Eddy an influential supporter in the press.

On January 27, 1908, newspaper magnate William Randolph Hearst, whose competition with Joseph Pulitzer jump-started yellow journalism, welcomed a newborn son and namesake. The infant, dubbed "Weeyum" by his older brother George, was diagnosed with a bowel defect. Unable to retain food of any kind, he "wasted away to an actual skeleton," according to his parent.

Distraught, Hearst consulted two of the finest physicians in New York.

"The doctors did all in their power, but without the slightest result," he later recounted in his column in the *Los Angeles Examiner*. Finally, he was told that the only option was surgery, which his son was unlikely to survive.

Given until morning to make his decision, Hearst was visited that night by Jessamine Goddard, a family friend (and wife of *American Weekly* editor Morrill Goddard) whose child had been healed of double pneumonia. She brought along the Christian Science practitioner who had prayed for her baby, and in desperation Hearst gave permission for his son to have Christian Science treatment.

The practitioner prayed through the night. By morning, the infant was able to drink and retain milk. His recovery was swift.

"The child is now a little over six feet tall, and weighs 180 pounds and runs a newspaper considerably better than his father can," Hearst boasted some years later.

Impressed by this "miraculous rescue" of his son "from the very jaws of death," Hearst gave orders forbidding his newspapers from publishing attacks on Mrs. Eddy or on Christian Science.

prosperity of our Cause hangs in this balance."

The hardest part for Mrs. Eddy was the fact that her son, George, had put his name to the suit. "I love you my only child," she wrote to him. "Why do you allow yourself to be used to bring this great grief and trouble to your own aged mother?"

Calvin Hill soon arrived to join the band of trusted students and metaphysical workers who helped provide support that summer. Each day, he went to the courtroom so he could give Mrs. Eddy an update of the case from Frank Streeter, her chief legal counsel.

"I have a vivid picture of her, sitting quietly and listening to what I had to report," he later recalled. "She reminded me of a gray gull riding calmly, serenely, on a storm-tossed sea.... She

COURTESY OF THE BANCROFT LIBRARY, UNIVERSITY OF CALIFORNIA, BERKELEY

▲ William Randolph Hearst and "Weeyum"

once said to me, 'You cannot hurt anyone by telling the truth, and no one can hurt you by telling a lie.'"

Despite the ordeal, Mrs. Eddy didn't lose her sense of humor. She even signed one of her letters to Hill, "Your best friend, but not your 'next friend.'"

Nor did she ever lose her tender heart and generosity as a healer. At one point in the middle of all the hoopla, as reporters descended on Concord hoping to dig up dirt for their own newspapers, Mrs. Eddy asked Irving Tomlinson, a member of her staff, to relay a message to one of them in particular. Irving didn't know it at the time, but the individual in question—a hard-boiled New York newsman and heavy drinker—suffered from an extremely painful growth in his throat, and had difficulty speaking. In the time it took for the reporter to listen to the message relayed from Mrs. Eddy, he was completely healed. He and his astounded companions, who had believed Mrs. Eddy to be a fraud, packed up and left.

Years later, the newspaperman's nephew visited Irving in Boston and told him, "My uncle requested me to see you and to tell you in his last days he turned to Christian Science, and he knew that he owed a debt of gratitude to Mrs. Eddy for his healing in Concord."

By now, the lawsuit had moved to a wider stage. The entire nation was following the developments of the case with interest. Frank Streeter urged Mrs. Eddy to grant some proper interviews to the press. Not to a horde of reporters clamoring with questions, but on a one-on-one basis. He felt that the mystery surrounding her home and the false accusations that the *World* and *McClure's* were publishing must be refuted. Well-known journalists, he counseled, ones with no connection to Christian Science, as well as some psychiatrists, or "alienists" as they were then called, should meet with her and give their frank appraisal to the public. The clear statements of support in the *Concord Monitor* by the mayor, by Streeter himself, and by Mrs. Eddy's household members, were not enough.

Mrs. Eddy immediately saw the logic of this approach. Although work demanded her full attention—construction on the 3,000-seat Extension of The Mother Church had just been completed the previous year, along with another revision of *Science and Health*, among other things—she realized that it was time for her to step into the public arena. The attack had come by

PHOTO EZRA W. REID COURTESY TMBEC

▲ Construction of the Extension to The Mother Church (pictured here on dedication day in June of 1906) was completed the year before the Next Friends suit.

way of the press, and her defense must rest there also.

Over the long, hot summer, Mrs. Eddy spoke with two psychiatrists, as well as four prominent reporters from Boston, Philadelphia, Chicago, and New York. All six men gave positive reports.

Dr. Edward French, the first psychiatrist, found her "fully sane and above the average in intelligence and directness." He reported that "there was not the least evidence of mental weakness or incompetence."

The second, Dr. Allan McLane Hamilton, grandson of founding father Alexander Hamilton and a professor of clinical psychology at Cornell, had no love for Christian Science. In fact, he had testified against the religion in a court case in New York. Yet Streeter felt that his fairness and professional reputation were such that he would be a valuable voice for the defense.

"I was secretly to examine Mrs. Eddy as to her sanity, and subsequently to testify in her behalf if I could do so conscientiously," Hamilton later wrote, confessing that he'd gone to the interview prejudiced against her by the reports in the press. After his investigation, the doctor made his report, and gave an interview to the *New York Times* which included the following:

"I have now become candidly of the opinion that Mrs. Eddy is not only sincere in all she says and does, but I believe, also, that she unselfishly spends her money for the perpetuation of a church which, in her estimation, is destined to play an important part in the betterment of humanity....

"For a woman of her age I do not hesitate to say that she is physically and mentally phenomenal.... In this country everyone is entitled to hold whatever religious belief he or she may choose; and this being so, there seems to be a manifest injustice in taxing so excellent and capable a woman as Mrs. Eddy with any form of insanity."

The four journalists who interviewed Mrs. Eddy agreed.

Like his trio of colleagues, Edwin Park of the *Boston Globe* was highly regarded and commanded a wide audience. His was the first interview to be published, and his excitement at this honor bubbled over in his lead paragraph:

"At her beautiful home, Pleasant View, this afternoon, Mrs. Mary Baker G. Eddy, Discoverer and Founder of the Christian Science belief, for the first time

➤ "Captain of her ship": Mary Baker Eddy around the time of the Next Friends suit

PHOTO CALVIN A. FRYE © TMBEC

in six years gave a real newspaper interview, and for forty minutes talked not only entertainingly, but with animation and keen intelligence on a number of subjects in which she is concerned."

Some of his other comments: Mrs. Eddy talked fluently, incisively; she didn't use glasses to read; and as he was leaving her study, she showed no signs of fatigue.

Leigh Hodges of Philadelphia's *North American* noted "her whole manner was practical, forceful, unaffected," adding, "Who thinks she is not the captain of her ship should have been there to see her at that moment."

And William Curtis of the *Chicago Record-Herald* reported to his readers, "I have never seen a woman eighty-six years of age with greater physical or mental vigor."

The most famous interview was with Arthur Brisbane. One of the best-known American newspapermen of his day, Brisbane was editor of the *New York Evening Journal*, a Hearst publication, and his syndicated editorial column "Today" had a readership in the tens of millions. The August issue of *Cosmopolitan*—at that time a well-respected

COURTESY HEATHER VOGEL FREDERICK

COURTESY OF THE LIBRARY OF CONGRESS, PRINTS AND PHOTOGRAPHS DIVISION

➤ Journalist Arthur Brisbane, circa 1906. His interview with Mary Baker Eddy appeared in this issue (August 1907) and helped turn the tide of public opinion in her favor.

literary magazine also under the Hearst umbrella—in which his interview with Mrs. Eddy ran, sold out completely, and later appeared in book form as *What Mrs. Eddy Said to Arthur Brisbane.*

"It is quite certain that nobody could see this beautiful and venerable woman and ever again speak of her except in terms of affectionate reverence and sympathy," wrote Brisbane.

"Women will want to know what Mrs. Eddy wore," he continued. "The writer regrets that he cannot tell. With some women you see the dress; with Mrs. Eddy you see only the face, the very earnest eyes, and the beautiful, quiet expression that only age and thought can give to a human face."

Among the many other points he made:

"She is able to manage her affairs as much as she may choose to do, and if she were not, no greater crime could be committed against her than to take her from the surroundings that she loves and the friends that make her happy. Very few women of seventy have the business intelligence, power of will, and clearness of thought possessed by Mrs. Eddy at eighty-six."

When Brisbane asked her why the lawsuit had been started, "Mrs. Eddy replied in a deep, earnest voice that could easily have been heard all over the biggest of her churches: 'Greed of gold, young man. They are not interested in me, I am sorry to say, but in my money, and in the desire to control that. They say they want to help me. They never tried to help me when I was working hard years ago and when help would have been so welcome.'"

Brisbane continued, "Mrs. Eddy said in her interview, 'Young man, I made my money with my pen, just as you do, and I have a right to it.' Mrs. Eddy not only has a right to it, but she has the mind to control it."

As the two said good-bye, Mrs. Eddy rose from her chair and took his hand in both of hers. "She presented a very beautiful picture of venerable womanhood," Brisbane reported. "Her face, so remarkably young, framed in the beautiful snow-white hair and supported by the delicate, frail, yet erect, body, seemed really the personification of that victory of spirit over matter to which her religion aspires."

By now, the tide of public opinion had definitely turned.

One further hurdle awaited Mrs. Eddy. When the Next Friends suit was first filed back in March, Robert Chamberlin was the presiding justice.

The case had gained such prominence by late June that he made an unusual decision. He asked Judge Edgar Aldrich to serve as Master (an officer of court appointed to assist a judge). Aldrich agreed, on the condition that he be allowed two co-Masters, and attorney Hosea Parker and Dr. George Jelly, a psychiatrist, were duly appointed. First, this trio of Masters would listen to arguments from both sides at the courthouse. Then, in deference to Mrs. Eddy's age, they would go to Pleasant View. By interviewing her themselves in person, they could report back to Judge Chamberlin, who would decide whether she was competent to manage her business affairs.

The session opened at the courthouse on August 13th. William Chandler, chief counsel for the "next friends," tried to show that Mrs. Eddy suffered "delusions" and was the puppet of her staff, who had stolen her money.

On the following day, the chief Master, Judge Aldrich, stopped the arguments and accusations from the prosecution. "This hearing is not for the purpose of disestablishing the Christian Science faith," he noted sternly. "It is a question whether [Mrs. Eddy] is now in a condition to manage, control, and direct her financial affairs and property rights."

At two o'clock that afternoon, the Masters, the court stenographer, and Chandler and Streeter, the lawyers for each side, found themselves in Mrs. Eddy's private study, a large, comfortable room with a bay window looking out over the Merrimack Valley to the distant hills of her birthplace in Bow. When all were seated, Judge Aldrich began with a

EVERYDAY LIFE

MRS. EDDY'S HIGH-TECH HOUSEHOLD

Long before today's iPods and MP3 players, there was the Victrola. Considered cutting-edge technology in its day, the Victrola was the trademarked name of an improved version of Thomas Edison's original phonograph. While the phonograph used tinfoil-covered cylinders to reproduce sound, and the Graphophone which followed it used wax-coated cylinders, the Victrola made the leap to flat discs called "records" made of rubber, a shellac compound, or plastic. These were the forerunners of vinyl records, which were largely replaced by magnetic tape recordings, which in turn gave way to today's digital music formats.

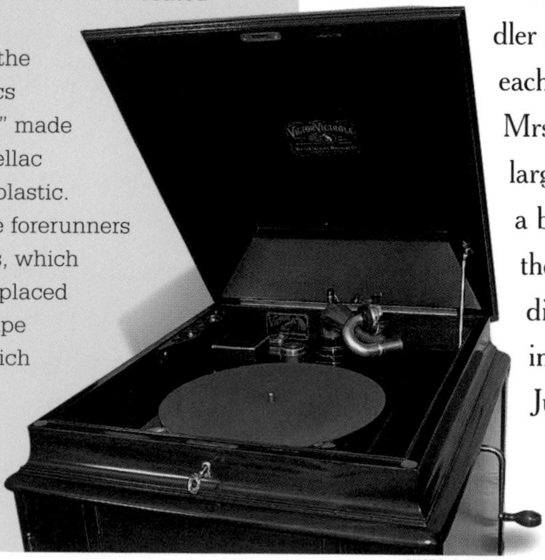

PHOTO © TMBEL

Mrs. Eddy owned a Victrola (she called it an "artificial singer") like this one.

American Red Cross founder Clara Barton, shown here circa 1904, had this to say about Mary Baker Eddy in a *New York American* interview a few months after the Next Friends suit: "Love permeates al the teachings of this great woman.... How beautifully she has managed her own unfortunate trials! Without malice, always with a kindness and charity that is almost beyond human comprehension, has this woman fought antagonism and that only with love." Miss Barton also noted that she had read *Science and Health*, and was "much comforted by its teachings."

COURTESY OF THE LIBRARY OF CONGRESS, PRINTS AND PHOTOGRAPHS DIVISION

few opening questions about her home, how long she had lived in Concord, and so on.

The questions came thick and fast. The Masters asked Mrs. Eddy about her finances and investments, about how she had come to discover Christian Science, about her everyday affairs, her daily drive, her work. Did she see all the letters that went out in her name? Did she like to read, to listen to music?

Mrs. Eddy responded fully to each question, and when asked about music, she told them: "I have an artificial singer in my house." She rang the bell and asked Calvin Frye to show it to their guests.

As they were leaving the room to listen to it, Judge Aldrich commented: "I want to say before going that my mother is still living and she is 87 years of age."

"Give my love to her," Mrs. Eddy replied, adding, "God bless her. She is not a day older for her 87 years if she is growing in grace.... Now, my thought is, that if we keep our mind fixed on Truth, God, Life and Love, He will advance us in our years to a higher understanding...."

The group left to follow Calvin. A few minutes later, Mrs. Eddy sent Judge Aldrich a message. Might she finish explaining her footsteps to Christian Science? The Judge said they hadn't pursued the subject as they didn't want to tire her. Also, they did not want to make it appear that they were attacking her doctrines, and that she had to defend them.

"Not at all," Mrs. Eddy replied. "I shall regard it as a great favor if you will condescend to hear me in this."

She went on to elaborate more about Christian Science and its healing mission. When she was finished, she thanked the group for their kindness and attention.

William Chandler, the chief prosecuting attorney, had never met Mrs. Eddy in person before that afternoon. After the interview, even he had to admit her competency. His comment? "She's as sharp as a steel trap."

A week later, he filed for dismissal of the suit. He was finished.

When Mrs. Eddy heard that the defense had triumphed and the lawsuit was dismissed, she raised her hands from the arms of her chair, then dropped them again and lifted her thoughts in prayer. With characteristic love and Christian spirit, she turned to her desk and immediately wrote to one of the "nexters" a letter full of forgiveness.

She was free to go forward.

23
A Bold Venture

No one was prepared for Mrs. Eddy's next move.

No one except her household and staff, that is. Plans had been quietly in the works for some time now at Mrs. Eddy's direction. On a calm, clear January day in 1908 she went for her usual afternoon carriage ride, but instead of going home, she drove to the Concord railroad depot. A special train was waiting for her. Some of her household were already aboard, and as soon as Mrs. Eddy was seated, the train chugged out of the station. Where was she headed? After nearly 16 years at her beloved Pleasant View, Mary Baker Eddy was leaving her native state of New Hampshire and returning to Massachusetts.

There were several reasons for the move. First and foremost, the decision was the result of prayer, as was always the case with Mrs. Eddy. In addition, she felt that New Hampshire's laws had failed to protect her, and that the Massachusetts courts would offer a stronger shield should there be any legal action in the future. And there was quite simply the matter of space. By this time, her household had physically outgrown Pleasant View. Visitors, including the church's Board of Directors and Trustees, were reduced to sleeping on cots in the parlor or the hallway when they came to call. Relocating to a larger residence closer to Boston would give her household the room they needed, while also allowing Mrs. Eddy to be on hand for the next big project she was planning.

As for the secrecy, the previous year *Human Life* magazine had dubbed Mary Baker Eddy "the most famous, interesting and powerful woman in America, if not the world, today." As such, she was front-page news, and her

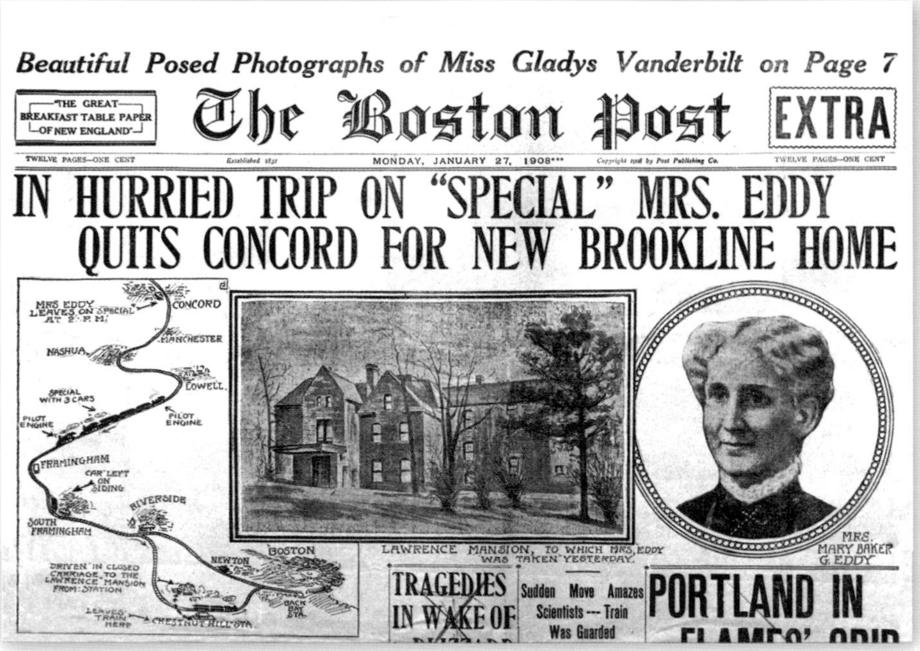
Beautiful Posed Photographs of Miss Gladys Vanderbilt on Page 7

THE GREAT BREAKFAST TABLE PAPER OF NEW ENGLAND

The Boston Post

EXTRA

TWELVE PAGES—ONE CENT | Established 1831 | MONDAY, JANUARY 27, 1908*** | Copyright 1908 by Post Publishing Co. | TWELVE PAGES—ONE CENT

IN HURRIED TRIP ON "SPECIAL" MRS. EDDY QUITS CONCORD FOR NEW BROOKLINE HOME

MRS EDDY LEAVES ON SPECIAL AT 2 P.M.
CONCORD
MANCHESTER
NASHUA
LOWELL
SPECIAL WITH 3 CARS
PILOT ENGINE
PILOT ENGINE
FRAMINGHAM
CAR LEFT ON SIDING
RIVERSIDE
SOUTH FRAMINGHAM
BOSTON
NEWTON
DRIVEN IN CLOSED CARRIAGE TO THE LAWRENCE MANSION FROM STATION
LEAVES TRAIN HERE
CHESTNUT HILL STA.
BACK BAY STA.

LAWRENCE MANSION, TO WHICH MRS. EDDY WAS TAKEN YESTERDAY.

MRS. MARY BAKER G. EDDY

TRAGEDIES IN WAKE OF

Sudden Move Amazes Scientists --- Train Was Guarded

PORTLAND IN

PHOTO © TMBEL

Mary Baker Eddy's move was front-page news.

movements were closely watched by the press. Sure enough, word of her departure traveled like wildfire. A crowd of reporters and cameramen rushed to Boston's North Station. In anticipation of this, the train was switched to a different track that led directly to Chestnut Hill, a neighborhood west of the city where Mrs. Eddy's new home was located. Some of the paparazzi got wind of the move and crowded round the entrance to the house at 400 Beacon Street.

Mrs. Eddy's carriage, along with six other vehicles holding her household members, swept up the drive. As the reporters surged forward, Mrs. Eddy turned to John Salchow, her groundskeeper and handyman, who had run to her side. "Can you get me out of this, John?"

Scooping her up in his arms, he carried her past the jostling newsmen, into the house, and up the stairs. She laughed as they made their escape, but the laughter faded as she saw her new house for the first time.

"A great barn of a place," she called it. The rooms were so big! Archibald McLellan, a Director and editor of the Christian Science periodicals, had done his best to find a suitable home, one that could provide space for the growing number of workers in her household. In October 1907, he'd settled on this 15-room, three-story mansion on 12 acres of wooded land.

Only five miles from her church's headquarters in the city, the estate had the feel of the countryside. Jersey cows grazed in pastures nearby, and two were purchased later that spring by Mrs. Eddy (there would be ice cream at 400 Beacon Street, too!).

From the front of the house you could see out to the street—something Mrs. Eddy liked to do. The top floors offered views of the Blue Hills and Boston. In spite of its size, however, the house had already been enlarged, with a new wing added in order to accommodate Mrs. Eddy's staff (which now numbered about 20).

After the tight quarters at Pleasant View, Mrs. Eddy's workers welcomed the extra space. Mrs. Eddy, on the other hand, felt that the grand stone house was too showy. The rich décor, with its dark wallpaper and rose-patterned carpet, wasn't to her taste, and her rooms in particular were too large. She disliked having to wait while her secretary made his way across her study over "all those roses," as she put it. She missed her lovely, light rooms back in Concord—the simplicity, the coziness.

Mary Baker Eddy's home at 400 Beacon Street, Chestnut Hill

COURTESY OF LONGYEAR MUSEUM CHESTNUT HILL, MASSACHUSETTS

EVERYDAY LIFE
A PET FOR 400 BEACON STREET

When a scruffy little squirrel missing most of her fur showed up at the kitchen door of Mrs. Eddy's home in Chestnut Hill, she quickly scurried her way into the hearts of the residents. The staff promptly adopted her, naming her "Spiketail" in honor of her near-hairless tail. Lavished with food and affection, Spiketail soon fattened up, and once her fur filled in again and her tail fluffed out, she was renamed simply "Spike."

"Everybody loved Spike for her gentleness and friendliness," recalled Margaret Macdonald, one of the household workers. "She was very proud of her name and would always come when called by it." In fact, Spike was so tame that she would scamper in and out of the men's pockets hunting for the treats they hid for her.

Left: Irving Tomlinson coaxes Spike to take a leap. Right: Success! Spike sits atop Irving's shoulder, nibbling on her reward.

But Mrs. Eddy wasn't one to lament for long. She moved up to her dressmaker's quarters on the top floor while her rooms were remodeled to a smaller, more comfortable size. Swiftly, her suite at Chestnut Hill took on more of the modesty that she valued.

Although Pleasant View would always tug at her heart as home, eventually "she grew to love her rooms, and her drives around the reservoir very much," reported Adelaide Still, her personal maid.

At 86, Mrs. Eddy had reached a time of life when most people had long since retired. But just six months earlier, she'd told a reporter from the *New York American*, "I have much work to do.... I trust in God, and He will give me strength to accomplish those things which have been marked out for me to do."

Now, at 400 Beacon Street, she kept largely to the same daily schedule as she had at Pleasant View. Rising at 6:00 in the summer and 7:00 in

COURTESY TMBEC

COURTESY OF LONGYEAR MUSEUM, CHESTNUT HILL MASSACHUSETTS

the winter, she arrived in her study by 8:30, after breakfast and time spent quietly reading and praying. Mornings were reserved for correspondence and other tasks, dinner was served promptly at noon, after which Mrs. Eddy went for her daily drive. More work and meetings with church officials took place in the afternoons. Supper was at six, often followed by time with her household—singing, perhaps, or reading together or reminiscing. Though leisure hours were few, the staff still managed to squeeze in some recreation, including bird watching (one worker spotted 90 species of birds in the neighborhood in 1910), bicycle riding, and even star-gazing with a telescope, which the amateur astronomers in the group carried up to the roof on clear nights, now and then.

In March 1908, Mrs. Eddy received a letter from John Wright, a Boston newspaperman and student of Christian Science, asking what she thought of the possibility of a newspaper run by Christian Scientists?

"I believe there is need of daily newspapers that will place principle before dividends, and that will be fair, frank and honest with the people on all subjects and under whatever pressure; that will not compromise with evil," he wrote in part. "It seems to me that a newspaper should be active in the interests of civic righteousness."

Mrs. Eddy had actually been considering this very idea for some time now. She jotted a reply: "Beloved Student: I have had this newspaper scheme in my thought for quite a while and herein send my name for our daily newspaper *The Christian Science Monitor.* This *title* only clarifies the paper and it should have departments for what else is requisite."

Although there is no record that the note was ever sent, it brought into focus Mrs. Eddy's next project. After the Next Friends suit and all that she had suffered over the years at the hands of the press, she told a reporter from Philadelphia's *North American* that she felt "newspapers should be edited with the same reverence for Truth, God, as is observed in the administration of the most serious affairs of life."

The Christian Science Monitor would be such a paper. Mrs. Eddy notified the Board of Directors of her intent, then in August of 1908 wrote to the Trustees of the Publishing Society:

"Beloved Students:

It is my request that you start a daily newspaper at once, and call it the

Christian Science Monitor. Let there be no delay. The Cause demands that it be issued now."

The Trustees were bowled over. They were just completing construction of the Publishing House, home to the other periodicals the church published, and here was another huge assignment!

Three days after receiving her letter, they wrote back explaining that, as starting a daily paper "is a very large enterprise," they had to "gain advice from men in that work." On the 12th and 13th, they met with newsmen from Pittsburgh and Chicago and with friends at the *Boston Herald,* then reported back to Mrs. Eddy with their findings.

They calculated they would need the following: a new building; two presses and ten linotype machines; 90 to 100 employees. They estimated the costs to be $105,000 ($2.5 million in today's dollars) to purchase and set up the printing plant and $125,000 (roughly $3 million in today's dollars) for payroll. The Publishing Society revenue at that time was about $90,000 (just over $2 million in 2013 dollars) a year, which was used by The Mother Church for its operations.

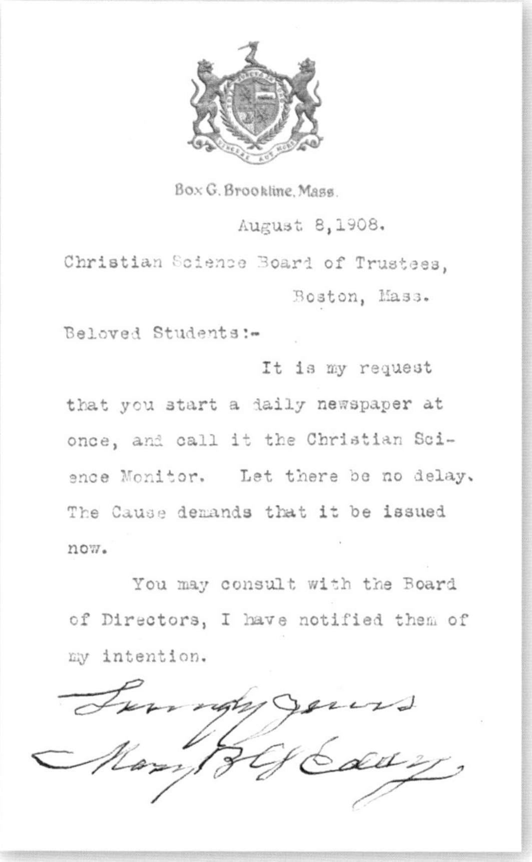
Box G. Brookline, Mass.

August 8,1908.

Christian Science Board of Trustees,
Boston, Mass.

Beloved Students:-

It is my request that you start a daily newspaper at once, and call it the Christian Science Monitor. Let there be no delay. The Cause demands that it be issued now.

You may consult with the Board of Directors, I have notified them of my intention.

Lovingly yours
Mary B. G. Eddy

PHOTO © TMBEL

The letter that Mary Baker Eddy wrote to the Board of Trustees, requesting them to start a newspaper

"We have no larger fund to draw upon if we are to keep the business in the proper state of solvency," they told Mrs. Eddy. "Nevertheless we know the newspaper can be financed, since you see it to be the right time for the enterprise."

Mrs. Eddy was surprised at the expense. Her intention was modest—not metropolitan greatness but something smaller, an eight-page paper with a circulation of about 50 to 60,000, perhaps. But she wanted to give her Trustees free reign, so she urged them to "go ahead with wisdom and economy as your guide."

Meanwhile, there was another sticking point.

Who would buy a newspaper called *The Christian Science Monitor*? Why not just call it the *Monitor*? That would raise less opposition from the public, was the general feeling of the Trustees. Archibald McLellan, who would soon take the helm as editor of the newspaper, tried to bring up this point and got nowhere.

"God gave me this name and it remains," Mrs. Eddy told him firmly.

Once that question was settled, the church officers swung into action. The Board of Directors had two months to move tenants, demolish old brick buildings, build new foundations, and extend the Publishing House to accommodate the new printing presses and typesetting machinery. The Trustees had to order all this equipment, and they also had to assemble a staff of newsmen as well as compositors, those who physically put the paper together. A notice in the *Christian Science Sentinel* of October 17th brought more than 1,000 responses from editors, writers, reporters, printers, typesetters, pressmen—all Christian Scientists eager to help with the new venture. The Trustees were pleasantly surprised to discover so large a pool of expertise.

Among them was John Wright, who had so recently written to Mrs. Eddy. He left the *Boston Globe* to become the *Monitor's* first city editor. Later promoted to editorial writer, he would remain on the staff until 1922.

Another key figure was Alexander Dodds, day editor of the *Pittsburgh Sun* and one of the handful of knowledgeable newsmen with whom the Trustees initially consulted back in August. Dodds had worked his way up through the ranks and knew the newspaper business inside and out. He was described by one of his colleagues as "a man with smiling eyes, an amiable disposition, and an exceptional working knowledge of the mechanics of a newspaper."

A few years earlier, Alexander had been told he was incurably ill with a heart condition, and had just a few months to live. A woman who was hoping to see Christian Science treated fairly by the press gave him a copy of *Science and*

COURTESY TMBEL

▲ Alexander Dodds, the *Monitor*'s first managing editor

Health to read, not knowing he was ill. Although he initially disagreed with what it set forth, Alexander read and re-read the book. In less than two months, his friends started commenting on his improved health, and to his amazement he found himself healed not only of the heart condition, but also of a number of other ailments and debilities, including the need for glasses. Addictions to alcohol and tobacco also fell away.

Dodds became an ardent Christian Scientist, one who fully understood Mrs. Eddy's observation that, "The press unwittingly sends forth many sorrows and diseases among the human family. It does this by giving names to diseases and by printing long descriptions which mirror images of disease distinctly in thought."

Dodds later wrote: "Crime, scandal, disaster are the three common features in the display headings of the daily press. The reverse are law-abiding, good tidings and the opposite of disaster or destruction which is construction. This was the key which would unlock the great mine of unpublished news of the world and should be the standard established."

Mrs. Eddy's first question to him: How long before they could be ready to operate? Dodds told her a year.

"She replied that six months was sufficient," he recalled. "Then it came to me we could be ready in three months and I promised her a paper by Thanksgiving Day—1908.... Many times the evidence of the senses was so strong that it seemed that the work could not be completed in time. Never-the-less we all knew that Mrs. Eddy in seeing the *Monitor* foresaw its completion; and to me, this was a sufficient assurance that our demonstration would be made."

Erwin Canham, who decades later would become the paper's longest-serving editor to date, described the process: "Within little more than a hundred days, spurred by their Leader's ringing mandate and inspired by the feats of organization and construction which had recently been performed in erecting the Original Mother Church and its Extension, and which they had found to be habitual and normal in Christian Science, these men carried out what [half a century later] would be considered a total impossibility."

Construction work began on September 16th.

"The building was ready for occupancy in exactly nine weeks," Dodds noted. "The presses were installed before the roof was on; the type-setting machines were placed ... before the walls were up; and various other expediencies were employed."

The newsmen who gathered to work for the paper were instructed in their work by editor Archibald McLellan. A native of Canada working in Chicago as an attorney, McLellan was called to Boston in the summer of 1902 to take the helm of the Christian Science periodicals. The following winter Mrs. Eddy expanded the church's four-person Board of Directors, adding him to the fifth spot.

COURTESY TMBEL

Archibald McLellan, first editor of *The Christian Science Monitor*. "All the news it is worth while reading" he told a Chicago audience in October of 1910, describing the *Monitor*'s goal—perhaps a wink and a nod at *The New York Times*, whose owner Adolph Ochs had created the slogan "All the News That's Fit to Print" for the paper's masthead a decade earlier.

Instead of emphasizing the sensational, with headlines about vice and crime, McLellan told his staff they were to record the important and constructive developments in the news, be it local, national or international. They were not to suppress crime or disaster, but rather to put it in perspective. Big headlines and large space were to be given to events of long-range importance.

"There is a field, and a wide one, for a clean newspaper, and it is this field which the *Monitor* is entering," McLellan assured them.

In spite of the speed at which the *Monitor* moved forward, it wasn't without setbacks. All the composing room equipment—the type, steel cabinets, metal make-up tables, etc.—sank when the boat carrying the cargo from New Jersey to Boston collided with another vessel en route. Fortunately, the foreman of the composing room heard of the collision right away, knew that his equipment was on board, and immediately

COURTESY TMBEC

Artist's rendering of Mary Baker Eddy and some of her staff on the *Monitor*'s first publication day.

informed the American Type Founders Company. In no time, a new shipment was on its way.

In the meantime Forrest Price, the *Monitor's* newly appointed financial editor, had a close call with the wire service. In 1908, long before the Internet and cell phones, the nerve center for a newspaper was its wire service, which connected foreign correspondents to the newsroom and provided news bulletins and the stock ticker service and such. No paper could operate without it. Just days before start-up, Price was staggered to discover that Western Union's telegraphic service stopped short a block and a half from the Publishing House. All wires had to be laid underground, but there was no time to dig a conduit for them before the presses were due to roll.

"We simply had to have the wire service," Price later wrote. "The Monitor could not come out without it."

The Trustees were informed and quickly began to pray. Means were soon found to run the wires temporarily overhead, and the wire service was in place before press time.

Publication day, November 25, 1908, was so murky that ships in both New York and Boston were not allowed to dock. Mrs. Eddy called her

PHOTO © TMBEL

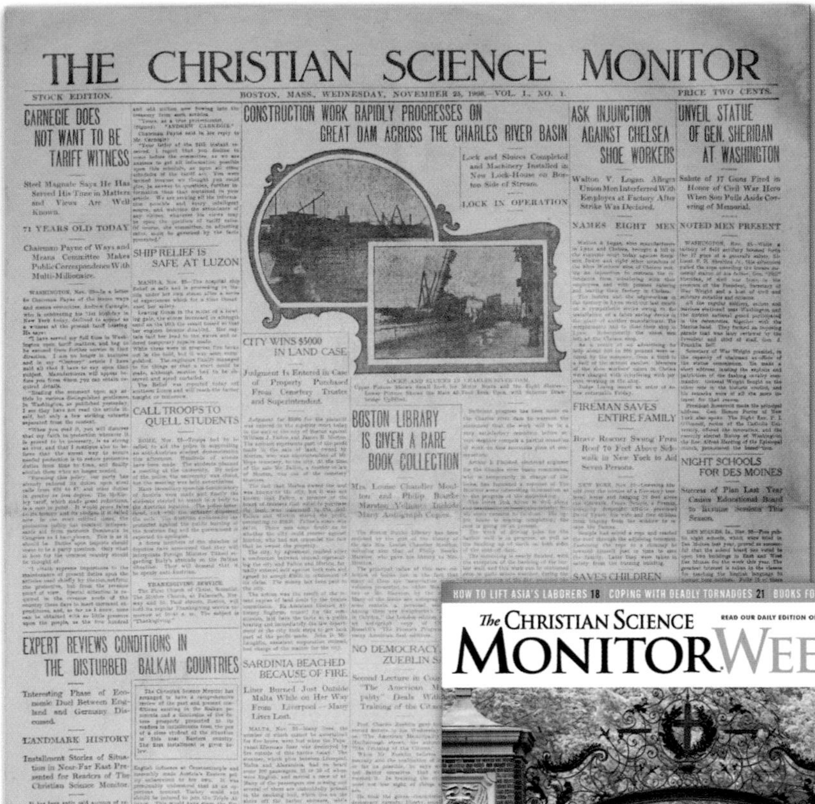

THE CHRISTIAN SCIENCE MONITOR

STOCK EDITION. BOSTON, MASS., WEDNESDAY, NOVEMBER 25, 1908.—VOL. 1., NO. 1. PRICE TWO CENTS.

CARNEGIE DOES NOT WANT TO BE TARIFF WITNESS

Steel Magnate Says He Has Served His Time in Matters and Views Are Well Known.

71 YEARS OLD TODAY

Chairman Payne of Ways and Means Committee Makes Public Correspondence With Multi-Millionaire.

CONSTRUCTION WORK RAPIDLY PROGRESSES ON GREAT DAM ACROSS THE CHARLES RIVER BASIN

Lock and Sluices Completed and Machinery Installed in New Lock-House on Boston Side of Stream.

LOCK IN OPERATION

ASK INJUNCTION AGAINST CHELSEA SHOE WORKERS

Walton V. Logan Alleges Union Men Interferred With Employes at Factory After Strike Was Declared.

NAMES EIGHT MEN

UNVEIL STATUE OF GEN. SHERIDAN AT WASHINGTON

Salute of 17 Guns Fired in Honor of Civil War Hero When Son Pulls Aside Covering of Memorial.

NOTED MEN PRESENT

SHIP RELIEF IS SAFE AT LUZON

CITY WINS $5000 IN LAND CASE

Judgment Is Entered in Case of Property Purchased From Cemetery Trustee and Superintendent.

CALL TROOPS TO QUELL STUDENTS

BOSTON LIBRARY IS GIVEN A RARE BOOK COLLECTION

FIREMAN SAVES ENTIRE FAMILY

NIGHT SCHOOLS FOR DES MOINES

SAVES CHILDREN

EXPERT REVIEWS CONDITIONS IN THE DISTURBED BALKAN COUNTRIES

Interesting Phase of Economic Duel Between England and Germany Discussed.

LANDMARK HISTORY

Installment Stories of Situation in Near-Far East Presented for Readers of The Christian Science Monitor.

SARDINIA BEACHED BECAUSE OF FIRE

NO DEMOCRACY

37,000 TURKEYS FOR HOME MARK

© CSPS

▲ Inaugural edition of *The Christian Science Monitor*, whose motto is "To injure no man, but to bless all mankind."

➤ Winner of seven Pulitzer prizes and more than a dozen Overseas Press Club awards, *The Christian Science Monitor* has undergone a number of changes to its format over the years. Today, it's on the cutting edge of digital publishing, with news available 24/7 through its website, as well as through daily news briefings, e-mail newsletters, e-reader and tablet editions, and a weekly print edition.

household to her study and they spoke about the weather.

"A heavy fog makes it darker than usual," commented one.

"Yes, but only according to sense," Mrs. Eddy answered. "We know the reverse of error is true. This, in Truth, is the lightest day of all days. This

COURTESY © TMBEC

▲ *Monitor* trucks, circa 1911, ready to deliver "A Daily Newspaper for the Home"

is the day when our daily paper goes forth to lighten mankind."

When her copy of the first *Monitor* arrived, Mrs. Eddy "clasped it to her heart," according to Daisette McKenzie. At last, a newspaper to bring comfort and hope! In the lead editorial of that inaugural edition, she outlined the mission of each of her publications—the *Journal*, the *Sentinel*, and *Der Herold*, the German edition of the *Herald*. Then she spoke of the newest family member, the newspaper which was to "spread undivided the Science that operates unspent. The object of the Monitor is to injure no man, but to bless all mankind."

Musing on this editorial, Erwin Canham later noted, "Here is the essence of the *Monitor*, in a brief phrase. It is the paper's mandate.... 'To injure no man' has not inhibited the paper from uncovering evil in whatever guise, for it is clear that such exposure can be impersonal and constructive.... It is a mandate which is not easy to fulfill, but it keeps the *Monitor's* flag nailed high on the masthead."

What did the *Monitor* cover on its first day of publication? Among other things, the battle being waged in the House Ways and Means Committee over tariffs; the Balkan crisis; conservation of natural resources (so important to then U.S. President Theodore Roosevelt); the Transcontinental Canadian Railroad; and the arms budget. It also reported on a telescope that might tell of life on Mars, and the invention of an electric hair dryer.

The following day was Thanksgiving in the United States, and everyone at the paper was given the day off. Mrs. Eddy wrote to congratulate the men in the composing room, and sent them a basket of pansies. The men were surprised that they were getting the holiday off with full pay, as this was not common practice at that time. They sent a letter of thanks to the Trustees, feeling truly appreciated.

The first sheet off the press was sent to Mrs. Eddy each day, and the editorials and religious articles, which at that time ran anonymously in the paper, were rubber-stamped with the name of the writer so that she knew who was writing what. She read the paper with care, forwarding any comments she had along to the writers or the editor.

Mrs. Eddy told her household, "When I established *The Christian Science Monitor,* I took the greatest step forward since I gave *Science and Health* to the world."

24

Journeying On

As the first decade of the 20th century drew to a close, Mary Baker Eddy's leadership took a quieter form. Her students expected her to continue as commander-in-chief, fighting the day-to-day battles of the movement, but she began to disengage herself and spend more hours behind the scenes in reflective study and prayer. As she had told a journalist a few years earlier, "All that I ask of the world now is that it grant me time, time to assimilate myself to God."

As early as the 1880s, she had begun turning her students and the officers of her church away from her personally to the Bible and to her writings, including the *Church Manual*, for guidance. She wanted them to be able to stand on their own feet spiritually, and learn to pray their way through challenges just as she had had to do. Meanwhile, she continued to strengthen the Christian Science movement through the *Manual*, making a number of changes, including adding a provision for the office of Christian Science nurse, one who has "a demonstrable knowledge of Christian Science practice, who thoroughly understands the practical wisdom necessary in a sick room, and who can take proper care of the sick."

Many of the other By-laws came about because of a woman named Augusta Stetson.

"Almost all of my rules in the Manual have been made to prevent her injuring my students and causing me trouble in my church," Mrs. Eddy had written to her student Laura Lathrop back in 1897.

As was her custom, Mrs. Eddy tried for years to keep Augusta in the fold, encouraging her strong points—Augusta was by all accounts an effective speaker and healer, among other things—while at the same time rebuking her weaknesses.

➤ Augusta Stetson, pictured here in the 1880s, lavished Mary Baker Eddy with praise and gifts while at the same time plotting to take control of the church as her successor.

COURTESY TMBEL

A practitioner and teacher based in New York City, Augusta saw herself as "divinely" appointed to be Mrs. Eddy's successor, and held her students and the large branch church she dominated in an iron grip. A controversy ensued, and once again Mrs. Eddy found herself and her church in the headlines as the *New York World* and other newspapers rushed to report on the story.

In typical fashion, Mrs. Eddy reached out to Augusta with love, inviting her in December 1908 to come for a carriage ride. Augusta was quick to respond. Mrs. Eddy spoke with her as the two of them rode together, warmed by a shared lap robe, and Augusta agreed to give up the idea of spinning off her own branch churches.

Ambitious Augusta didn't stop jockeying for leadership, however—or trying to injure those who opposed her—and by the end of the following year the Board of Directors was forced to excommunicate her. In the wake of all this, Mrs. Eddy added this By-law as a warning to all teachers of Christian Science: "The less the teacher personally controls other minds, and the more he trusts them to the divine Truth and Love, the better it will be for both teacher and student." Likewise, Mrs. Eddy saw each branch church as self-governing and democratic, not under the control of any one teacher, or that teacher's students.

Some people wondered what would happen when Mrs. Eddy was no longer around to lead the movement. Should she appoint a successor? What about certain By-laws in the Manual that required her signature? Mrs. Eddy's lawyer cousin, General Henry Baker, had the answer to that. In common law, when an individual cannot fulfill certain conditions, the next in authority fills that place. The next in authority, in this case, was the Board of Directors. The *Manual* would remain the guiding principle for the Board and for the church, just as Mrs. Eddy intended. The By-laws requiring her consent underlined their importance for the Board, and obliged them to pay special attention before they acted.

In the summer of 1909, Mrs. Eddy set aside work on *The First Church of Christ, Scientist, and Miscellany*, a compilation begun in 1906. Another collection of her articles, notices, and letters that had appeared in print, it chronicled the building of the Extension, among other things. Assembled and published posthumously, it would cap a writing career that spanned some sixty years, from modest beginnings in small-town newspapers to a best-selling book that changed forever not only the lives of many of its readers, but also, with its focus on healing as Jesus did, the landscape of Christianity.

Science and Health with Key to the Scriptures went through over 400 printings and nine major editions in Mrs. Eddy's lifetime. The process of revising and perfecting the book she called "my best witness, my babe! the new-born of Truth … that will forever testify of itself, and its mother," was the core of her life's work.

"Spiritual ideas unfold as we advance," she explained in its pages, adding in *Footprints Fadeless*, an autobiographical work that wouldn't be published for nearly a century, "in my revisions of Science and Health, its entire keynote has grown steadily clearer, and louder, and sweeter."

Some critics scoffed that a woman who professed to be a "scribe under orders," and one whom God had "called … to proclaim His Gospel to this age" surely should have produced something that didn't need revision. To this Mrs. Eddy calmly countered, "Was Newton capable of satisfactorily stating the laws of gravitation when first he discovered that ponderous principle? Much less could I, at first, formulate and express the infinite Principle and the divine laws of which God gave me the first faint gleam in my hour of physical agony and mental illumination."

Increasingly, Mrs. Eddy stepped back from the day-to-day running of her church. William McKenzie, who by now was serving as a lecturer and Trustee of the Publishing Society, noticed the change. In April 1910, he went to visit some of the household at Chestnut Hill. Unexpectedly, Mrs. Eddy invited him into her office. They hadn't met for several years.

As they spoke, McKenzie later recalled, "My whole heart went out to her in gratitude ... and once more I saw the light from her eyes which made her face shine as I told her of my appreciation and affection."

He also told her of the problems that the Publishing Society was facing, including the demands that came with publishing a newspaper, and commented on how much the Trustees wished her to advise and direct them. In fact, he added, "we had asked her for this help a good many times, but she had not elected to give it and so to the best of our ability we had to seek earnestly for the guidance of Mind."

Mrs. Eddy smiled, then replied, "That is just what I wanted you to do."

Others in her household noticed an increasing sense of peace, including William Rathvon, one of Mrs. Eddy's correspondence secretaries at that time. In a diary entry in July 1910 he wrote: "The nights are quieter than for years and years, I am told, and the days are full of rest and quiet...."

Mrs. Eddy's relationship with her son George had also become more tranquil. She sent him a three-year subscription to *The Christian Science Monitor* in May 1909, and that October he signed a settlement agreement, resolving the question of her will. In exchange for his promise not to contest her plans to leave the bulk of her fortune to her church (a promise he would not keep), George received $120,000 plus another $125,000 in trust—nearly $6 million in today's dollars. George no longer needed to ask his mother for money, but he still looked to her for approval.

Dec. 11, 1909

My dear Mother:

I am very glad that any money differences between us are ended and I hope that your feelings toward me are kind.

He made reference to the recent Next Friends lawsuit, saying he feared she was "grossly deceived by men about you who were for some reason hostile to me. This is now all in the past and I trust you will hereafter have nothing to complain of against me or my children. I assure you that Mary and the boys are worthy of your kindness and affection, and I do not think there ought longer to be any cloud between you and me and my family."

PHOTO MARK THAYER © TMBEL

▲ This pin's exquisite details include the distinctive Black Hills Gold jewelry motif of grape leaves, grape clusters, and vines, though a 24-karat finish obscures the traditional red and green color. A gold nugget rests on the point of the pick, and gold flakes can be seen on the shovel and in the pan. A gift from her son, it was presented to Mary Baker Eddy by her grandsons on her 89th birthday.

▼ George Glover III (l.) was the "little chubby darling" who had so charmed his grandmother years earlier. He and his brother Andrew (r.) are holding the copies of *Science and Health* that Mrs. Eddy gave them, inscribed "Lovingly Grandmother Mary Baker Eddy."

COURTESY TMBEL

George signed the typewritten letter, "Affectionately, your son."

It did not occur to George that perhaps he was the one who had been "grossly deceived by men who were for some reason hostile" to his mother. He didn't realize how much he had helped her enemies, nor the suffering that he had brought her. Now that he had money to spare, he gave up mining, bought a store, and set up his son and namesake as manager.

In 1910, William Chandler, George's lawyer, invited both of the younger Glover boys to spend the summer in New Hampshire. It wasn't exactly the vacation they'd been expecting—young George and his brother Andrew were set to work repairing Chandler's boats most of the time—but they did get to pay their grandmother a surprise visit at her home in Chestnut Hill on July 16th for her 89th birthday. She was very pleased to see them. She had last seen her grandson George when he was four; now he was 21. She had never met 19-year-old Andrew. She remarked on George's wavy auburn hair, and how much he looked like his grandfather, Wash Glover.

The boys brought a present for her from their father, a pin made with gold from the Glover mine, depicting all the prospector's tools—shovel, pickaxe, miner's pan—that her son had once used.

The young men felt stiff in their unaccustomed suits. George let Andrew do most of the talking, but while he sat silently beside his grandmother he realized, "Why—she loves me!" It was a recollection that would still bring tears to his eyes when recounting it decades later.

At some point during the visit, Mrs. Eddy gave her grandsons each a signed copy of *Science and Health*. Afterwards, the brothers were given a tour of the house and served sherbet, cake, and lemonade. Reporters were waiting with a camera and took their picture with the garden wall as background. A few days later, they sent a copy to Mrs. Eddy, who framed it and displayed it proudly in her room.

The following month, she sent each of the boys a complete set of her other works, trusting they would read them carefully. Young George responded with many thanks and the glad news that "We are preparing for school this fall." Mrs. Eddy's son also wrote a reply:

> *My dear Mother,*
>
> *Words cannot express the pleasure I have in receiving a few lines from you, and knowing that you was alive. I will come and see you some day, and would like to correspond with you in the meantime, if I could do so with out my letters being opened before you received them. From your loving son,*
>
> *As ever,*
>
> *George W. Glover*

His mother reassured him that his letters would come directly to her, but there is no record of further correspondence. This concluded almost 50 years of interchange, which began with George's first letter home in 1861 to let his mother know he was alive and fighting for the Union army. Their relationship, though full of genuine affection, had been at cross-purposes ever since, partly because each expected what the other could not give.

As summer waned and the trees surrounding Chestnut Hill covered themselves in autumn glory, there were still times when Mrs. Eddy answered letters, shot off telegrams, and issued orders as briskly as she once had, but on the whole her life grew more contemplative. She was overheard praying one night by Irving Tomlinson, who recorded the scene afterward:

"She would voice her inmost desire for a realization of God's presence and power and follow it with a declaration that that presence and power was an eternal manifestation and fully realized by His children. She would petition that no temptation could assail; and follow [it] by the declaration that the real man was free from temptation. She affirmed that there was no lack in God's provisions for His offspring and asserted that this truth was realized by all."

At the conclusion of her prayer, Irving spoke. "She asked 'Who is it dear?' and when I told her that the prayer was heard, she answered, 'Yes, dear it is,' and fell sound asleep."

At the end of November, Mrs. Eddy became ill with a cold. She continued to take her drive every day, although on December 1st she had to be carried back into the house. Rallying, she asked for her writing tablet and wrote, "God is my life." On Saturday December 3rd, she stayed in bed all day, but was alert, sent messages to her household staff, and prayed for herself. That night, Adelaide Still, Mrs. Eddy's personal maid, helped her get ready to retire while Laura Sargent and one of the secretaries sat by her side.

"I have all in divine Love, that is all I need," was the last thing she said to her faithful staff.

The next morning, when Adelaide came on duty at 7:00 a.m., she saw Calvin Frye sitting outside Mrs. Eddy's door.

"Mother has gone, Adelaide," he told her. So peaceful had been her passing that those sitting with her didn't hear a sound.

At the conclusion of the Sunday service that morning in The Mother Church, Judge Clifford Smith, the First Reader, read a passage from a letter Mrs. Eddy had written back in 1891:

"My Beloved Students:—You may be looking to see me in my accustomed place with you, but this you must no longer expect. When I retired from the field of labor, it was a departure, socially, publicly, and finally, from the routine of such material modes as society and our societies demand. Rumors are rumors,—nothing more. I am still with you on the field of battle, taking forward marches, broader and higher views, and with the hope that you will follow.... All our thoughts should be given to the absolute demonstration of Christian Science. You can well afford to give me up, since you have in my last revised edition of *Science and Health* your teacher and guide."

Wondering what was coming next, the congregation waited as Judge

Smith paused and then told them: "Although these lines were written years ago, they are true to-day, and will continue to be true. But it has become my duty to announce that Mrs. Eddy passed from our sight last night at a quarter before eleven o'clock, at her home on Chestnut Hill."

Calvin Frye telegraphed George Glover, and he, his daughter Mary, and young George, who had just recently seen his grandmother, came east from South Dakota for the private funeral, which was held December 8th at Mrs. Eddy's home.

For two months after Mrs. Eddy's passing, special articles and editorials about her life appeared in the press. These spontaneous tributes were so extensive, ranging from well-known metropolitan papers to small-town broadsheets, that the Christian Science Publishing Society put out a slim bound volume containing nearly 200 of them.

The *Chicago Tribune*, *Houston Chronicle*, *Spokane Inland Traveler* and countless others called her "a remarkable woman." *Harper's Weekly* lauded her as "a pioneer—one of the most extraordinary of whom there is a record." The *Boston Traveler* heralded her as "one of the world's great benefactors," while the *Asheville Citizen* described her as "a woman of rare moral courage."

From Baltimore to Butte, Hartford to Honolulu, the accolades to Mrs. Eddy's life flowed freely. "She was the moving spirit in and the chief exemplar of a religious and spiritual phenomenon affecting in some degree nearly the whole of the civilized world," noted the *Kansas City Star*. "This Boston woman's life was as beautiful as it was devoted, and as sublime as were her teachings," remarked the Bemidji, Minnesota *Pioneer*.

Mrs. Eddy's steadfast devotion to the Bible was central to many of the testimonials. "No woman ever lived who did more to strengthen faith and direct the footsteps of humanity toward the Master," said Alaska's *Fairbanks Daily Times*, while the Rockford, Illinois *Morning Star* noted, "She knew the Bible as few knew it, indeed to her its meanings and teachings were as sure and understandable as the alphabet."

Ultimately, concluded the *Los Angeles Express*, "The work she did endures and will endure." The *Salt Lake Tribune* agreed: "The church she founded will be her ever-present and most splendid memorial for all time. That work is a marvel, amazing to whoever will consider it candidly for what it is, and in its inception and growth. It is now one of the mighty factors in American life, and is still pushing on."

That her lifework helped and healed many was almost universally recognized in these tributes, as was the fact that Mary Baker Eddy's selflessness and love touched and transformed lives. In a flash of poetic insight, the *Chicago Journal* summed this up beautifully, noting that her passing "well might serve as inspiration for a new beatitude: Blessed are they who need no monument; their names are graven on many hearts."

Epilogue

How did Mary Baker Eddy herself sum up her life?

"What I am is for God to declare in His infinite mercy," she once wrote. "As it is, I claim nothing more than what I am, the Discoverer and Founder of Christian Science, and the blessing it has been to mankind which eternity enfolds."

As a child, Mary sensed her God-impelled purpose, "a hunger and thirst after divine things,—a desire for something higher and better than matter, and apart from it," as she put it. As an adult, she found and fulfilled that purpose, patiently persisting through decades of adversity as she sought "diligently for the knowledge of God as the one great and ever-present relief from human woe."

NEW HAMPSHIRE HISTORICAL SOCIETY

"I have faced the destiny of a discoverer and pioneer from first to last." —Mary Baker Eddy

The girl who took to heart Christ Jesus' counsel, "It is more blessed to give than to receive," and gave away her winter coat to a schoolmate, later made a promise to God during a time of desperate need. God answered her prayer and Mary kept her promise, leaving a lasting legacy of love to the world as she dedicated her life to helping and healing others.

In 1896, looking back on the extraordinary trajectory of the preceding decades, she noted, "The discovery and founding of Christian Science has cost more than thirty years of unremitting toil and unrest; but, comparing those with the joy of knowing that the sinner and the sick are helped thereby, that time and eternity bear witness to this gift of God to the race, I am the debtor."

Mary Baker Eddy's remarkable life overflowed with accomplishments. Pastor Emeritus of her church and, through her writings, its forever leader, she was also a healer, teacher, author, poet, journalist, lecturer, editor, publisher, pastor, wife, mother, grandmother, and philanthropist. As bold a pioneer as any of her stalwart forebears, she broke barriers of gender and age, founding a worldwide religion and church, a newspaper, a publishing company, and a college at a time when women didn't even have the right to vote.

Born in obscurity in a tiny New Hampshire town, she rose to international prominence, and the schoolgirl who wanted to write a book ended up writing 17 of them, including *Science and Health with Key to the Scriptures*, a perennial best-seller that has sold more than 10 million copies to date, been translated into 16 languages and English Braille, and inspired and healed countless readers.

Working right into her ninth decade, Mary Baker Eddy unselfishly and tirelessly sought to share the vision revealed to her of a "world more bright," the spiritual reality that Jesus proved was a present possibility, bringing hope and healing.

She spoke again of her life's purpose in an interview with the *New York American* in August of 1907, when she said, "I know that my mission is for all the earth, not alone for my dear devoted followers of Christian Science.... All my efforts, all my prayers and tears are for humanity, and the spread of peace and love among mankind."

Mary Baker Eddy found the answers to her search for truth in the Bible. She saw *Science and Health*, the book she called "my most important work," as the key to unlocking its treasures, and encouraged readers to test the revelation her textbook contained for themselves.

"The divine Principle of healing is proved in the personal experience of any sincere seeker of Truth," she affirms, inviting those who open its pages: "You can prove for yourself, dear reader, the Science of healing, and so ascertain if the author has given you the correct interpretation of Scripture."

Mary Baker Eddy's invitation still stands.

Acknowledgements

Every biographer stands on the shoulders of those who have gone before. Isabel and I owe an enormous debt of gratitude to the efforts of many who have traveled this path ahead of us, from journalist Sibyl Wilbur, who penned the very first biography of Mary Baker Eddy, to the "cloud of witnesses"—those who knew Mrs. Eddy and took the time to record their recollections—to historian Robert Peel and all the other fine scholars who have left a rich trail of breadcrumbs for future writers to follow.

This book would not exist without the enthusiasm and dedication of Isabel Ferguson. In the more than two years that have elapsed since her passing, there were innumerable times when I came across new information, photographs or other colorful details that I knew would delight her as well as enrich the manuscript, and I so wanted to be able to pick up the phone and share these discoveries. Isabel was a joy to work with, and her generous spirit and keen intellect are greatly missed.

Many hands went into the making of *A World More Bright*. At the Christian Science Publishing Society, Jennifer McLaughlin was an early champion of the project, and Phebe Bergenheim was invaluable in carefully shepherding it through to completion, earning my eternal gratitude in the process. Trustees Linda Kohler, Michael Pabst, and Judy Wolff offered their whole-hearted support as the book progressed, while design and production whizzes Jerry Rutherford and Sal Giliberto helped ensure it would be a thing of beauty. At The Mary Baker Eddy Library, senior research archivist Judith Huenneke's eagle eye and probing questions prompted additional research that raised the level of scholarship. Her colleagues were also a great resource, in particular Mike Davis, Amanda Gustin, Mark Montgomery, and Kurt Morris. Heartfelt thanks, too, are due Senior Curator Alan K. Lester and Mark Thayer, Director of Creative Services.

At the Longyear Museum, Sandy Houston and Cheryl Moneyhun patiently assisted us in our endeavors, answering our many questions and sifting through their collection for pertinent materials. And kudos to the whole museum staff for their work in preserving and interpreting Mary Baker Eddy's historic homes, which allow 21st-century visitors to trace the footsteps of her remarkable life.

Archivists and reference librarians at Old Sturbridge Village, the Lynn Museum, and the Weston Public Library aided in the preliminary stages of research. Susan Hill Long's editorial comments on an early draft were immensely helpful in getting things off to a good start, while Marjorie Kehe provided a welcome vote of confidence as the finish line drew near. Lynn Tennant was our intrepid proofreader, and I can't thank Lark Smith enough for her diligence in serving as "boots on the ground" for an out-of-state writer in need of a Boston-based fact checker.

Neither Isabel nor I could have undertaken this project without the full support of our families, and in particular our husbands. I know Isabel would have wanted to thank her dear Joe for his love and encouragement, just as I want to thank my dear Steve for his. And last but by far from least, I want to thank Isabel herself for trusting me as her co-pilot on what has been the project of a lifetime. It was a privilege to work side by side with her in telling Mary Baker Eddy's story, and in the end, I think that a poet-practitioner and a journalist-turned-novelist made a very good team indeed.

Heather Vogel Frederick
June 2013

Key Dates

1821	July 16	Mary Morse Baker is born in Bow, New Hampshire.
1836	January 11	The Baker family moves to Sanbornton Bridge (later renamed Tilton).
1838	July 26	Mary joins the Congregational Church at Sanbornton Bridge.
1841	October 17	Albert Baker dies.
1843	December 10	Marries George Washington ("Wash") Glover.
1843	December 25	Sails with Wash for their new home in Charleston, South Carolina.
1844	February	The Glovers move to Wilmington, North Carolina.
1844	June 27	Wash dies of yellow fever; Mary returns to her parent's home in Sanbornton Bridge.
1844	September 12	Mary's son George Washington Glover II ("Georgy") is born.
1846		Mary starts a kindergarten in Sanbornton, one of the first in New Hampshire.
1848	Summer	Attends graduation of John Bartlett from Harvard Law School.
1849	November 21	Abigail Ambrose Baker, Mary's mother, dies.
1849	December 11	Mary's fiance John Bartlett dies in Sacramento, California.
1850	December 5	Mark Baker (Mary's father) marries Elizabeth Patterson Duncan.

1851	May 9	Georgy is sent to live with Mahala and Russell Cheney in North Groton, New Hampshire.
1853	June 21	Marries Daniel Patterson, an itinerant dentist.
1855	April	The Pattersons move to North Groton to be near Mary's son Georgy.
1856	April	Georgy is taken to Minnesota by the Cheneys.
1860	March 19	The Pattersons move to Rumney Depot, New Hampshire, after Mary's sister Martha forecloses on their house in North Groton.
1861	October 10	Mary hears from Georgy, now a Union soldier, for the first time since 1856.
1862	March	Daniel Patterson is captured by Confederate soldiers.
1862	September 20	Daniel Patterson escapes from prison.
1862	October 10	Mary visits Dr. Phineas P. Quimby.
1863	September 12	Daniel Patterson opens a dental practice in Lynn, Massachusetts.
1865	October	The Pattersons move to Swampscott, Massachusetts.
1866	February 1	Mary falls on the ice while going to a temperance meeting in Lynn, Massachusetts, and is not expected to live.
1866	February 4	Healed of injuries by turning to God in prayer.
1866	March	Daniel Patterson deserts Mary.
1866	Autumn	Mary begins notes on Genesis, which she titles "The Bible in Its Spiritual Meaning."
1867	July	Mary is called to Sanbornton Bridge to help her dying niece Ellen Pilsbury, who is healed by Mary's prayers.
1870	August	Teaches her first class in Lynn, Massachusetts.
1872	January	Begins writing *Science and Health*.

1875	March 31	Buys house at 8 Broad Street in Lynn, Massachusetts, where she finishes writing *Science and Health*.
1875	October 30	*Science and Health* is published; first printing is 1000 copies.
1877	January 1	Marries Asa Gilbert Eddy at her home in Lynn.
1878	November 24	Begins preaching Sunday sermons at venues in Boston.
1879	April 12	Mary's students vote to organize a church.
1879	August 16	Mary is ordained pastor of the church.
1881	January 31	The Massachusetts Metaphysical College is chartered in Boston.
1882	January 21	The Eddys travel to Washington, D.C., where Mary teaches and lectures while Gilbert researches copyright law.
1882	June 2	Husband Gilbert Eddy dies at home in Boston.
1883	April 14	First issue of the *Journal of Christian Science* published.
1884	August 8	Mary teaches the first Normal class at the Massachusetts Metaphysical College, authorizing these and subsequent students to teach Christian Science.
1887	November	Mary's son George and his family come to Boston for six months.
1887	December 24	Moves into her new home at 385 Commonwealth Avenue in Boston.
1889	June	Moves to 62 North State Street in Concord, New Hampshire.
1889	October	Closes Massachusetts Metaphysical College.
1889	December 2	At her request, Church of Christ (Scientist), Boston, dissolves its congregational organization, although it continues to hold services as a voluntary association.

1891	January 19	The 50th edition (a major revision) of *Science and Health* is published.
1892	June 20	Mary moves to Pleasant View in Concord, New Hampshire. It will be her home for the next 16 years.
1892	September 23	The Church of Christ (Scientist) is reorganized as The Mother Church, The First Church of Christ, Scientist in Boston, Massachusetts.
1893	October 1	Groundbreaking for building the church edifice.
1894	December 19	Mary ordains the Bible and *Science and Health* as Pastor of The Mother Church.
1894	December 30	The first service is held in the Original Edifice.
1895	January 6	The Original Edifice is dedicated.
1895	April	In the April Journal, Mary ordains the Bible and *Science and Health* as Pastor for all branch churches.
1897	July 5	Addresses 2,500 members of The Mother Church by invitation at Pleasant View.
1898	September	*The Christian Science Weekly* is established, renamed *Christian Science Sentinel* four months later.
1898	November 20-21	Teaches her last class in Concord, New Hampshire.
1901	June 25	Welcomes some 3,000 Christian Scientists to Pleasant View at her invitation.
1903	June 29	Addresses some 10,000 Christian Scientists and others at Pleasant View by invitation.
1907	March 1	The "Next Friends" lawsuit begins in Concord.
1907	September 30	The "Next Friends" lawsuit is formally dismissed
1908	January 26	Moves to Chestnut Hill, near Boston.
1908	August 8	Requests the Trustees of the Christian Science Publishing Society to start a newspaper.
1908	November 25	First issue of *The Christian Science Monitor* is published

1910	July 16	Mary's grandsons George and Andrew visit her at Chestnut Hill.
1910	December 1	Mary's last written words are "God is my life."
1910	December 3	She dies at home in Chestnut Hill.

Selected Bibliography

In researching this book, the authors relied as much as possible on primary sources (letters, diary entries, eyewitness accounts, newspaper accounts, and the like). In cases where this was not possible, we were grateful for the scholarship of others. The following is a list of books we found helpful.

Armstrong, Joseph. *The Mother Church* (Boston: The Christian Science Publishing Society, 1897).

Bancroft, Samuel Putnam. *Mrs. Eddy As I Knew Her in 1870* (Boston: Press of Geo. H. Ellis Co., 1923). (abbreviated *As I Knew Her*)

Brisbane, Arthur. *What Mrs. Eddy Said to Arthur Brisbane* (New York: M. E. Paige, 1930). (abbreviated *What Mrs. Eddy Said*)

Canham, Erwin D. *Commitment to Freedom: The Story of The Christian Science Monitor* (Boston: Houghton Mifflin, 1958).

Eddy, Mary Baker and Gilman, James F. *Painting a Poem: Mary Baker Eddy and James F. Gilman Illustrate Christ and Christmas* (Boston: The Christian Science Publishing Society, 1998). (abbreviated *Painting a Poem*)

Editorial Comments on the Life and Work of Mary Baker Eddy (Boston: The Christian Science Publishing Society, 1911)

Eicher, David J. *The Longest Night: A Military History of the Civil War* (New York: Simon & Schuster, 2001).

Gottschalk, Stephen. *Rolling Away the Stone: Mary Baker Eddy's Challenge to Materialism* (Bloomington: Indiana University Press, 2006).

Grossberg, Michael. Governing the Hearth: Law and the Family in Nineteenth-Century America (Chapel Hill, N.C.: University of North Carolina Press, 1985).

Hamilton, Allan McLane. *Recollections of an Alienist* (New York: George H. Doran Company, 1916).

Hartog, Hendrik. *Man and Wife in America: A History* (Cambridge, Mass.: Harvard University Press, 2000).

Hearst, William Randolph, Jr. with Casserly, Jack. *The Hearsts: Father and Son* (Colorado: Roberts Rinehart, 1991).

Howard, Stephen R. *Homeward II: Chestnut Hill* (Longyear Museum Press, 2008).

Hufford, Kenneth. *Mary Baker Eddy and the Stoughton Years* (Brookline, Mass.: Longyear Foundation, 1963). (abbreviated *Stoughton Years*)

In My True Light and Life (Boston: The Mary Baker Eddy Library for the Betterment of Humanity, 2002). (abbreviated *In My True Light*)

Larkin, Jack. *The Reshaping of Everyday Life: 1790-1840* (New York: HarperCollins, 1988).

Longyear, Mary Beecher *The Genealogy and Life of Asa Gilbert Eddy* (Boston: Press of Geo. H. Ellis Co., 1922). (abbreviated *Geneaology and Life*)

Meehan, Michael. *Mrs. Eddy and the Late Suit in Equity* (Concord, N.H.: Michael Meehan, 1908). (abbreviated *Late Suit in Equity*)

Older, Cora Baggerly. *William Randolph Hearst: American* (New York: D. Appleton-Century Co., 1936).

Orcutt, William Dana. *Mary Baker Eddy and Her Books* (Boston: The Christian Science Publishing Society, 1950).

Peel, Robert. *Mary Baker Eddy: The Years of Authority* (New York: Holt, Rinehart and Winston, 1977); *Mary Baker Eddy: The Years of Discovery* (New York: Holt, Rinehart and Winston 1966); *Mary Baker Eddy: The Years of Trial* (New York: Holt, Rinehart and Winston, 1971); *Spiritual Healing in a Scientific Age* (San Francisco: Harper & Row, 1987). (abbreviated *Years of Authority, Years of Discovery, Years of Trial*)

Pinkham, Margaret M. *The Miracle in Stone* (Santa Barbara: Nebbadoon Press, 2009).

Powell, Lyman P. *Mary Baker Eddy: A Life Size Portrait* (New York: Macmillan, 1931). (abbreviated *Portrait*)

Procter, Ben. *William Randolph Hearst: The Early Years, 1863-1910* (New York: Oxford University Press, 1998).

Smaus, Jewel Spangler. *Mary Baker Eddy: The Golden Days* (Boston: The Christian Science Publishing Society, 1968). (abbreviated *Golden Days*)

Smith, Clifford P. *Historical Sketches from the Life of Mary Baker Eddy and the History of Christian Science* (Boston: The Christian Science Publishing Society, 1934).

The Human Life Articles on Mary Baker Eddy (Chestnut Hill, Mass.: Longyear Museum Press, 2000

Tomlinson, Irving C. *Twelve Years with Mary Baker Eddy: Recollections and Experiences, Amplified Edition* (Boston: The Christian Science Publishing Society, 1994). (abbreviated *Twelve Years*)

von Fettweis, Yvonne Cache and Warneck, Robert Townsend. *Mary Baker Eddy: Christian Healer, Amplified Edition* (Boston: The Christian Science Publishing Society, 1998). (abbreviated *Christian Healer*)

We Knew MBE: Expanded Edition Vol. I (Boston: The Christian Science Publishing Society, 2011). (abbreviated *We Knew MBE Vol. I*)

We Knew MBE: Expanded Edition Vol. II (Boston: The Christian Science Publishing Society, 2013). (abbreviated *We Knew MBE Vol. II*)

Wilbur, Sibyl. *The Life of Mary Baker Eddy* (New York: Concord Publishing Co., 1908). (abbreviated *Life of MBE*)

Winkler, John K. *William Randolph Hearst: A New Appraisal* (New York: Hastings House, 1955).

Woo, Ilyon. *The Great Divorce: A Nineteenth-Century Mother's Extraordinary Fight Against Her Husband, the Shakers, and Her Times* (New York: Atlantic Monthly Press).

Works Mentioned, written by Mary Baker Eddy, and published by The Christian Science Publishing Society

Christ and Christmas

*Christian Healing** (abbreviated *Healing*)

Manual of The Mother Church The First Church of Christ, Scientist in Boston, Massachusetts (abbreviated *Manual*)

Message to The First Church of Christ, Scientist of The Mother Church Boston, June 15, 1902* (abbreviated *'02*)

Miscellaneous Writings: 1883-1896* (abbreviated *Miscellaneous*)

Poems

*Pulpit and Press** (abbreviated *Pulpit*)

*Retrospection and Introspection** (abbreviated *Retrospection*)

*Rudimental Divine Science** (abbreviated *Rudimental*)

Science and Health with Key to the Scriptures (abbreviated *S&H*)

*The First Church of Christ, Scientist, and Miscellany** (abbreviated *Miscellany*)

*These works are included in the compilation *Prose Works* other than *Science and Health with Key to the Scriptures.*

Source Notes

Dates for events and publications in Mary Baker Eddy's life were cross-referenced with "Mary Baker Eddy: A Chronology," available in The Mary Baker Eddy Library in Boston, Massachusetts. Historical documents cited courtesy of The Mary Baker Eddy Collection and The Mary Baker Eddy Library (TMBEL) are generally indicated with an "L," "A," "IC," "EOR," "SB," "SF," or "Rem," and can be accessed by an alphanumeric notation with assistance from the Library's research staff. Historical documents from Longyear Museum (LM) in Chestnut Hill, Massachusetts, are indicated in the Source Notes. The Chandler papers can be found at the New Hampshire Historical Society, Manuscript Collection.

Chapter 1: EARLY DAYS

p. 7 Hats, scarves, mittens—even hair ribbons—all had disappeared before… TMBEL, A11809; *Twelve Years*, p. 4.

p. 7 "You must not give away your clothes…" *Twelve Years*, p. 4.

p. 7 "… remember the words of the Lord Jesus, how he said, It is more blessed to give than to receive." Acts 20:35.

p. 7 Mary may have given her coat to one of the White children. TMBEL, L13544 (October 9, 1905).

p. 8 Caption: Artist's depiction of the Baker homestead. In later life, Mary would draw on recollections of her childhood home to collaborate on this illustration with her cousin Rufus H. Baker. "Accept my thanks for the well executed engraving of the Baker homestead," she wrote to him. "Around the memory thereof clusters the golden days of my childhood." TMBEL, L12649 (December 28, 1899).

p. 8 "Here is another invalid for Mary." *Twelve Years*, p. 3.

p. 8 Sidebar/Words of Wisdom: TMBEL, A11058.

p. 9 "Mary, get down and pick up that corn…" This anecdote was related by Mrs. Eddy to several of her household members, including Adelaide Still and Clara Shannon, who later recorded it in their reminiscences, TMBEL.

p. 9 "Her presence, like the gentle dew and cheerful light, was felt by all around her." *Retrospection*, p. 5, quoting from *New Hampshire Patriot and State Gazette* (December 6, 1849).

p. 9 "… always thinking of ways that she could help an ailing friend or neighbor." *Twelve Years*, p. 15.

p. 10 Mary's childhood fondness for particular Bible stories, as well as the anecdote about marking her prayers on the woodshed wall, were related to numerous students, including Irving Tomlinson (see *Twelve Years*, p. 7), Julia Bartlett, and Adam Dickey, who later wrote about it in their reminiscences, TMBEL.

p. 10 "What are you going to do when you are grown up?" TMBEL, L10106; TMBEL, Rem: Clara Shannon.

p. 11 The walk home from school… TMBEL, L09579.

p. 11 Sidebar/One Room Schoolhouses: *Golden Days*, pp. 30-34, 172; http://oneroomschoolhousecenter.weebly.com; http://www.npr.org/series/5178603/america-s-one-room-schools; http://en.wikipedia.org/wiki/One-room_school; http://www.osv.org/explore_learn/village_tour.html?S=L-33

p. 12 "keep shaking the table and making me laugh…" LM, Baker letters (May 1, 1836).

p. 12 Mary "was devoted to her grandmother," according to Clara Shannon's reminiscence, TMBEL. See also *Retrospection*, p. 2.

p. 12 Mary's grandmother told her about the American side of her family, too… *Retrospection*, pp. 2-3

p. 12 The battle in which Mary's great-great-grandfather John Lovewell was killed is the subject of "Lovewell's Fight," a popular ballad written shortly after the 1725 skirmish. It's also featured in Nathaniel Hawthorne's short story "Roger Malvin's Burial," as well as Henry Wadsworth Longfellow's very first published poem, "The Battle of Lovell's Pond," written when he was 13 (http://www.hwlongfellow.org/poems_poem.php?pid=2095).

p. 13 "the playground…" *Years of Discovery*, p. 13.

p. 13 The story of Mary and her cousin Mehitable is related in *Retrospection*, pp. 8-9, as well as in Janette E. Weller's reminiscence, TMBEL.

p. 14 "I shall wait for *you* to be *my* wife!" *Retrospection*, 1st edition, p. 24; *Twelve Years*, p. 12; TMBEL, A11976 (November 12, 1909).

p. 14 The family doctor told Mr. Baker that his daughter's brain was "too large" for her body… *Ret.*, p. 10, *Portrait*, p. 60.

p. 14 One of Mary's favorite spots to write was under an apple tree… TMBEL, Rem: Julia Bartlett.

p. 15 *Resolutions for the Morning.* Mary Baker's girlhood notebook (later revised and included in *Poems*, p. 32).

Chapter 2: WHAT'S RIGHT?

p. 16 Mark Baker … was a man of strong character. *Miscellany*, pp. 308-309; *Twelve Years*, p. 14; TMBEL L01707; *Years of Discovery*, p. 9.

p. 16 "At Christmastime, father would fill the democrat wagon…" *Twelve Years*, p. 14.

p. 17 "… it is the duty of heads of families to train up the children…" LM, Records of the Union Church of Christ in Bow, New Hampshire, 1806-1829.

p. 17 Years later, Mary would recount with amusement how she made her escape in the confusion that followed. TMBEL, Rem: William Rathvon.

p. 17 "My childhood's home, I remember as one with the open hand." *Retrospection*, p. 6.

p. 18 Mary recounts her healing of a fever and the events leading up to it in *Retrospection*, pp. 13-14.

p. 18 "the dear old farm…" TMBEL, L13544 (October 9, 1905).

p. 18 "the golden days of childhood…" TMBEL, L07681 (June 27, 1902).

p. 18 "We like to had a dreadful fight about it…" LM, Baker letters (January 20, 1836).

p. 19 "a gentleman from New York…" Ibid.

p. 19 "It is extremely mortifying, to my pride…" LM, Baker letters (April 24, 1836).

p. 19 "Father is as happy as a clam…" LM, Baker letters (August 23, 1836).

p. 19 "French Twist" hairstyle… *McClure's Magazine* (January 1907).

p. 19 "Balls and dancing schools we have not frequented…" LM, Baker letters (April 24, 1836).

p. 19 "he did not forbid us and of course we went…" LM, Baker letters (November 20, 1836).

p. 19 "We find society very agreeable and refined…" LM, Baker letters (April 24, 1836).

p. 20 "Hopeing [sic] time still continues to glide smoothly as in former years…" TMBEL, F00026, Baker letters (May 2, 1836).

p. 20 "The young gentlemen have not been slow in their attentions." LM, Baker letters (April 24, 1836).

p. 20 "Let all conversation and pleasure be in harmony with the will of God." *Twelve Years*, p. 8.

p. 20 "Bright, good, and pure, aye brilliant!" Wilbur, *Life of MBE*, p. 33. A noted investigative journalist and foreign correspondent, Sibyl Wilbur attended Hamline University in St. Paul, Minn., and later wrote for newspapers in Minneapolis, Chicago, Washington, D. C., Boston, and New York. Her series of articles on Mrs. Eddy in *Human Life* magazine, published in 1906-1907, formed the basis for the biography she would publish the following year. Sibyl had previously interviewed Mrs. Eddy for the *Boston Herald* on June 11, 1905, which was reprinted in the CSS (June 17, 1905). In an introduction to the CSS article, Mrs. Eddy said in part, "I confess to having yielded reluctantly to meet the occasion for quieting the billows of public opinion…. But what a grand, calm call was hers, what a short time it took for us to talk when touched by the truth of an honest purpose! … Will Miss Wilbur accept my thanks for her kind courtesy, for leaving me with not one hour less in which to put my mite with hers into the vast treasure-troves of eternity…? May she, because of her goodness, broaden her range of usefulness…." Sibyl graciously complied when Mrs. Eddy asked her to hold off publishing the biography she'd spent several years researching and writing, and was much relieved when she eventually got the green light. (Published in October 1908, the book was read to Mrs. Eddy by Irving Tomlinson a few months later, a fact he notes in his reminiscences.) Mrs. Eddy's written approval appeared in the CSS (March 10, 1910), and was reprinted in *Miscellany*, p. 298: "I thank Miss Wilbur and the Concord Publishing Company for their unselfed labors in placing this book before the public, and hereby say that they have my permission to publish and circulate this work."

p. 20 "Mary, some day you will be a distinguished author." *Twelve Years*, p. 11.

p. 20 "I never before had a pupil with such depth and independence of thought." *Life of MBE*, p. 33.

p. 21 She framed her protest in the words of the Psalmist… *Retrospection*, pp. 14-15.

p. 21 "She always wore clothes we admired." *Life of MBE*, p. 34.

p. 21 She was especially fond of the stories of Sir Walter Scott, and she read Charlotte Brontë's novels as they rolled off the press. TMBEL, A11001A; *Years of Discovery*, p. 83.

p. 22 "If you knew how much satisfaction I take in reading your letters…" LM, Baker letters (January 29, 1840).

p. 23 Caption: "TO GEN. FRANKLIN PIERCE," by Mary M. Glover. *New Hampshire Patriot and State Gazette* (October 20, 1852).

p. 23 Sidebar/Reading Law in the 19th Century: http://en.wikipedia.org/wiki/Reading _ law; http://www.monticello.org/site/research-and-collections/jeffersons-formal-education; http://showcase.netins.net/web/creative/lincoln/speeches/law.htm

p. 23 "I am very anxious to hear again from my dear father." LM, Baker letters (December 31, 1838).

p. 23 Albert himself entered politics in 1839… *Retrospection*, pp. 6-7; *Twelve Years*, p. 16; *Longyear Museum Quarterly News* (Summer 1968).

p. 24 "I have some eight or ten jury trials…" LM, Baker letters (January 29, 1840).

p. 24 "Your health is of paramount importance." LM, Baker letters (January 24, 1840).

p. 24 By 1841, his political star was on the rise. *The Bench and Bar of New Hampshire* (Cambridge, Mass.: The Riverside Press, 1894) by Charles H. Bell, p. 11.

p. 24 "Your lamented brother was emphatically one of the best friends of the rights of the people." LM, Baker letters (December 18, 1841).

p. 24 He was no stickler for expediency…" *New Hampshire Patriot and State Gazette* (November 4, 1841).

p. 24 Mr. Baker was a young man of uncommon promise…" *New Hampshire Patriot and State Gazette* (October 21, 1841).

Chapter 3: MOUNTAINS AND VALLEYS

p. 25 "The Bible and I are inseparable." *Twelve Years*, p. 105.

p. 26 "As to my being married..." TMBEL, L02679.

p. 27 "soulful..." John Lathrop in *We Knew MBE Vol. I*, p. 265; "brilliant..." *Years of Discovery*, p. 41, quoting letter from Russell Ambrose (April 9, 1876); "expressive..." *Stoughton Years*, p. 20; "luminous..." Abigail Thompson in *We Knew MBE Vol. I*, p. 147; also *New York American* interview with Mrs. Eddy, reprinted in the CSS (August 31, 1907).

p. 27 John Bartlett and the Young Ladies' Literary Society. *Years of Discovery*, p. 325/n36.

p. 27 "We had a fine time..." TMBEL, F00028 (April 17, 1837).

p. 27 "Oh, you're dressed up!" TMBEL, Rem: Gilbert Carpenter Sr..

p. 27 Sidebar/Dear Penpal: "In this way we got acquainted..." *Twelve Years*, p. 13.

p. 27 The sore point for Mark Baker wasn't Wash necessarily... LM, Baker letters (February 6, 1844). As Mary later recalled: "It was not that my father disliked Major Glover that he did not want me to marry him, but father did not want me to go so far away from home." TMBEL, A11976 (November 12, 1909).

p. 28 "The lonely night-wind sighs a dull requiem to my spirits..." TMBEL, A09002.

p. 28 "much better health and spirits." TMBEL, A09002.

p. 28 "such a sky rocket adventure I never had..." TMBEL, F00033 (July 21, 1843).

p. 28 "I beleve [sic] among 7 Builders I am Duing [sic] one half the Buiseness [sic] in the Citty [sic]..." LM, Baker letters (May 19, 1841).

p. 29 "I married young the one I loved." TMBEL, L08338.

p. 29 "some cloudy..." *New Hampshire Historical Society*, diary of Joseph Moody, cited in "Family: The Carolina Glovers, Part IV," by Jewel Spangler Smaus, *Longyear Museum Quarterly News* (Fall/Winter 1989/90). Smaus's article offers a colorful glimpse of holiday and wedding customs of this era.

p. 29 Wash had joined the Freemasons... Freemasonry is a fraternal organization dating back to the Middle Ages. Some notable Freemasons include Johannes Brahms, Davy Crockett, Henry Ford, Benjamin Franklin, Paul Revere, Booker T. Washington, George Washington, and John Wayne.
For more information, see: http://web.mit.edu/dryfoo/Masons/

p. 29 "... brilliant in conversation and most gracious in her manner." TMBEL, Rem: Elizabeth Earl Jones, p. 57.

p. 30 "She had no sooner come to Wilmington than she began contributing rhymes to the local paper..." *Years of Discovery*, p. 322/n130, quoting Greensboro, N.C. *News* (1906).

p. 30 Mary wrote a glowing review of the play *The Death of Rolla*... TMBEL, A09002 (June 1, 1844 - Mary Baker Glover notebook).

p. 30 "The Old Man of the Mountain," by Mrs. G. W. Glover, *The Floral Wreath* (July 1844).

p. 31 "little fat beautiful Daughter..." LM, Baker letters (May 6, 1844).

p. 31 "Dear Child, Are you happy as anticipated?" LM, Baker letters (February 6, 1844).

p. 31 Yet there was something that troubled her... In the coming years, Mary would speak of her aversion to slavery to a number of her students, including Irving Tomlinson (*Twelve Years*, pp. 18-20). On August 12, 1861 she wrote a letter of thanks to Union Army General Benjamin Butler, a fellow New Hampshire native who had famously refused to return runaway slaves to their Southern owners. "You as we all 'hold freedom to be the normal condition of those made in God's image,'" Mary told him (TMBEL, V03472), quoting from his own widely published letter to Secretary of War Simon Cameron. Mary would also later write, "I could never believe that a human being was my property." (*'02*, p. 15.)

p. 31 The house that Wash had built... *Longyear Museum Quarterly News* (Autumn 1987).

p. 31 "My father was a strong believer in States' rights..." *Miscellany*, p. 309.

p. 31 "The Liberty Bells," *Lynn Reporter* (February 3, 1865).

p. 32 "To-day, by order of Governor Andrew, the bells are ringing..." *Poems*, p. vi.

p. 32 "The Emigrant's Farewell," by Mrs. Mary M. Glover, *The Covenant* (May 1846).

p. 32 With his parting breath ... *Retrospection*, p. 19.

p. 33 "Dead is he who loved me dearly..." *Miscellany*, p. 189.

p. 33 "What would your husband say to you..." TMBEL, Rem: Clara Shannon

Chapter 4: TWO GOODBYES

p. 34 "We will go to Mrs. Glover..." *Years of Discovery*, p. 81; Mary also referenced this incident in a *CSJ* article (January 1907), later reprinted in *Miscellany*, p. 312.

p. 34 "Tall, slender, exceedingly graceful..." TMBEL, Rem: Sarah Clement Kimball.

p. 35 "I feel as if I must *begin* something this summer..." TMBEL, L11150.

p. 35 "The Bible," by Mary M. Glover, *The Covenant* (October 1846).

p. 35 "Emma Clinton, or a Tale of the Frontiers," by Mrs. Mary M. Glover. *The Covenant* (August 1846).

p. 35 "The Test of Love," by Mary M. Glover. *The Covenant* (June 1847).

p. 35 "'Tis like looking down through the transparent waters of the sea of life..." TMBEL, F00032 (March 20, 1848).

p. 35 "There has been some sleigh riding…" TMBEL, L11150.

p. 36 Sidebar/Poorhouse Blues: For more information on women's rights in the 19th century, see *The Great Divorce: A Nineteenth-Century Mother's Extraordinary Fight Against Her Husband, the Shakers, and Her Times* (New York: Atlantic Monthly Press) by Ilyon Woo, pp. 16, 24, 65, 163, 171, 344; Man and Wife in America: A History (Cambridge, Mass.: Harvard University Press, 2000) by Hendrik Hartog, pp. 115-122; Governing the Hearth: Law and the Family in Nineteenth-Century America (Chapel Hill, N.C.: University of North Carolina Press, 1985) by Michael Grossberg; www.poorhousestory.com/history.htm; http://en.wikipedia.org/wiki/Poorhouse; http://mshistorynow.mdah.state.ms.us/articles/6/betsy-love-and-the-mississippi-married-womens-property-act-of-1839; http://www.nwhm.org/; http://memory.loc.gov/ammem/awhhtml/awlaw3/property _ law.html; http://www.britannica.com/EBchecked/topic/366305/Married-Womens-Property-Acts

p. 37 Sidebar/Poorhouse Blues: "Our laws are not impartial, to say the least…" *S&H*, p. 63.

p. 37 Sidebar/Poorhouse Blues: "If a dissolute husband deserts his wife…" Ibid., p. 63.

p. 37 "This morning looks on us bereft of a Mother!" TMBEL, F00031 (November 22, 1849). Many years later, Mary would have these words inscribed on the headstone at her mother's grave: "Her life the grand realities impart that fix their records deeply in the heart." TMBEL, P00338.

p. 37 Mr. Baker threatened to send Georgy to the poorhouse… LM, Baker letters (late November, 1850).

p. 38 "Oh! How I miss him already!" TMBEL, F00030.

p. 38 Mary's brief but touching account of her forced separation from her son Georgy can be found in *Retrospection*, p. 20.

p. 38 "Go, little voyager, o'er life's rough sea…" TMBEL, A09002 (Mary's notebook, May 9, 1851).

Chapter 5: ANOTHER MARRIAGE

p. 40 He rode his horse from town to town in his black silk top hat and kid gloves… *Human Life*, February 1907. *Human Life* (subtitled "The Magazine About People") was a popular magazine of its day, reporting annual circulation figures of just under two million in 1907. It featured a monthly series of articles on Mary Baker Eddy by Sibyl Wilbur from December 1906 through December 1907. More information can be found in *The Human Life Articles on Mary Baker Eddy* (Chestnut Hill, Mass.: Longyear Museum Press, 2000). For an account of Wilbur's meeting with Mrs. Eddy, see the CSS (June 17, 1905).

p. 41 "dark things…" TMBEL, L16249 (April 10, 1853).

p. 41 "I beg you to remember that we will be friends…" TMBEL, L08903.

p. 41 "It seems I have lost you at last…" TMBEL, L16250 (April 11, 1853).

p. 42 A sawmill in which Daniel purchased part-ownership… According to Myra Smith Wilson's reminiscence, Mary's sister Martha lent Daniel the money for this venture, as well as for the mortgage on their house. TMBEL.

p. 42 Mahala had taken him from time to time to visit Mary… "Family: From New England to the Black Hills Part II," by Jewel Spangler Smaus, *Longyear Museum Quarterly News* (Winter 1982-83). Smaus's interview with George W. Glover III (Mary's grandson) provides fascinating background information about George Glover II's life.

p. 43 Furious to find his stepson in the yard… George W. Glover III reminiscence, *Longyear Museum Quarterly News* (Winter 1982-83).

p. 44 She felt as if the family was plotting against her. *Retrospection*, p. 20; *Years of Discovery*, p. 118.

p. 44 "Every means within my power was employed to find him…" *Retrospection*, p. 21.

p. 44 "fine looking woman, intellectual and stately in appearance…" TMBEL, Rem: Daniel Kidder.

p. 45 "I remember well her beautiful eyes, her soft voice and how she would put down her book…" *Human Life* (February 1907).

p. 45 "Oh, you dear little girl." TMBEL, Rem: Marcia A. Wilson Swett.

p. 45 "poor sick lady…" Ibid.

p. 45 around this time she made a solemn promise to God… TMBEL, L10106; *Twelve Years*, p. 43.

Chapter 6: PRISON BREAKS

p. 46 Desperately seeking a way to cure herself and others… *S&H*, p. 370; *Miscellaneous*, pp. 378-379; *Retrospection*, p. 24; TMBEL, Rem: Elmyra Smith Wilson; *Years of Discovery*, p. 99.

p. 46 "I prescribed the fourth attenuation of *Argentum nitratum*…" *S&H*, p. 156.

p. 46 "It then occurred to me to give her unmedicated pellets…" *S&H*, p. 156.

p. 47 "a mental standpoint not understood…" *Miscellaneous*, p. 379.

p. 47 The experience "was a falling apple to me…" *Late Suit in Equity*, p. 161. Author Michael Meehan was editor of the *Concord [NH] Patriot*, and well-acquainted with Mrs. Eddy.

p. 47 "… my first discovery of the Science of Mind." Ibid.

p. 47 "Very Dear Wife…" TMBEL, L16251 (February 17, 1857).

p. 47 Mary had to auction off some of her possessions… TMBEL, Rem: Elmyra Smith Wilson; *Human Life* (February 1907).

p. 48 "It was spring and the roads were very bad…" TMBEL, Rem: Elmyra Smith Wilson.

p. 49 "Ode to Adversity," *Years of Discovery*, p. 143.

p. 49 She'd grown disenchanted with homeopathy, telling Myra "not to mind as they were no good anyway…" TMBEL, Rem: Elmyra Smith Wilson.

p. 49 "I gave the infant no drugs…" TMBEL, A10402.

p. 49 a twenty-year effort "to trace all physical effects to a mental cause…" *Retrospection*, p. 24.

p. 50 George Glover II's enlistment is detailed in the *Longyear Museum Quarterly News* (Spring 1983), and *Years of Discovery*, p. 144.

p. 52 "The Heart's Unrest," TMBEL, A09001 (written in Rumney, December 13, 1861).

p. 53 Sidebar/Bull Run: For more information on this Civil War battle, see the National Park Service website: www.nps.gov/mana; http://en.wikipedia.org/wiki/First_Battle_of_Bull_Run; and The Longest Night: A Military History of the Civil War (New York: Simon & Schuster) by David J. Eicher.

p. 53 Sidebar/Bull Run: "Today will be known as BLACK MONDAY." Eicher, Ibid., p. 100.

p. 53 "You will be amazed to learn that I am in prison…" TMBEL, L16248 (April 2, 1862).

p. 53 "To a Bird Flying Southward," by Mary A. [sic] Patterson. *The Independent Democrat* (July 3, 1862).

p. 54 Abi insisted on sending her to Dr. William T. Vail's Hydropathic Institute… *In My True Light*, p. 125.

p. 54 "I have been at this Water Cure between 2 and 3 months…" Ibid., p. 125.

p. 54 "and in a few weeks returned apparently well…" *Miscellaneous*, p. 378.

p. 55 "in a loud voice demanded that each patient look him straight in the eye…" TMBEL, Rem: Charles A. Quincy Norton.

p. 55 "I well remember the fearful tangle which Mrs. Patterson's hair was in after her treatments…" TMBEL, Rem: Martha J. Hinds.

p. 56 "the essence of quackery…" TMBEL, A10402. In this vigorous letter of defense on Mary's behalf written years later, her sister-in-law Mary Cook Baker (wife of Mary's older brother Samuel) would also have this to say: "I am acquainted with the birth and growth of Christian Science, and know that the claim that it originated with Phineas P. Quimby is absurd, and without foundation. I can state positively that Mrs. Eddy never received any instructions or suggestions from him in regard to Metaphysical healing or Christian Science. I know whereof I speak, because I accompanied her to Dr. Quimby: at that time she was too feeble to go unattended. His treatment consisted of manipulations in cold water, and was wholly material, and entirely devoid of metaphysics or spirituality."

p. 56 "assiduously pondering the solution…" *Miscellaneous*, p. 379.

p. 56 those "dark things" Mary's father had heard years ago about his character had proved true… TMBEL, L16249 (April 10, 1853); *Years of Discovery*, p. 185.

p. 58 Mark's three daughters received only $1.00... In his will, Mr. Baker also left Mary and Abigail each a piece of furniture, and he forgave Mary and Daniel any debts that they may have owed him. In addition, the will called for the division of whatever remained of Mr. Baker's estate amongst all of his children after his second wife's eventual death. TMBEL, SF: Mary Baker Eddy Family – Bakers – Mark Baker.

p. 58 "God had been graciously preparing me during many years…" *S&H*, p. 107.

Chapter 7: A TURNING POINT

p. 59 Mary shared her own account of this healing in detail in *Science and Health,* third edition (1881). See also *Years of Discovery,* pp. 195-198; interview with Dr. Alvin Cushing, *The Sunday Herald* (December 24, 1899); *Lynn Reporter* (February 3, 1866); *Human Life* (May 1907).

p. 59 The next day, Mary "came to consciousness…" TMBEL, L07796 (February 15, 1866).

p. 59 Caption: In winter, Mary liked to feed the birds… *Lynn Reporter* (April 4, 1866); *Human Life* (May 1907).

p. 60 Sidebar/Temperance Movement: She "had a quiet way about her of commanding attention…" *Human Life* (May 1907); *Life of MBE,* p. 118. For more information on the temperance movement, see *The Reshaping of Everyday Life: 1790-1840* (New York: HarperCollins, 1988) by Jack Larkin; *Historical Notes on Temperance Reform in the Early 19th Century* (Old Sturbridge Village, 2001) by Jack Larkin; http://www.osv.org/explore _ learn/document _ viewer.php?DocID=1991; National Women's History Museum (http://www.nwhm.org/online-exhibits/progressiveera/wctu.html).

p. 60 TMBEL, Rem: George Newhall (George attended the same church and temperance society that Mary did); TMBEL, Rem: Arietta Mann.

p. 61 "As I read, the healing Truth dawned upon my sense…" *Miscellaneous,* p. 24:11.

p. 61 "I am the way, the truth, and the life…" John 14:6; see also *CSJ* (August 1885—Lilian Whiting's interview with Mary Baker Eddy for the July 2, 1885 *Ohio Leader);* and *S&H,* 3rd edition (1881).

p. 61 "What! Are you about!" *S&H,* 3rd edition (1881).

p. 61 "namely, Life in and of Spirit…" *Miscellaneous,* p. 24.

p. 61 "it all seemed to come to me again…" TMBEL, SF: Henry Robinson — "Memorandum of an Interview with Mrs. Dr. Eddy" (August 31, 1890).

Chapter 8: I FOUND HIM

p. 62 "into a new world of light and Life…" *Retrospection,* p. 27.

p. 62 "I am constantly wishing that <u>you</u> would step forward…" TMBEL, L07796 (February 15, 1866).

p. 62 "I do not even help my wife out of her trouble." TMBEL, IC 632.64.008 (March 2, 1866).

p. 62 There'd been too much "disappointment and tears…" TMBEL, L11153 (April 28, 1867).

p. 62 "if he had done as he ought…" TMBEL, R. D. Rounsevel affidavit (February 3, 1900).

p. 63 "I'm Sitting Alone," *Lynn Reporter* (September 12, 1866).

p. 63 Dorr Phillips' healing is recounted in *Life of MBE,* pp. 140-141.

p. 63 "Nor would it be if it had been a broken wrist or a withered arm…" Ibid.

p. 64 Sidebar/Red Rock: "the shoreline's famous red-hued outcropping was a favorite spot of Mary's..." TMBEL, Julia Bartlett reminiscence; *Human Life* (January, June & October 1907); Walter W. Watson, quoted in *In My True Light*, p. 603, also recalls being told by Julia that "sometimes she [Mary] had become so lost in thought that she had not noticed the incoming tide until it was almost upon her."

p. 64 "the average life expectancy for a female born in 1821 was 37." *Years of Discovery*, p. 124.

p. 64 "Abi's offer must have been tempting, but Mary couldn't accept it." *Human Life* (May 1907); James F. Gilman diary entry (August 19, 1893), quoted in *Painting a Poem*, p. 133. Mary may have been referring in part to this incident when she wrote in a *CSJ* article (January 1907), later reprinted in *Miscellany*, p. 313: "My oldest sister dearly loved me, but I wounded her pride when I adopted Christian Science, and to a Baker that was a sorry offence."

p. 65 "Later, a family friend wrote down the boy's description of what happened." Mrs. James Norton, mother of young George Norton, recounted this healing to Margaret E. Harding, who recorded it in her reminiscence. TMBEL, Rem: Margaret E. Harding.

p. 65 "When I came to the point that it was mind that did the healing..." *Late Suit in Equity*, p. 165.

p. 65 Mary grew more confident that "the Divine Mind was the Healer." Ibid.

p. 65 "After these experiments you cannot be surprised that we resigned the imaginary medicine altogether..." *Healing*, p. 13.

p. 65 "holy, uplifting faith..." *S&H*, p. 109.

p. 65 "I must know the Science of this healing..." Ibid., p. 109.

p. 66 "I sought God diligently..." TMBEL, A10125.

p. 66 "But the Scriptures had a new meaning, a new tongue..." Mary Baker Eddy, *Historical Sketch of Metaphysical Healing* (1885), p. 7.

p. 66 "divinely natural and possible to understand..." Ibid., p. 7.

p. 66 "would read the pages to Mother and me..." TMBEL, Rem: Fred O. Ellis.

p. 66 "cherished remembrance of those precious evenings..." TMBEL, IC 471.54.001 (November 16, 1901).

p. 66 "Do you forget your Christmas present to me..." TMBEL, L05670 (January 21, 1903).

Chapter 9: A SHOEMAKER LEARNS A NEW TRADE

p. 67 Mary thought it would take "centuries of spiritual growth" before she could teach others... *Miscellaneous*, p. 380.

p. 67 Hiram Crafts, a young shoemaker... *Human Life* (May & July 1907); *Portrait*, p. 111, 121.

p. 67 In November of 1866, the Crafts invited Mary to come back to East Stoughton… TMBEL, A10402, p. 100.

p. 68 Sidebar/Shoe Capital Of The World: "her jack-of-all-trades father once made shoes for a needy family…" TMBEL, L13544 (October 9, 1905). For more information on the city of Lynn's role in the shoe trade, see Lynn Museum & Historical Society (http://lynnmuseum.org/); Lynn Heritage Park website (http://www.mass.gov/dcr/parks/metroboston/lnhp.htm); City of Lynn website (http://www.ci.lynn.ma.us/aboutlynn _ history.shtml); "A Look at Mary Baker Eddy's Years in Lynn 1870-1881," by Susan E. Schopp, *LM Historical Review,* Vol. 36, #1, pp. 3-4.

p. 68 "We used nothing outside of the New Testament…" TMBEL, SF: Hiram Crafts, (February 23, 1902).

p. 69 *"I can cure you."* Advertisement in *Taunton Daily Gazette* (May 14, 1867). According to Howard Hathaway's "History of Christian Science in Taunton, Massachusetts" (TMBEL), the ad also appeared weekly in the *Union Gazette and Democrat*.

p. 69 "I had not received her attention but a short time…" *S&H,* first edition (1875), p. 338.

p. 69 "Metaphysics, as taught in Christian Science, is the next stately step beyond homœopathy." *S&H,* p. 156.

p. 69 "All that come to him sick he cures." TMBEL, L11153.

p. 69 Ellen's case had been given up by three doctors… Martha Rand Baker account, published in *S&H,* third edition (1881), pp. 152-153. *Years of Discovery* notes on pp. 215-217 that this account was mistakenly attributed to Elizabeth P. Baker, Mary's step-mother, but later confirmed to be Martha by her son George Baker in a letter of April 22, 1924 to Mary B. G. Billings (Mary's granddaughter).

p. 69 "I am glad to see you, Aunty." Ibid.

p. 70 "Such a change came over the household…" TMBEL, Rem: Addie Towns Arnold.

p. 70 "I have my private opinion that in the end no real good will result…" LM, Baker letters (August 4, 1867).

p. 70 Mrs. Crafts was tired of "doing" for her houseguest… *Human Life* (May 1907); *Years of Discovery,* p. 216.

p. 70 "I should be willing to do all you ask if I was in different circumstances…" TMBEL, IC 056.16.001 (November 27, 1868).

p. 71 "sweet, calm, and buoyant with hope…" *S&H,* p. 109.

p. 71 Mary was evicted—turned out in the rain with her trunk. *Human Life* (May 1907).

p. 72 "Christ My Refuge." *Lynn Reporter* (February 15, 1868); *Amesbury Villager* (August 20, 1868). Between February and August, Mary changed the wording of the last line in the second stanza from "with love perfumed" to "by love perfumed" (and would later permanently change it back again). Also, the seventh stanza originally read: "I am no reed to shake at scorn/Or hate of man;/I am no medium but Truth's, to warn/The creedish clan."

p. 73 "When Hiram Crafts brought her to our fireside, we just felt as if an angel had come into our home..." LM, Lucy Wentworth Holmes letter (November 12, 1936); *Stoughton Years*, p. 5.

p. 73 Additional information on Mary's healings of various members of the Wentworth family can be found in *Christian Healer*, pp. 79-88; *Life of MBE*, p. 174; and *Stoughton Years*, p. 28.

p. 73 Mary called 13-year-old Lucy "little Lue..." TMBEL, Rem: Lucy Wentworth Holmes (February 10, 1922).

p. 73 "Her manners were beautiful..." *Human Life* (May 1907).

p. 74 Charles later described Mary as cheerful and sprightly, "a woman of culture and refinement..." *Stoughton Years*, p. 36, quoting Alfred Farlow's unpublished manuscript *Incidents in the Life of* Mrs. Eddy, p. 108.

p. 74 "one of the brightest spots in my life..." TMBEL, Rem: Alfred Farlow p. 102.

p. 74 "She was lively and entered heartily into our fun..." TMBEL, Rem: Lucy Wentworth Holmes (February 10, 1922).

p. 74 "a sort of graceful glide..." Ibid.

p. 74 "it made no difference what she wore, there always seemed to be a certain style about her." Ibid.

p. 74 "a faraway look..." Ibid.

p. 75 The Bible remained her "chart and compass..." From Mary's early poem "The Bible," published in *The Covenant* (October 1846).

p. 75 "The revelation of Truth in the understanding came to me gradually..." *S&H*, p. 109.

p. 75 "I won my way to absolute conclusions through divine revelation..." *S&H*, p. 109.

p. 75 "The question, What is Truth, is answered by demonstration..." *S&H*, p. viii.

p. 76 Mary loved to discuss her discoveries... *Stoughton Years*, pp. 29-30, quoting Alfred Farlow's unpublished manuscript *Incidents in the Life of* Mrs. Eddy, p. 107-108.

p. 76 The healing of William Scott's father John in 1869 (as told by William to A. H. L. Cobb in a letter of January 10, 1907), recounted by Mrs. Eddy in *Miscellaneous*, p. 69, has an interesting postscript. In an article published in the *Boston Traveller* in 1900, Mrs. Eddy told how Mr. Scott's wife came to her a few days after this healing and said that she'd never seen her husband hug his children "as other fathers did," and that his character had been transformed as well. Mrs. Scott thanked Mrs. Eddy not only for restoring him to health, "but more than all, I am grateful for what you have done for him morally and spiritually." *Twelve Years*, p. 56.

p. 76 there may have been some relief mixed with genuine regret at her departure... "There was a coolness grew up in the family," Lucy Wentworth later recalled. "My father thought she absorbed my mother too much and took her away from him..." *Human Life* (May 1907).

Chapter 10: WRITING HER BOOK

p. 77 [Mary] had been persuaded to move to Lynn and go into partnership with Richard Kennedy... *Life of MBE*, pp. 186-187; *Christian Healer*, p. 85.

p. 77 "What is God?" Mary Baker Eddy, *The Science of Man, by which the Sick are Healed, or Questions and Answers in Moral Science* (1876), p. 3. Multiple versions of this work existed in manuscript form as well as in published pamphlets.

p. 78 "If sickness was truth Christ would not have destroyed it..." Ibid., p. 4.

p. 78 A catechism is a summary of religious principles in question and answer form. Mary noted (*Retrospection*, p. 10) that every Sunday as a child she had to recite from the *Westminster Catechism*. Written in the 17th century, it was the chief catechism for English-speaking Presbyterians and some Congregationalists and Baptists.

p. 78 "while we may have been unable to fully grasp the truths she uttered..." *As I Knew Her*, p. 59.

p. 78 "then we admit that effect is superior to cause..." *Science of Man*, p. 4.

p. 78 "discord is not caused by the principle of music..." Ibid.

p. 78 "the sunlight that melts away darkness..." Ibid., p. 13.

p. 78 "Ye shall know the truth, and the truth shall make you free." John 8:32.

p. 79 Mary's course consisted of twelve lessons... *As I Knew Her*, p. 2.

p. 79 Sidebar/What is God? Mary ... always began her classes by giving her students a clear understanding of God... *S&H*, p. 465. "GOD. The great I AM..." *S&H*, p. 587.

p. 79 Initially, she wasn't sure what to charge "for an impartation of a knowledge of that divine power which heals..." *Retrospection*, p. 50.

p. 79 "we learned that our success or failure in healing depended on the purity of our lives..." *As I Knew Her*, p. viii.

p. 79 Mary expected her students to obey the Ten Commandments and the Beatitudes, and to follow Jesus' example... *Science of Man;* see also *As I Knew Her*, pp. 55, 102. Mary would later write: "The lecturer, teacher, or healer who is indeed a Christian Scientist ... keeps unbroken the Ten Commandments, and practises Christ's Sermon on the Mount." *Rudimental Divine Science*, pp. 11-12.

p. 79 "Many, many times each day I ask myself..." TMBEL, IC 327.44.003 (April 26, 1875).

p. 79 "the printed page of a musical score..." *Years of Discovery*, p. 247.

p. 80 "To be happy and useful is in your power..." TMBEL, L09012.

p. 80 Caption: "the term 'mother' was also sometimes used by Civil War soldiers for their nurses..." *Years of Discovery*, p. 278. A good example of this is Union Army hospital administrator Mary Ann "Mother" Bickerdyke. In 1903, "owing to the public misunderstanding of this name," Mrs. Eddy added a by-law to the *Manual* (p. 64) requesting all Christian Scientists "to drop the word *mother* and to substitute Leader."

p. 81 "enables us to determine good from evil..." *Lynn Transcript* (February 3, 1872). TMBEL, SF: Mary Baker Eddy—Writings—Articles and Pamphlets

p. 81 "Mrs. Glover and her Science [are] practically dead and buried..." *Lynn Transcript* (February 24, 1872).

p. 81 Mary ... confided to her old friend Mrs. Ellis that she felt keenly the mental anguish of the very public debate. TMBEL, L05663 (February 6, 1872).

p. 81 She told her students to stop this practice. TMBEL, L09662; *Years of Discovery*, pp. 265-266.

p. 81 Richard Kennedy's refusal to comply and subsequent dissolution of business partnership with Mary are detailed in *As I Knew Her*, p. 3, and *Years of Discovery*, pp. 266-268.

p. 81 "Now go, write it before them..." Isaiah 30:8.

p. 81 "There was no good reason for my moving..." James F. Gilman diary entry (August 19, 1893), quoted in *Painting a Poem*, p. 132.

p. 82 "He was reduced to almost a skeleton..." *S&H* (first edition), p. 353. In her reminiscence, Helen Nixon adds a postscript to this healing. By the time Mary left the house, not only was the baby well, but the woman's husband (who was suffering from rheumatism) and young daughter (who was deaf) were also healed. TMBEL, Rem: Helen Nixon.

p. 82 "could not understand it, and would not attempt to publish it..." *Twelve Years*, p. 40; *As I Knew Her*, p. 46.

p. 82 "Its title, Science and Health, came to me in the silence of night..." *Message for 1902*, p. 15.

p. 83 "to drop both the book and the title..." Ibid., p. 15.

p. 83 "and pointed out that identical phrase..." Ibid., p. 16. See Luke 1:77 of the Wycliffe Bible.

p. 83 "I named it *Christian*, because it is compassionate..." *Retrospection*, p. 25.

p. 83 "Such a flood tide of truth was lifted upon me..." TMBEL, A10934.

p. 83 "a scribe under orders..." *Miscellaneous*, p. 311.

p. 83 "After two years and a half incessant labor seven days in a week..." *As I Knew Her*, p. 47.

p. 83 "Although she was writing ..." Ibid., p. 34.

p. 84 "I have known her when nearly crushed with sorrow, but she wrote on..." Ibid., p. 127.

p. 84 At one point, with no explanation, Brown stopped work altogether. *Retrospection*, p. 38.

p. 85 On the wall was a framed copy of her favorite Bible verse... *Human Life* (July 1907); *S&H*, p. 340.

p. 85 "the divine purpose that this should be done..." *Retrospection*, pp. 37-38.

p. 86 "had learned that this Science must be demonstrated by healing..." *S&H*, p. ix; *Retrospection*, p. 35.

p. 86 "This book is indeed wholly original, but it will never be read." *Retrospection*, p. 37.

p. 86 "The book is certainly original and contains much that will do good." *Christian Advocate* of Buffalo, quoted in *As I Knew Her*, p. 51.

p. 86 "Accept my thanks for your remarkable volume…" TMBEL, SF: A. Bronson Alcott (January 17, 1876).

p. 86 "I have come to comfort you…" *Pulpit*, p. 5; TMBEL, Rem: Clara Shannon.

p. 86 "I hail with joy your voice…" *Miscellaneous*, p. 455.

p. 87 "Love, meekness, charity or patience with everybody…" TMBEL, L07808.

p. 87 "get students into the field as practitioners…" TMBEL, L07816.

Chapter 11: A WEDDING

p. 88 a festive spread of cake and lemonade… *Lynn Reporter* (February 10, 1877).

p. 88 True, he had a "reserve force…" Arthur Buswell, quoted in *The Genealogy and Life of Asa Gilbert Eddy* by Mary Beecher LM, p. 19.

p. 89 Christiana Godfrey's healing is recounted by her daughter Mary Godfrey Parker in *We Knew MBE Vol. I*, pp. 11-13.

p. 89 "He was calm, clear and strong and so kind…" TMBEL, L09897.

p. 89 "any opposition or ridicule of the truth…" *Genealogy and Life*, p. 19.

p. 89 "He was not easily ruffled." TMBEL Rem: Clara Choate.

p. 90 Sidebar/Gilbert Eddy: "red cheeks, and quite a dandy…" *Genealogy and Life*, p. ix. It was Gilbert who would later organize the first Christian Science Sunday School… *Retrospection*, p. 42. "the sweetest disposition…" L02059 (June 27, 1882). "He was always the kind husband and friend…" Julia Bartlett in *We Knew MBE Vol. I*, p. 47. For more information on Gilbert Eddy, see *Human Life* (July 1907), *MBE: Christian Healer*, and *Longyear Museum Quarterly News* (Autumn 1969).

p. 90 "buoyant hopefulness…" *Genealogy and Life*, p. 35.

p. 90 "He was ever on the alert…" Ibid., p. 34.

p. 90 Caption: "wore his hair more naturally…" Mary Godfrey Parker in *We Knew MBE Vol. I*, p. 8.

p. 91 "Why, your child was all right all the time…" *Genealogy and Life*, p. 41.

p. 91 "good exercise after sitting at the writing-table so long…" Ibid., p. 30.

p. 91 "unworthy to be the standard bearer…" TMBEL, IC 327.44.006 (May 30, 1877).

p. 92 Caption: "at one time stones were thrown through her windows…" *What Mrs. Eddy Said*, p. 57.

p. 92 "little band of earnest seekers after Truth…" *Manual*, p. 17.

p. 92 "To organize a church designed to commemorate the word and works of our Master…" Ibid.

p. 93 Sidebar/Hymn of Christian Science: "The history that you celebrate …" TMBEL, L09607.

p. 93 "I have lectured in parlors 14 years…" TMBEL, L02463.

p. 94 Caption: "sweeping up bits of stray trash and orange peel…" TMBEL, Rem: Clara Shannon.

p. 94 A selected list of Mary's early lecture and sermon titles can be found in the *MBEL Magazine* (Winter/Spring 2002).

p. 94 "the book of books…" TMBEL, A10360A.

p. 94 "Christian Science is proof not profession…" TMBEL, A10585C.

p. 94 "Christian Scientists should so live that they will not need to tune themselves like a violin…" *In My True Light*, p. 602.

p. 94 "instead of serving Christianity on ice…" LM, *"First Impressions of* Mrs. Eddy *in the Pulpit"* by Arthur Buswell, pp. 2-3.

p. 94 "one of restful serenity…" TMBEL, Rem: Clara Choate.

Chapter 12: GEORGE GLOVER COMES TO TOWN

p. 95 Before North Dakota and South Dakota became states, they were part of what was called the Dakota Territory. (The name "Dakota" refers to a branch of the Sioux tribes who occupied the area at the time.) Officially created by Congress on March 2, 1861, the Territory of Dakota included much of present-day Montana and Wyoming. The territory was reduced in size over the next few years, then divided in two and admitted to the Union as the 39th and 40th states on November 2, 1889. More information can be found on the Library of Congress website (http://memory.loc.gov/ammem/award97/ndfahtml/ngp _ nd _ terr.html).

p. 95 A wealth of information about George Glover II's early years, his service for the Union Army during the Civil War, and his life on the frontier can be found in the eight-part series "Family: From New England to the Black Hills," by Jewel Spangler Smaus, *Longyear Museum Quarterly News* (Spring 1983, Autumn 1983, Summer 1984, Autumn 1984).

p. 96 "very jolly and a good honest man…" TMBEL, Rem: Jessie Hughes Roberts.

p. 96 "When he'd walk, he'd step right out…" George Glover III reminiscence, *Longyear Museum Quarterly News* (Summer 1984).

p. 96 George decided to try his hand at freighting. TMBEL, IC 197.32.002 (January 14, 1878).

p. 96 Two of the more colorful characters in the history of the American West are Wild Bill Hickock and Calamity Jane. Like Mary's son, George, Hickock fought (and reportedly spied) for the Union Army during the Civil War. Later he, too, became a frontiersman, and gained notoriety as a lawman, scout, marksman, and professional gambler. He also worked briefly as an actor with Buffalo Bill Cody's company. (Library of Congress website: http://memory.loc.gov/ammem/today/may27.html - scroll to bottom of page) Born Martha Jane Canary, Calamity Jane was a frontierswoman, a crack shot and a fearless rider. She worked as an Army scout in the 1870s and later for the Pony Express, riding the dangerous route between Deadwood and Custer City, South Dakota. Like Hickock, she also worked in Buffalo Bill Cody's

Wild West Show. (National Women's History Museum website: http://www.nwhm.org/education-resources/biography/biographies/martha-jane-cannary/)

p. 97 Sidebar/The Gold Rush Of 1876: For more information, see The Newberry Library website (http://publications.newberry.org/lewisandclark/newnation/miners/blackhills.html); the City of Deadwood website (www.cityofdeadwood.com); and Wikipedia (http://en.wikipedia.org/wiki/Black _ Hills _ Gold _ Rush).

p. 97 "The [Black] Hills are immensely rich in gold…" TMBEL, IC-197.32.003 (August 12, 1879).

p. 98 George had kept his mother's picture with him all during the war. George Glover III reminiscence, *Longyear Museum Quarterly News* (Spring 1983).

p. 98 George looked every inch the frontiersman. Mary Godfrey Parker in *We Knew MBE Vol. I,* pp. 24-25.

p. 99 His mother explained these constant upsets as the result of "animal magnetism…" The chapter "Animal Magnetism Unmasked" (pp. 100-106 in *S&H*) gives a fuller explanation of this subject. See also *Miscellaneous,* p. 97, and *S&H* pp. 484 and 584.

p. 99 "The carnal mind is enmity against God: for it is not subject to the law of God, neither indeed can be." Romans 8:7.

p. 100 "I will search you out and shoot you like a mad dog…" George Glover II interview in the *World* (March 3, 1907).

p. 100 "loved him dearly, and was very proud of him…" *As I Knew Her,* p. 53.

p. 100 "I got the dear child into my class…" TMBEL, L03477 (July 20, 1891).

p. 100 "home being so far away…" TMBEL, EOR10 Minutes of the Christian Scientist Association (November 22, 1879); *Years of Trial,* p. 70.

p. 100 "We came very near being all burnt up…" TMBEL, IC 197.32.006 (January 11, 1880).

p. 101 "My father expressed much concern about my eyes…" TMBEL, Rem: Mary Glover Billings.

Chapter 13: LOSS IS GAIN

p. 102 "My boy, you will be ruined for life…" *As I Knew Her,* p. xi.

p. 102 "my dear friend … sort of an adopted mother." Ibid., p. vii.

p. 102 In the summer of 1880, Mary was hurt… TMBEL, L02095.

p. 102 He was busy testing his "attraction…" TMBEL, IC 197.32.008 (April 24, 1881).

p. 102 "Tell Father that my attractions for minerals are perfect…" Ibid.

p. 103 "As your wife says much has gone into those mines but what has come out of them?" TMBEL, L02082 (May 4, 1881).

p. 103 "When God called the author to proclaim His Gospel to this age…" *S&H,* p. xi.

p. 103 "Jesus mapped out the path for others." *S&H,* p. 38.

p. 103 "Mrs. Eddy's works are the outgrowths of her life…" From Gilbert Eddy's foreword to *S&H* (third edition, 1881), p. xii.

p. 104 "I have worked harder here than ever…" TMBEL, L02499.

p. 104 "I have awakened a ripple of interest…" TMBEL, L02498.

p. 104 "He had no sense of his crime…" *Miscellaneous*, p. 112.

p. 104 "I said to him briefly, that this was an excellent opportunity to put to test our talk of the afternoon…" TMBEL, A11418; *Twelve Years*, p. 83.

p. 105 Accounts of Gilbert's passing can be found in Julia Bartlett's reminiscence in *We Knew MBE Vol. I*, p. 63, and *Human Life* (October 1907).

p. 105 "I never shall master this point of missing him all the time…" TMBEL, L04089.

p. 106 "It is beautiful here the hills vales and lakes are lovely…" TMBEL, L07691.

p. 106 "Thou … shalt not remember the reproach of thy widowhood any more." Isaiah 54:4. (The verse that follows this begins: "For thy Maker is thine husband.")

p. 106 "I would like more than ever to be myself again…" TMBEL, L10643.

p. 106 "I have on hand the largest class I ever had…" TMBEL, L04885.

p. 107 Caption: "The light that shone into my thought has never left me…" TMBEL, Rem: Janet Colman. For more information on Janet Colman, see *Longyear Museum Quarterly News* (Autumn 1977).

p. 107 "There were fourteen in my class when I studied in 1883…" Ibid.

p. 108 "Dear reader, the purpose of our paper is the desire of our heart…" *CSJ* (April 1883).

p. 109 Caption: "Why is Adam the patron saint of Western pork raisers?" *CSJ* (February 1884).

Chapter 14: SONS OLD AND NEW

p. 111 "Dear Mother, I beliv [sic] you owe me a letter…" TMBEL, L18984 (October 23, 1887).

p. 111 By the end of the decade, parlor lectures… In her article "Broader Bounds" (CSS August 7, 2006), Judy Huenneke traces the evolution of the Wednesday evening testimony meetings held in Christian Science churches around the world today. The popular Victorian tradition of parlor (or living room) lectures, she explains, were "not too formal, definitely interactive, and spiced with an element of spontaneity that was probably very intriguing to audiences." In January of 1895, Mrs. Eddy sent a rousing letter (TMBEL, L05043) to Judge Septimus Hanna, then First Reader of the church, requesting that he read it aloud at the next Friday evening meeting (whose gatherings had faded by this time from public sharing to semi-private sessions focused on Bible study): "My dear Students, Make broader your bounds for blessing the people. Have Friday evening meetings to benefit the people. Learn to forget what you should not remember viz. self, and live for the good you do.

Conduct your meetings by repeating and demonstrating practical Christian Science. Tell what this Science does for yourself and will do for others. Speak from experience of its Founder—noting her self sacrifice as the way in Christian Science. Be meek, let your mottoes for this meeting be, Who shall be least and servant and 'Little children love one another.'"

p. 111 "I am daft with business..." TMBEL, L11014.

p. 112 "Feed My Sheep," *CSJ* (March 1887).

p. 113 Sidebar/"Captain, why don't you heal your wife yourself?" Joseph Eastaman recounts this series of events in the May 1892 issue of the *CSJ* ("The Travail of My Soul"). For more background information on Captain Eastaman and his wife, Mary, see *We Knew MBE, Vol. II.*

p. 114 "Since 'Science and Health' was published, I have been constantly in receipt of letters..." *Historical Sketch of Metaphysical Healing*, p. 15.

p. 116 Mrs. Eddy wrote back, urging them to postpone their journey. TMBEL, L02085 (October 31, 1887).

p. 116 "sweet" Gershom ... TMBEL, L02105; "bright" Evelyn ... TMBEL, L02102; "my dear little namesake" Mary ... TMBEL, L02081.

p. 116 "I want your children educated!" TMBEL, L02089.

p. 116 George Glover III recounts his father's longing for "a regular mother" in *Longyear Museum Quarterly News* (Winter 1983-84).

p. 116 "Hope you are happy and safe at home..." TMBEL, N00011.

p. 117 Sidebar/CSA & NSA: "to meet the broader wants of humanity..." *Retrospection*, p. 52.

p. 117 "but if Christian Science is better, I want it..." TMBEL, IC 205a.34.003 (June 24, 1887).

p. 118 "My Dear Spiritual Mother..." TMBEL, IC 205a.34.004 (November 30, 1887).

p. 118 "Sunday the 8th ... was a most glorious day to me..." TMBEL, Rem: E. J. Foster Eddy, "My Revelation Night of July 8th, 1888."

p. 118 "in business, home life, and life work..." SF: E. J. Foster Eddy—Adoption petition of November 1888.

p. 119 "my son in Dakota is a victor at law..." TMBEL, L02256 (September 22, 1890).

p. 119 "I should think you would be the terror of the West in such matters." TMBEL, L02099.

p. 119 "Science and the senses are at war..." *CSJ* (August 1888). This passage would be amended slightly for inclusion in *Miscellaneous* (p. 101) to read: "Christian Science and the senses are at war. It is a revolutionary struggle. We already have had two in this nation; and they began and ended in a contest for the true idea, for human liberty and rights. Now cometh a third struggle; for the freedom of health, holiness, and the attainment of heaven."

p. 120 "When the speaker concluded the audience rose en masse..." *Chicago Times* (June 15, 1888).

p. 121 Caption: More information on Susan B. Anthony's connection to Christian Science and the copy of *Science and Health* that she owned can be found on the Mary Baker Eddy Library website: (http://www.marybakereddylibrary.org/collections/research/objects/item/susan-b-anthony).

p. 121 "I remember of hearing you speak in the Chicago Music Hall…" TMBEL, IC 519.56.005 (June 19, 1903).

Chapter 15: GENERAL-IN-CHIEF

p. 122 "huge conspiracy in our midst…" TMBEL, V01111.

p. 122 "I bless Him for the faithful ones…" TMBEL, V03390.

p. 122 "I never felt my Father so near…" TMBEL, V01069.

p. 123 "Our Cause has had a great propulsion…" TMBEL, L04491.

p. 123 "O, the love that was expressed in our Leader's face…" TMBEL, Rem: Clara Shannon.

p. 123 "Love will meet and destroy every claim of error." TMBEL, EOR10 Minutes of the Christian Scientist Association (October 3, 1888).

p. 123 "examining the situation prayerfully and carefully…" *Retrospection*, p. 44.

p. 123 "the headquarters of Christian Science…" TMBEL, L04129; TMBEL, L10677. *CSJ* (November 1893), later reprinted in *Miscellaneous*, p. 156.

p. 124 "I was simply astounded…" TMBEL, IC 363 (August, 1889).

p. 124 "They said as far as spiritual things were concerned…" Julia Bartlett recounts this anecdote in her reminiscence, and an abbreviated version appears in *We Knew MBE Vol. I*, pp. 81-83.

p. 125 "I have had little else this year but loss and cross…" TMBEL, L13959 (November 2, 1889). Two months later, Mrs. Eddy would echo this sentiment in another letter: "The test of my dear students this year in following by faith the order of Science is so sweet so comforting to me that but for this it would have seemed insupportable to have borne the cross of the old year." TMBEL, L05736 (January 2, 1890).

p. 125 "Be it understood that I do not require…" *CSJ* (December 1889).

p. 125 "She had previously been the Teacher…" William Lyman Johnson letter to the Board of Directors (July 1, 1925), quoted in *Years of Trial*, p. 256.

Chapter 16: THE 50TH EDITION AND A "SWEET HOME"

p. 126 Peace was what Mary longed for… "Many times I wish I could go to some place where I was not known and find the peace that I long for," wrote Mrs. Eddy to a friend on May 12, 1889 (V03101), shortly before she left Boston. And around this same time she wrote to her son George, "I want quiet and a Christian life alone with God, when I can find intervals for a little rest." TMBEL, L02085 (October 31, 1887).

p. 126 "God has given me new lessons…" TMBEL, L04139 (December 15, 1890).

p. 126 "women may become mothers…" Josephine Woodbury, "Christian Science and Its Prophetess," *The Arena Magazine* (May 1899).

p. 127 "Be patient as you can with her shortcomings…" TMBEL, L07752.

p. 128 "I and my students greatly desire…" TMBEL, L02215.

p. 128 "the new volume seems to take us back to the College…" Lanson P. Norcross's lead article in the *CSJ* of March 1891 was reprinted in full, again as a lead article, the following month, as an editor's note explains, "by request of the readers."

p. 128 "It gives me joy unspeakable…" TMBEL, L03475. On April 18, 1891, Mrs. Eddy would also write to Edward and Caroline Bates, "I made it a special point … to so systematize the statement of Science as to compel the scholar to see it is demonstrably true, and can be understood on the basis of proof." TMBEL, L08229.

p. 129 "Many happy New years to you all…" TMBEL, L02098 (January 3, 1892).

p. 129 "My Dear Grandmother…" TMBEL, IC 197.32.014 (December 11, 1889).

p. 129 "Now dear one, I have a request to make…" TMBEL, N00074 (January 3, 1892).

p. 130 "You seem to know just what I want…" TMBEL, L03403 (August 31, 1891).

p. 130 Sidebar/Home Sweet Home: "The strongest tie I have ever felt…" *Twelve Years*, p. 213. William Rathvon would also recall this quote, in slightly different words, in his reminiscence. "Oh! The singing birds and glorious view from my 'sweet home'…" TMBEL, L06073 (August 2, 1892). "well-ordered, well-kept country residence…" Sibyl Wilbur, "An Interview with Rev. Mary Baker G. Eddy," CSS (June 17, 1905). Wilbur's delightful eyewitness account is just one of many sources for information on life at Pleasant View. See also reminiscences of numerous household workers including Clara Shannon, Joseph Mann and Calvin Hill (TMBEL), as well as *Twelve Years*, pp. 211-233.

p. 130 Caption: "as though they were great pets…" Wilbur, CSS (June 17, 1905).

p. 132 "my 'pigeon' …" TMBEL, L05990. Mrs. Eddy once said of Laura, "She is the best, the kindest and dearest girl in all the world to me" (TMBEL, L07855). Laura's fellow household workers sang her praises as well. Adelaide Still, Mrs. Eddy's maid, noted in her reminiscence, "Of her love, gratitude, and self-sacrifice for our Leader, I cannot say enough. . . . No one could have been more faithful in the performance of her duties, or have fulfilled them more lovingly." And in his reminiscence, William Rathvon added, "The world may some day know of the debt it owes this woman, but it never can repay her."

p. 132 "Has Mrs. Eddy lost her power to heal?" *CSJ* (June 1884), later republished in *Miscellaneous*, p. 54.

p. 132 "I am healed…" TMBEL, IC 275.41.028 (September 30, 1891).

p. 133 "my life-purpose…" *CSJ* (August 1892), later reprinted in *Miscellaneous*, p. 207.

p. 133 "My fourth of July boy is as fat as a pig..." TMBEL, IC 197.32.016 (December 16, 1891).

p. 133 "Accept my more than thanks for your heart..." TMBEL, L02100 (January 16, 1892).

p. 134 Sidebar/Always Speak to the Horses: "This is my time for communion with God..." TMBEL, Rem: Maurine Campbell. "I have uttered some of my best prayers in a carriage." TMBEL, Rem: William Rathvon. "Always speak to the horses..." Wilbur, CSS (June 17, 1905). "When she returned from her drive..." TMBEL, Rem: Clara Shannon.

p. 134 "Except [sic] my thanks..." TMBEL, L02100.

p. 134 "Roses are red..." TMBEL, IC 197.32.01 (April 1892).

p. 135 Caption: "little chubby darling..." TMBEL, L02117.

p. 135 He trundled his small wheeled toy... George Glover III reminiscence, *Longyear Museum Quarterly News* (Autumn 1984).

p. 135 Though Mary would have loved to see all of her grandchildren more often... TMBEL, N00155 (November 26, 1897).

p. 135 "That was always the difference between George and myself..." Eugenie Paul Jefferson heard about this incident from Mary's son, and later recorded it in her reminiscence. TMBEL, Rem: Eugenie Paul Jefferson.

p. 135 "If you can help him at this time..." TMBEL, IC 197.32.025 (March 30, 1894).

Chapter 17: A "PRAYER IN STONE"

p. 136 Mrs. Eddy asked the newly-formed board to appoint Rev. Easton... TMBEL, L00043 (February 20, 1893).

p. 136 Mrs. Eddy ... deeded this land over to the Board of Directors in September of 1892... *The Mother Church*, p. 2.

p. 137 Mrs. Eddy wrote to a select number of her students... TMBEL, Rem: Septimus J. Hanna; Mary Baker Eddy, "Laying the Corner Stone," *CSJ* (June 1894).

p. 137 "The church must be built in 1894..." TMBEL, L03294.

p. 137 "Our church edifice must be built in 1894..." *CSJ* (December 1893). The punctuation was amended slightly for inclusion in *Miscellaneous*, p. 319.

p. 138 "The Mother's Evening Prayer." In his reminiscence (p. 59), Adam Dickey records an interesting conversation with Mrs. Eddy that occurred when she edited the final stanza: "She made a change in the words 'mother finds her home and far-off rest' by erasing 'far-off' and inserting the word 'heavenly' as it now reads. She asked me what I thought of the change. I told her that to me it conveyed a much better thought than as it was then written. I said that 'her home and far-off rest' carried the impression that she had a long and toilsome way ahead of her. She said, 'That is just the thing I want to get rid of.'" TMBEL, Rem: Adam H. Dickey.

p. 138 For more background information on the Bateses involvement in the building project, see *The Miracle in Stone* by Margaret M. Pinkham, and also the reminiscences of Edward Bates and Caroline Bates (TMBEL).

p. 139 "all things are possible..." Mark 10:27.

p. 139 "Finish the tower and plaster the church." TMBEL, Rem: Caroline Bates.

p. 140 "We will go up and find a way to do it." Ibid.

p. 140 "Woman, true to her instinct..." *Pulpit,* p. 9.

p. 141 "I have all this force of men to put this plaster on..." TMBEL, Rem: Edward Bates.

p. 143 "and gave instructions as to particular points..." TMBEL, Rem: Caroline Bates.

p. 143 "the work progressed rapidly..." TMBEL, Rem: Edward Bates.

p. 143 William Johnson, one of the Directors, slept on a pile of burlap bags... *Rolling Away the Stone,* p. 216.

p. 144 Caption: "our prayer in stone..." *Miscellaneous,* pp. 141 & 320.

p. 144 Sidebar/A Church of Her Own: "I shall have a church of my own some day!" *As I Knew Her,* p. 15; *Years of Discovery,* p. 288. Joseph Armstrong's *The Mother Church* is a good place to start for a closer look at the building's details and the story of the construction project. TMBEL, L02720.

p. 145 "but we were not the army of retreat..." TMBEL, Rem: Edward Bates.

p. 145 "Mrs. Eddy's demonstration was complete to the minute." Ibid.

Chapter 18: THE *CHURCH MANUAL* AS GUIDE

p. 146 Mrs. Eddy's first visit to The Mother Church is described by both Clara Shannon and Julia Bartlett in their reminiscences (TMBEL).

p. 146 "Ah, children, you are the bulwarks of freedom..." *Pulpit,* p. 9.

p. 146 Caption: Janet Colman's daughter Ruth was one of the early Busy Bees. TMBEL, SF: TFCCS, Edifices, Original–Mother's Room–"Busy Bees".

p. 147 "You simply feel as if she was your best friend..." *CSJ* (July 1895).

p. 147 A man visiting Boston that day also heard Mrs. Eddy preach... Laura Lathrop, "A Wonderful Transformation," *CSJ* (February 1897).

p. 147 This kind of healing was exactly what Mrs. Eddy expected... She was reported to have once said "that she longed for the day to come when no one could enter a Christian Science church, no matter how sick or how sorrowing that one might be, without being healed, and that this day can come only when every member of the church studies and demonstrates the truth contained in the Lesson-Sermon, and takes with him to the service the consciousness thus prepared " Florence Clerihew Boyd, "Healing the Multitudes," CSS (July I, 1916).

p. 147 "is designed to be built on the Rock, Christ..." *Manual,* p. 19.

p. 148 Sidebar/The Busy Bees: "I love children more than pen can tell..." TMBEL, L05797. "I asked God to direct my steps..." Rem: Maurine Campbell "*The Story of the Busy Bees: An Account of Pioneer Experiences in Christian Science*" by Maurine Campbell, offers a window into this engaging Chapter in the church's history.

p. 149 "were not arbitrary opinions nor dictatorial demands..." *Miscellaneous*, p. 148.

p. 150 Sidebar/Mary Baker Eddy's Definition of Church: "CHURCH. The structure of Truth and Love..." *S&H*, p. 583.

p. 150 Sidebar/The Cross and Crown: More information on the evolution of the Cross and Crown design, a legally protected trademark of The First Church of Christ, Scientist, can be found on the Mary Baker Eddy Library website (http://www. marybakereddylibrary.org/collections/research/ask-aresearcher/how-did-cross-and-crown-emblem), and in an article by Archibald McLellan in the *Christian Science Journal* (June 1908). McLellan notes: "To those of our readers who have been searching for some hidden significance in the larger cross, we may say for their reassurance that the cross which we are called upon to bear as Christian Scientists in no larger or heavier than heretofore. What we most need to impress upon our thought is that the crown has been brought nearer than ever through the ministry of Mrs. Eddy."

p. 150 "I was compelled by a sense of responsibility to put up the bars for my flock." TMBEL, L04777.

p. 150 "My students were preaching and were sending me copies of their sermons..." Daisette McKenzie in *We Knew MBE Vol. I*, p. 252.

p. 151 Sidebar/Evolution of the Tenets of The Mother Church: "important points..." *S&H*, p. 497. An additional line appears below the 1879 tenets: "We give no credence to spiritualism or mediumship and never in any case give or take medicine." TMBEL, EOR13.

p. 152 "This will tend to spiritualize thought..." TMBEL, L02748.

p. 152 "Humbly, and as I believe, Divinely directed..." Mary Baker Eddy, "Church and School," *CSJ* (April 1895), later reprinted in *Miscellaneous*, p. 313.

p. 152 "Could a church replace an eloquent preacher with two Readers..." *Twelve Years*, p. 183.

p. 152 Sidebar/The Bible Lesson-Sermon: "It was understood that these topics covered the course of instruction..." William P. McKenzie, "Preaching Universal and World Wide," *CSJ* (April 1916). "The Readers of The Mother Church and of all its branch churches..." *Manual*, p. 31. Term limits would eventually be set at three years for Readers in The Mother Church.

Chapter 19: THE CENTER BUT NOT THE BOUNDARY

p. 155 She wanted to go "like everything..." Alice Noble Converse diary, quoted in *Golden Days*, p. 167 and 186/n21.

p. 156 "We must hear Mrs. Eddy..." Ibid., p. 167 and 186/n18.

p. 156 She was a good civic neighbor... *Twelve Years*, pp. 244-247; TMBEL, Rem: Clara Shannon; *Longyear Museum Quarterly News* (Winter 1970-71).

p. 157 Henry Morrison's healing is recounted in a letter from his daughter Adelaide Morrison Mooney (June 19, 1943). TMBEL, Rem: Adelaide Morrison Mooney.

p. 157 There were countless other similar incidents over the years… TMBEL, Rem: Minnie Ford Mortlock describes her healing of tuberculosis in her reminiscence; TMBEL, Rem: Clara Shannon tells of the dry well filling overnight in hers; TMBEL, Rem: Ludie M. Waldron recounts the healing of the lineman; and *Years of Authority*, p. 468-469/n2, describes Rev. Larmour's healing.

p. 158 "I rise at about 6 o'clock …" TMBEL, L12892 (July 10, 1907).

p. 158 "Three times a day, I retire to seek the divine blessing…" *CSJ* (April 1885), later reprinted in *Miscellaneous*, p. 133.

p. 158 Caption: "intended to hold guard over Truth, Life, and Love…" "Something in a Name," by Mary Baker Eddy, *The Christian Science Monitor* (November 25, 1908). This was later reprinted in *Miscellany*, p. 353.

p. 158 "talk with God…" TMBEL, Rem: Eleanor Winslow.

p. 159 "alone with God…" TMBEL, L02085 (October 31, 1887).

p. 159 "Home is the dearest spot on earth…" *S&H*, p. 58.

p. 159 "To-day I have entertained letters from Congo Free State…" *Boston Journal*, June 21, 1899, reprinted in the *CSS* (June 29, 1899). The "minister" Mrs. Eddy referred to was Edwin Hurd Conger, who held the rather splendid title "Envoy Extraordinary and Minister Plenipotentiary to China."

p. 159 "Just one more surprise…" TMBEL, Rem: Michael Meehan (quoting William E. Curtis).

p. 160 So important did she consider this book that she requested via the next month's *Journal*… "Notice," by Mary Baker Eddy, included this statement: "'Miscellaneous Writings' is calculated to prepare the minds of all true thinkers to understand the Christian Science Text-book more correctly than a student can." *CSJ* (March 1897).

p. 160 "practical teachings indispensable to the culture and achievements…" *Miscellaneous*, dedication page.

p. 160 "I have wrought day and night this year…" TMBEL, L02402 (December 20, 1898).

p. 161 "We were all very happy to be called…" Emma Easton Newman in *We Knew MBE Vol. I*, p. 242.

p. 161 a gift designed "to spiritualize the Field…" *Twelve Years*, p. 99.

p. 161 "Only two lessons!" Septimus J. Hanna, "An Important Event," *CSJ* (December 1898). The editorial ran anonymously, but Emma Shipman attributes it to Hanna in *We Knew MBE Vol. I*, p. 312.

p. 161 Their teacher was "perfectly natural. She was ever alert…" Emma Shipman in *We Knew MBE Vol. I*, p. 309.

p. 161 "fresh impulse" Ibid., p. 307; *Miscellany*, p. 244.

p. 162 "because I want my teaching carried on..." Emma Shipman in *We Knew MBE Vol. I*, p. 313.

p. 162 "a world more bright..." Mary Baker Eddy, "Christ My Refuge," *Miscellaneous*, pp. 396-397.

p. 162 Mrs. Eddy would later amend her poem "Christmas Morn" slightly, changing the fourth line of the first stanza to "Nor dawn nor day!"; the third line of the third stanza to "Beloved, replete, by flesh embound"; the fourth stanza to "Thou gentle beam of living Love,/ And deathless Life!/ Truth infinite, —so far above/ All mortal strife,"; and adding "cruel" before "creed" in the first line of the final stanza.

Chapter 20: SONS NEAR AND FAR

p. 163 She urged her namesake Mary to learn to type... TMBEL, L02123.

p. 163 "I have got the machine and it is a very fine one..." TMBEL, L16995.

p. 163 "Georgie speaks a patriotic piece..." Ibid.

p. 164 "I was only ten years old ..." George Glover III reminiscence. *Longyear Museum Quarterly News* (Spring 1984). A wealth of interesting detail about this surprise Christmas present from Mary to her son George and his family can be found in this issue, as well as in the one for Summer 1984. See also "A Beautiful Christmas Gift," CSS (January 1, 1900); *Life of MBE*, p. 349; *Years of Authority*, p. 275.

p. 165 "one of the most elegant and beautiful gifts..." A news item from the *Lead City Call* about the Glovers' new mansion was picked up by the *St. Joseph (Mo.) Daily Gazette*, and reprinted in the CSS (January 1, 1900).

p. 165 "I am alone in the world..." TMBEL, L02127.

p. 165 "sharper than vinegar to the teeth..." TMBEL, L11047.

p. 165 "see that you start rightly in publishing this year..." TMBEL, L01806. In another letter to her adopted son a few days later, Mrs. Eddy underlined the importance of this work, noting, "You are, in your office as publisher of my works, next to their author the most important Teacher of Christian Science on earth." TMBEL, L01808.

p. 165 "Your books could not be audited..." TMBEL, L01962 (July 12, 1895).

p. 166 "We found in him an agreeable personality..." *Mary Baker Eddy and Her Books* (Boston: The Christian Science Publishing Society, 1950) by William Dana Orcutt, p. 47.

p. 166 "If ever I wear out from serving students..." "Advice to Students" *CSJ* (August 1891), later reprinted in slightly revised form in *Miscellaneous*, p. 303.

p. 166 In the summer of 1896, Mrs. Eddy finally took the publisher's work away... More information on the break with Foster Eddy can be found in *Rolling Away the Stone*, pp. 161-162, and *Years of Authority*, p. 113.

p. 167 "persistent unswerving fidelity..." TMBEL, IC 205b.34.048 (February 28, 1901).

p. 167 "I will have Mrs. Eddy's place..." TMBEL, Rem: Antoinette M. Mosher, quoted in *Years of Authority*, p. 354/n68.

p. 167 Mrs. Eddy ... felt keenly the toll of this bid for revenge. *Years of Authority*, pp. 159, 170; TMBEL, L08531.

p. 167 Mary Baker G. Eddy, "Satisfied," *CSJ* (February 1900).

p. 168 "Forgive, be unselfish, meek and Christlike..." TMBEL, L14525.

p. 168 Frederick Peabody unexpectedly rested his case... This is what is sometimes referred to today as a "motion for a directed verdict." At the judge's request, a verdict was returned, even though the defense had made no case and the case did not go to the jury.

p. 168 Night and day he was at her service... John Salchow in *We Knew MBE Vol. I*, pp. 386-387; *Years of Authority*, p. 244; a brief description of Calvin can also be found in "Mrs. Eddy in Good Health," a March 5, 1905 article from the *New York Herald* that was reprinted in the *CSJ* (April 1905).

p. 168 Sidebar/Calvin Frye: "I don't know how he does as much as he does..." TMBEL, Rem: Calvin Hill. Hill was also present, along with Lewis Strang, when Calvin Frye made the following statement: "There is no blood relationship between Mrs. Eddy and Mr. Frye; but having been in her employ and lived in her family for over twenty years, he has an affection for her as a son would have for his mother in caring for her interests and in trying to promote her comfort." TMBEL, A11532. "... a quiet, earnest man with a clear and placid countenance..." *Human Life* (November 1907). "... honest devotion to Mrs. Eddy..." TMBEL, Rem: Minnie B. Weygandt. For additional background information on Calvin Frye, see *Human Life* (November 1907); *Christian Healer*, pp. 446-447; Joseph Mann's reminiscence; *Years of Trial*, pp. 136-137; "Calvin A. Frye," by Kathleen Wagner Starrett, *Longyear Museum Quarterly News* (Autumn 1990).

p. 170 Caption: "He has done more practical work in my behalf..." TMBEL, L00352. In this letter to the Board of Directors, Mrs. Eddy mentions having given Calvin a "token of gratitude." That "token" was a check for $1,000—worth more than $25,000 in today's dollars—given as a thank you for standing by her side for 21 years to help the Cause of Christian Science.

p. 170 While he was there, he made derogatory remarks... TMBEL, IC 152a.24.030 (April 4, 1903).

p. 170 "Your remarks about me are so unjust..." TMBEL, V00392.

p. 170 Eva Thompson, a friend of his two daughters... TMBEL, Rem: Irving Tomlinson includes a letter from Eva (August 7, 1905).

p. 171 "We have two aims in our work here..." TMBEL, Rem: William Rathvon.

p. 171 "Glover naturally believed he was shut out from his mother..." TMBEL, SF: Mary Baker Eddy–Lawsuits–"Next Friends"–Miscellaneous Documents, untitled document attributed to Calvin Frye.

Chapter 21: THE HOUSE OF MYSTERY

p. 172 On Sunday, October 14, 1906, there was a sharp knock on the front door... TMBEL, L16215. Lewis Strang memorandum (October 26, 1906).

p. 172 "House of Mystery" *New York American* (August 26, 1907), reprinted in the CSS (August 31, 1907).

p. 173 "Of all the history of lies every written..." TMBEL, L01707.

p. 173 "She is certainly a well-preserved woman for her years..." TMBEL, L16215.

p. 174 "The report of my death was an exaggeration." *Bartlett's Familiar Quotations* (New York: Little, Brown and Co., 2002), p. 562. Mark Twain's fascination with Mary Baker Eddy and Christian Science makes for an interesting historical footnote. What began as poking fun in typical Twain style evolved into open criticism, and he went so far as to write a derogatory book on the subject in 1907. Yet he seemed to experience at least a slight change of heart at some point, for in writing to a friend he called Mrs. Eddy "the benefactor of the age." For more about Mark Twain and Christian Science, see "Mrs. Eddy Replies to Mark Twain," originally published in the *New York Herald* and reprinted shortly afterwards in CSS (January 22, 1903), and later in *Miscellany*, pp. 302-303; *Rolling Away the Stone*, pp. 43-51, 85-87, 147, 439/n2; *Years of Authority*, pp. 201-206, 448/n95-97, 450/n108.

p. 174 "Good morning, Mr. Frost; I am so glad we are not all dead this morning." *Boston Sunday Post* (May 5, 1907).

p. 175 He turned them down flat. TMBEL, SF: Mary Baker Eddy–Lawsuits–"Next Friends"– Farlow, Alfred–Research, Ernest Gosselin affidavit (p. 9 of document titled "Relating to Suit in Equity–1907. Facts and rumors re Persons Concerned in Suit").

p. 175 Sidebar/Extra! Extra! Read All About It! For more information on the yellow kid and the rise of yellow journalism, see *The Hearsts: Father and Son* (Colorado: Roberts Rinehart, 1991) by William Randolph Hearst, Jr. with Jack Casserly, p. 41; *William Randolph Hearst: The Early Years, 1863-1910* (New York: Oxford University Press, 1998) by Ben Procter, pp. 85, 95-114; Ohio State University Library (http://cartoons.osu.edu/yellowkid/); PBS (http://www.pbs.org/crucible/frames/ _ journalism.html).

p. 176 "I had gone expecting to find a tottering old woman..." *Years of Authority*, p. 267; *Boston Herald* (October 30, 1906).

p. 176 "Are you in perfect bodily health?" Wilbur, "Mrs. Eddy Interviewed," CSS (November 3, 1906); *Years of Authority*, p. 268.

p. 176 "she stood before them..." *Years of Authority*, p. 269, quoting Fleta Campbell Springer's *According to the Flesh*, p. 414.

p. 177 Definition of *next friend:* "A person admitted to or appointed by the court to act for the benefit of a person (as an infant) lacking full legal capacity." *Webster's Online Dictionary,* 11th edition. For more information, see Cornell University Law School website (http://www.law.cornell.edu/wex/next _ friend).

p. 177 "If the son is willing to make a move all is plain sailing..." Chandler papers.

p. 177 "worn out, a confirmed invalid..." Letter from Chandler to Slaght at the *World* (March 2, 1907). Robert Peel notes that when the letter was published, the newspaper deliberately left off Slaght's name in order to cover its tracks in initiating the lawsuit. *Years of Authority,* pp. 277 and 480n89.

p. 178 "You can rest assured that the statements in the *Monitor* are correct." TMBEL, N00455 (November 5, 1906).

p. 178 "I know that [what] the *New York World* made is all a lie..." TMBEL, IC 197.32.048 (November 11, 1906).

p. 178 "Should I discover that my mother is infeebled [sic]..." Chandler papers, letter from George Glover to William Chandler (November 30, 1906).

p. 178 "Mission to Lead entirely successful." Chandler papers, Letter from Slaght to Chandler (December 5, 1906).

p. 179 "galvanic battery..." After his visit, Mary's son George reported hearing a noise from within his mother's room "which he attributed to a galvanic battery" (*New York World,* March 2, 1907). The existence of such a device was fabricated by the *World* on October 28, 1906 and refuted in a trio of affidavits by Calvin Frye (TMBEL, L15766), Lewis Strang (TMBEL, L16206), and Pamelia Leonard (TMBEL, L18528) on October 29, 1906.

p. 179 "You will come and see me again..." *New York World* (March 2, 1907).

p. 179 "It is sweet to me to recall my little visit from you..." TMBEL, L02141.

Chapter 22: TURNING THE TIDE

p. 180 "by seeking them out and taking them up and buoying them..." Chandler papers, letter from William Chandler to Ralph Pulitzer (February 7, 1907).

p. 180 "moral obligation ... that may have occurred..." Chandler papers, letter from Ralph Pulitzer to William Chandler (February 18, 1907).

p. 181 Peabody was the Boston-based lawyer... The lecture that Peabody gave and later published in pamphlet form was titled "A Complete Expose of Eddyism or Christian Science and the Plain Truth in Plain Terms Regarding Mary Baker Eddy."

p. 181 "Nothing could give me greater professional satisfaction..." Chandler papers, letter from Frederick W. Peabody to William Chandler (January 3, 1907).

p. 181 "I want the dear little Mother and the older members of 'the household,' to know..." TMBEL, IC 205b.34.054 (March 4, 1907).

p. 182 "I live with the Bible..." TMBEL, Rem: Lida Fitzpatrick (April 5, 1907).

p. 183 "My beloved Church..." TMBEL, L08375.

p. 183 "Come and hear what God said to me this morning..." TMBEL, Rem: Joseph Mann.

p. 183 "Lift your thought to God as you go about your work..." TMBEL, Rem: Minnie A. Scott. Minnie also noted that during this difficult time, Mrs. Eddy told her household "we are not worse for persecution. We are better for it, because it turns us more unreservedly to God."

p. 183 "Love your enemies..." Matthew 5:44.

p. 183 "Each day I pray: 'God bless my enemies..." *Miscellany*, p. 220.

p. 183 "Returning good for evil makes good real and evil unreal." TMBEL, L04757.

p. 183 Yet at times the tide of hate appeared so great that even Mrs. Eddy grew troubled... Adelaide Still and August Mann reminiscences. Adelaide noted that Mrs. Eddy "met this trial bravely, and trusted that divine Love would deliver her, but there were times when there would creep in the fear that her enemies might take her from her home and friends." TMBEL, Rem: M. Adelaide Still; TMBEL, Rem: August and Amanda Mann.

p. 183 "This hour is going to test Christian Scientists..." Calvin Hill in *We Knew MBE Vol. I*, p. 362.

p. 184 "I love you my only child..." TMBEL, L02149 (June 16, 1907).

p. 184 Sidebar/Allies In The Press: As a result of his newborn son's healing of a closed pylorus, Hearst allowed Bill Jr. and two of his brothers to attend a Christian Science Sunday School, despite the fact that he himself was Episcopalian. William Randolph Hearst's account of the healing of his son appeared in his syndicated column *In the News* on July 17, 1941 (which he would reprint in a booklet entitled *Faith*). The son in question later corroborated his father's account, but said there was one thing that wasn't true "and Pop knows it. Neither Pop nor I ever knew the day when I could run a newspaper better than he." ("Medical vs. Spiritual Care," by George R. Plagenz, *The Nashua Telegraph*, Sept. 26, 1987.) See also *The Hearsts: Father and Son* (Niwot, Colorado: Roberts Rinehart Publishers, 1991) by William Randolph Hearst, Jr. with Jack Cassidy, p. 23; *William Randolph Hearst: The Early Years 1863-1910* (New York: Oxford University Press, 1998) by Ben Procter, pp. 241 & 327n23; *William Randolph Hearst: American* (New York: D. Appleton-Century Co., 1936) by Cora Baggerly Older, p. 316; *William Randolph Hearst: A New Appraisal* (New York: Hastings House, 1955) by John K. Winkler, pp. 155-156; *Years of Authority*, p. 495n49, and *Spiritual Healing in a Scientific Age* (San Francisco: Harper & Row, 1987), pp. 125-127, both by Robert Peel.

p. 184 "I have a vivid picture of her, sitting quietly..." Calvin Hill in *We Knew MBE Vol. I*, p. 362.

p. 185 "Your best friend, but not your 'next friend'..." Ibid., p. 363.

p. 185 This healing of the newspaper reporter is recounted in *Twelve Years*, pp. 69-71, and *Christian Healer*, pp. 378-383.

p. 185 "My uncle requested me to see you..." *Twelve Years*, p. 71.

p. 185 Frank Streeter urged Mrs. Eddy to grant some proper interviews to the press... TMBEL, L16438 (June 8, 1907).

p. 185 Although work demanded her full attention... *Years of Authority,* pp. 272-273.

p. 186 "fully sane and above the average in intelligence..." TMBEL, SB23, p. 724 - Binghamton, N.Y. *Herald,* (August 26, 1907); *Years of Authority,* p. 487n118.

p. 187 "I was secretly to examine Mrs. Eddy as to her sanity..." *Recollections of an Alienist* (New York: George H. Doran Company, 1916) by Allan McLane Hamilton, p. 310. Like many before him, Hamilton, who noted Mrs. Eddy's "extraordinary vitality," was also struck by the "extraordinary intelligence shown in her eyes," noting that "in aged persons they are likely to appear dimmed, and lacking in expression; with Mrs. Eddy, however, they were dark, and at times almost luminous."

p. 187 "I have now become candidly of the opinion..." *The New York Times* (August 25, 1907).

p. 187 "At her beautiful home, Pleasant View..." *Boston Globe* (June 16, 1907).

p. 187 Caption: "Captain of her ship..." *North American* (July 14, 1907).

p. 188 "her whole manner was practical, forceful, unaffected..." *North American* (July 14, 1907).

p. 188 "I have never seen a woman eighty-six years of age with greater physical or mental vigor..." *Chicago Record-Herald* (July 19, 1907).

p. 189 "It is quite certain that nobody could see this beautiful and venerable woman..." "An Interview with Mrs. Eddy," *Cosmopolitan* (August 1907); reprinted in *What Mrs. Eddy Said To Arthur Brisbane*, p. 41. According to one Hearst biographer (Winkler, op. cit.), Brisbane often cited this interview with Mrs. Eddy as "his finest piece of reporting."

p. 189 One further hurdle awaited Mrs. Eddy... *Late Suit in Equity,* p. 127.

p. 190 "This hearing is not for the purpose of disestablishing the Christian Science faith..." Ibid., p. 149.

p. 190 Sidebar/Mrs. Eddy's High-Tech Household: Mrs. Eddy always enjoyed music, and singing with her household was a frequent and cherished part of her daily routine. Her Victrola recordings included classical music—Chopin, Shubert, and Handel, among others—as well as popular songs of the day. Lyman Powell's *Portrait* (p. 236) lists some of her favorite songs and gospel hymns, including "Nearer, my God, to Thee," "Jesus, Lover of My Soul," and "I Love to Tell the Story." Ella Rathvon cites "Watchman Tell Us of the Night" as the hymn most frequently sung when she was a member of Mrs. Eddy's household at Chestnut Hill.

p. 191 Caption: Clara Barton's interview with Viola Rodgers in the *New York American* (January 6, 1908—also published in the *Boston American*) was reprinted in the *CSS* (January 11, 1908) and the *CSJ* (February 1908). Barton's pioneering nursing work during the Civil War earned her the nickname "Angel of the Battlefield." She was generous in her praise of Mrs. Eddy, calling her the "nation's greatest woman" and Christian Science a "joyous, healing and comforting religion" and "the most potent factor in religious life." Clearly moved by these warm words, Mrs. Eddy wrote, "Miss

Clara Barton dipped her pen in my heart, and traced its emotions, motives, and object." *CSJ* (February 1908).

p. 191 "I have an artificial singer..." *Late Suit in Equity*, p. 163.

p. 191 "Give my love to her..." Ibid., p. 164.

p. 191 "Not at all..." Ibid., p. 165.

p. 192 "She's as sharp as a steel trap." TMBEL, Rem: John M. Tutt.

p. 192 When Mrs. Eddy heard the defense had triumphed... Calvin Hill in *We Knew MBE Vol. I*, p. 363.

Chapter 23: A BOLD VENTURE

p. 193 On a calm, clear January day in 1908... John Lathrop in *We Knew MBE Vol. I*, p. 268.

p. 193 "the most famous, interesting and powerful woman in America, if not in the world, today..." *Human Life* (February 1907).

p. 194 Mrs. Eddy's home was originally designated as 384 Beacon Street, but the city later renumbered it to 400.

p. 194 "Can you get me out of this, John?" TMBEL, Rem: M. Adelaide Still.

p. 194 "A great barn of a place..." TMBEL, Rem: M. Adelaide Still. Another source of background information about Mrs. Eddy's home at 400 Beacon Street is *Homeward II: Chestnut Hill* (Longyear Museum Press, 2008) by Stephen R. Howard.

p. 195 Jersey cows grazed in pastures nearby... Ibid., p. 48n76; TMBEL, EF079; TMBEL, Rem: William Rathvon.

p. 195 Mrs. Eddy ... felt that the grand stone house was too showy. TMBEL, Rem: M. Adelaide Still; John Salchow in *We Knew MBE Vol. I*, p. 414; *Years of Authority*, p. 299-300; *Homeward II: Chestnut Hill*.

p. 195 "all those roses..." TMBEL, Rem: M. Adelaide Still.

p. 196 Sidebar/A Pet For 400 Beacon Street: "Everybody loved Spike for her gentleness and friendliness..." Rem: Margaret Macdonald; Longyear Museum website (https://secure.LM.org/museum/image _ galleries/48-mary _ baker _ eddys _ household _ at _ chestnut _ hill _ part _ two#5).

p. 196 Although Pleasant View would always tug at her heart as home... John Salchow in *We Knew MBE Vol. I*, p. 414.

p. 196 "I have much work to do..." *New York American* (August 26, 1907), reprinted in the CSS (August 31, 1907).

p. 196 Now, at 400 Beacon Street, she kept largely to the same daily schedule... For these and other details about life at Chestnut Hill, see *Twelve Years*, p. 267; *Homeward Bound II*; John Salchow and Martha Wilcox in *We Knew MBE Vol. I;* and the numerous additional reminiscences of Mrs. Eddy's household workers, including Adam Dickey, Adelaide Still, and William Rathvon.

p. 197 In March 1908, Mrs. Eddy received a letter from John Wright... TMBEL, L06998 (March 12, 1908).

p. 197 "I believe there is need of daily newspapers…" Ibid.

p. 197 "Beloved Student: I have had this newspaper scheme in my thought…" Ibid.

p. 197 "newspapers should be edited with the same reverence for Truth…" *North American* (July 14, 1907).

p. 197 "It is my request that you start a daily newspaper at once…" TMBEL, L07268.

p. 198 Three days after receiving her letter, they wrote back… TMBEL, IC94b.21.036, 94b.21.038.

p. 198 "We have no larger fund…" TMBEL, IC94b.21.038.

p. 199 "go ahead with wisdom and economy as your guide…" TMBEL, L07269.

p. 199 "God gave me this name and it remains…" *Twelve Years*, p. 125.

p. 199 For more information on the founding of *The Christian Science Monitor*, see Canham's *Commitment to Freedom* and Dodds' *Autobiography and Story of the Founding of the Monitor* (unpublished original manuscript at LM), as well as Adelaide Still's reminiscence.

p. 199 "a man with smiling eyes, an amiable disposition, and an exceptional working knowledge of the mechanics of a newspaper…." Walter W. Cunningham, former city editor of the *Monitor*, quoted in "Your Periodicals and You," CSS (July 11, 1959.)

p. 199 A few years earlier, Alexander had been told he was incurably ill… Dodds, *Autobiography*; *Commitment to Freedom*, p. 78.

p. 200 "The press unwittingly sends forth many sorrows and diseases…" *S&H*, p. 196.

p. 200 "Crime, scandal, disaster are the three common features…" Dodds, *Autobiography*.

p. 200 "She replied that six months was sufficient…" Dodds, *Autobiography*. Dodds would later write a letter to Mrs. Eddy, published in the CSS (December 26, 1908), that concluded: "From my first introduction to this great project I have endeavored to keep constantly in mind that success can be gained only by "those leaning on the sustaining infinite" (Science and Health, Pref., p. vii.), and each succeeding day makes me more grateful that I am, even in this small way, identified with the *Monitor* and its mission."

p. 200 "Within little more than a hundred days…" *Commitment to Freedom*, p. 28.

p. 201 "The building was ready for occupancy in exactly nine weeks…" Dodds, *Autobiography*.

p. 201 Caption: "All the news that is worth while reading…" *Commitment to Freedom*, p. 74.

p. 201 "There is a field, and a wide one, for a clean newspaper…" Archibald McLellan, "The Christian Science Monitor," CSS (October 17, 1908).

p. 202 "We simply had to have the wire service…" Forrest Price reminiscence, quoted in *Commitment to Freedom*, p. 42.

p. 203 "A heavy fog makes it darker than usual…" *Twelve Years*, p. 125.

p. 204 Mrs. Eddy "clasped it to her heart..." Daisette McKenzie, whose husband William was a Trustee and present at the time, recalled Mrs. Eddy's delight on publication day: "They reported that the scene was most moving. Her great hope which she had cherished so long had at last found expression." *Commitment to Freedom*, p. 54.

p. 204 "spread undivided the Science that operates unspent..." Mary Baker Eddy, lead editorial in *The Christian Science Monitor* (November 25, 1908), later reprinted in *Miscellany*, p. 353.

p. 204 "Here is the essence of the *Monitor*..." *Commitment to Freedom*, p. 56.

p. 205 The first sheet off the press was sent to Mrs. Eddy... TMBEL, Rem: M. Adelaide Still; *Twelve Years*, p. 126. Additionally, Tomlinson notes that a daily article from a Christian Science perspective was one of Mrs. Eddy's specific requests for her newspaper. The first and third issues contained the names of the authors of the religious articles; after that, they ran anonymously.

p. 205 "When I established *The Christian Science Monitor*, I took the greatest step forward since I gave *Science and Health* to the world." *Years of Authority*, pp. 311 & 496n66.

Chapter 24: JOURNEYING ON

p. 206 "All that I ask of the world..." Wilbur, "An Interview with Rev. Mary Baker G. Eddy," CSS (June 17, 1905).

p. 206 "a demonstrable knowledge of Christian Science practice..." *Manual*, p. 49.

p. 206 "Almost all of my rules in the Manual..." TMBEL, L04373.

p. 207 Augusta saw herself as "divinely" appointed... *Years of Authority*, p. 332.

p. 207 In typical fashion, Mrs. Eddy reached out to Augusta with love... TMBEL, L13518.

p. 207 "The less the teacher personally controls other minds..." *Manual*, p. 87; *Retrospection*, p. 84.

p. 207 Mrs. Eddy's lawyer cousin, General Henry Baker, had the answer to that... In his reminiscence (pp. 256-267), William Rathvon recalls a conversation with Baker on this subject: "I well remember the load that was lifted from me when he assured me that if the validity of the Manual were questioned because it was impossible to obtain her signature and it should be taken into Court, there was not a high tribunal in the land but would recognize the Board of Directors as next in authority and therefore competent to administer the By-Laws when it was physically impossible to obtain her signature. That this opinion was shared by Judge Hanna I later learned from Mr. McLellan, who said at their last interview that the Judge expressed himself similarly and without reservation." For more information, see "Permanency of The Mother Church and Its Manual" (Boston: The Christian Science Publishing Society, 1942).

p. 208 "my best witness, my babe!" TMBEL, A10402.

p. 208 "Spiritual ideas unfold as we advance..." *S&H*, p. 361.

p. 208 "in my revisions of Science and Health, its entire keynote..." TMBEL, A10402, p. 107.

p. 208 "scribe under orders" *Miscellaneous*, p. 311.

p. 208 "called … to proclaim His Gospel to this age" *S&H*, p. xi.

p. 208 "Was Newton capable of satisfactorily stating the laws of gravitation…" TMBEL, A10402, p. 107.

p. 209 "My whole heart went out to her in gratitude…" Clifford P. Smith, *Historical Sketches from the Life of Mary Baker Eddy and the History of Christian Science* (Boston: The Christian Science Publishing Society, 1934), p. 100.

p. 209 "The nights are quieter than for years…" TMBEL, Rem: William Rathvon.

p. 209 that October he signed a settlement agreement… Mary's son George would later break his promise and contest her will.

p. 209 "My dear Mother…" TMBEL, L18296.

p. 210 Caption: More information on the pin that Mary's grandsons delivered to her on her 89th birthday can be found on the Mary Baker Eddy Library website (http://www.marybakereddylibrary.org/collections/research/objects/item/birthday-gift)

p. 210 George and his brother Andrew were set to work… George Glover III reminiscence, *Longyear Museum Quarterly News* (Autumn 1984).

p. 210 "Why—she loves me!" George Glover III reminiscence, *Longyear Museum Quarterly News* (Autumn 1984).

p. 211 "We are preparing for school this fall…" TMBEL, V03140.

p. 211 "My dear Mother…" TMBEL, I.C. 197.32.067 (August 21, 1910).

p. 211 "She would voice her inmost desire …" TMBEL, A12003 (September 5, 1910).

p. 212 "God is my life." TMBEL, Rem: M. Adelaide Still.

p. 212 "I have all in divine Love, that is all I need." TMBEL, L13841; TMBEL, Rem: Ella Rathvon.

p. 212 "Mother has gone, Adelaide." TMBEL, Rem: M. Adelaide Still.

p. 212 "My Beloved Students…" CSS (December 10, 1910); *CSJ* (January 1911). The letter read by Smith was one that had been reprinted in *Miscellaneous*, p. 135.

p. 213 Calvin Frye telegraphed George Glover… CSS (December 10, 1910); *CSJ* (January 1911). It's interesting to note that, according to the *CSJ* account, among the honorary pallbearers at Mrs. Eddy's funeral were Edward Bates, who had been so instrumental in the building of the Original Mother Church; Frank Streeter, Mrs. Eddy's faithful legal counsel for many years; and Arthur Brisbane, the renowned journalist who had helped turn the tide of opinion just a few years earlier during the Next Friends lawsuit.

p. 213 "remarkable woman…" *Editorial Comments on the Life and Work of Mary Baker Eddy* (Boston: The Christian Science Publishing Society, 1911), pp. 12, 23, 50.

p. 213 "pioneer…" Ibid., p. 68.

p. 213 "one of the world's great benefactors…" Ibid., p. 18.

p. 213 "a woman of rare moral courage..." Ibid., p. 28.

p. 213 "She was the moving spirit..." Ibid., p. 49.

p. 213 "This Boston woman's life was as beautiful as it was devoted..." Ibid., p. 113.

p. 213 "No woman ever lived who did more to strengthen faith..." Ibid., p. 73.

p. 213 "She knew the Bible as few knew it..." Ibid., p. 70.

p. 213 "The work she did endures and will endure..." Ibid., p. 37.

p. 213 "The church she founded..." Ibid., p. 43.

p. 214 "well might serve as inspiration for a new beatitude..." Ibid., p. 119.

EPILOGUE

p. 215 "What I am is for God to declare..." *Pulpit*, p. 74.

p. 215 "a hunger and thirst after divine things..." *Retrospection*, p. 31.

p. 215 "diligently for the knowledge of God..." Ibid.

p. 215 "It is more blessed to give than to receive." Acts 20:35.

p. 215 "The discovery and founding of Christian Science..." *Miscellaneous*, p. 382.

p. 215 Caption: "I have faced the destiny of a discoverer and pioneer..." TMBEL, A10402, p. 106.

p. 216 "I know that my mission is for all the earth..." *New York American* (August 26, 1907), reprinted in the CSS (August 31, 1907).

p. 216 "my most important work..." *Retrospection*, p. 37.

p. 216 "The divine Principle of healing..." *S&H*, p. x.

p. 216 "You can prove for yourself..." Ibid., p. 547.

Index

Page numbers in **bold** refer to images.

About the Authors

Born into a British family living in Shanghai, China, Isabel Ferguson spent part of her childhood as a prisoner of war in a Japanese internment camp during World War II. Boarding school in England followed, after which she earned a degree in history from Edinburgh University, as well as a graduate degree in education from Boston University. An accomplished poet with a keen eye for the natural world, Isabel was in the full-time public practice of Christian Science for thirty years. She lived with her husband and family in Weston, Massachusetts.

A graduate of Principia College and a former Fulbright scholar, Heather Vogel Frederick began her career at *The Christian Science Monitor*, where her favorite assignment was as children's book review editor. Later, after working as a contributing editor at *Publishers Weekly* for many years, Heather left journalism to fulfill a lifelong dream of writing for young readers. Today, she's the author of over a dozen books, and her work has been translated into a number of languages and honored both nationally and internationally. Heather lives with her husband and family in the Pacific Northwest.

SHR1307005